New Paths
for Interreligious Theology

New Paths
for Interreligious Theology

Perry Schmidt-Leukel's
Fractal Interpretation of Religious Diversity

Alan Race and Paul Knitter, editors

ORBIS BOOKS
Maryknoll, New York 10545

Founded in 1970, Orbis Books endeavors to publish works that enlighten the mind, nourish the spirit, and challenge the conscience. The publishing arm of the Maryknoll Fathers and Brothers, Orbis seeks to explore the global dimensions of the Christian faith and mission, to invite dialogue with diverse cultures and religious traditions, and to serve the cause of reconciliation and peace. The books published reflect the views of their authors and do not represent the official position of the Maryknoll Society. To learn more about Maryknoll and Orbis Books, please visit our website at www.maryknollsociety.org.

ISBN
LIC-CIP to come

Contents

Part Three
Multireligious Perspectives

Part Four
Continuing the Conversation

Introduction

Exploring What Looks Like "A New Paradigm" for Dealing with Religious Diversity

———

Paul Knitter

WHY THIS BOOK?

"Looks like he's on to something." That, basically, was the reaction that Alan Race and I shared after reading Perry Schmidt-Leukel's Gifford Lectures.[1] This historic and time-honored lecture series has a reputation for presenting forums where new paradigms for understanding religion and religious history have been launched. We felt that Schmidt-Leukel's lectures, now published by Orbis Books as *Religious Pluralism and Interreligious Theology*, may be such a site.

In his book, Schmidt-Leukel (SL) offers two broad perspectives on how to understand and deal with a phenomenon that perplexes not only scholars of religious studies and theologians but also spiritual seekers, and even politicians: the diversity of religions. One perspective is theological; the other is phenomenological.

Theological. SL is calling for a new way of doing theology. He calls it interreligious theology—which challenges any theologian or interpreter of religion to recognize that she cannot carry on her job of understanding her own tradition unless she is in conversation with other traditions. No religion is sufficient unto itself for carrying on the task of religious understanding. All religions must engage each other if they are to be true to their religious identities and experiences.

This sounds like what in the academy is known as comparative theology.

---

[1] I composed this introduction in full consultation with my coeditor, Alan Race. It represents our shared perspectives.

But SL is pushing the comparative envelope. He's not just saying that learning from other religious communities is a profitable pursuit for Christian theologians; he's saying that engaging the other is the only authentic way for *all* theologians or spiritual truth seekers to ply their trade. And he adds a further admonition to comparativists: such an interreligious theology is best carried out on the basis of a pluralistic theology of religions that would take the place of traditional exclusivist and inclusivist theologies by recognizing that there is truth in many religions and that none has the final truth.

To the oft-heard criticism that such a "pluralistic agenda" is really a Western or hegemonic imposition on religious communities, SL shows that *all* religions have within them resources to establish a "pluralistic attitude" toward other religions. Pluralism has the capability for becoming a homegrown product of all religions. SL has pleaded his case for a pluralistic theology before, and more extensively;[2] in his Gifford Lectures he presents this case clearly, succinctly, and therefore, it seems to us editors, all the more engagingly.

Phenomenological. It is especially in the final section of his Gifford Lectures, where he lays out what he calls a "Fractal Interpretation of Religious Diversity" that Alan Race and I felt that SL was on to something really different, really pioneering.

To offer a trimmed-down summary of SL's fractal proposal: when one takes a careful—both broad-reaching and deep-reaching—look at the world of religions, one finds vast differences. That's what one expects. But in looking more carefully, one can come to discover patterns of similarity within the differences. The geometry of fractals, applied to nature by Benoît Mandelbrot, seems to apply to the world of religions as well. The very same differences that one notes *between* the religions are repeated *within* the religions. And, SL adds, such differences can also be found within the religious experience and needs of individual human beings. In other words, the religions are neither all the same nor incommensurably different but similar in their internal diversity, which means that no religion is a total stranger to any other religion.

We felt that SL's proposal of a fractal theory of religions offered really "new paths for interreligious theology," but not just for interreligious theology—also for the wide and diverse ways of studying the phenomena of religion and spirituality. It's a perspective that can enlighten and enliven the conversations between the various approaches to the study of religion—sociological, psychological, neurobiological, comparative—but also for theological assessments of religion: comparative theology, theology of religions.

---

[2]See his magisterial *God beyond Boundaries: A Christian and Pluralist Theology of Religions* (Münster: Waxman, 2017).

So in order to try to determine whether SL really was on to something, we decided to call together, as it were, a jury of theological and religious studies experts and ask them if they could come up with some sort of verdict. The first hearing took place at a session of the annual meeting of the American Academy of Religion in November 2017. SL flew over from the University of Münster in Germany to present his case for a pluralistic interreligious theology and for a fractal interpretation of religious diversity. Many of the contributors to this volume were present at AAR to offer their initial responses, and then other interested scholars were further enlisted. In light of ensuing conversations on the value of SL's proposals, the "verdicts" were submitted to Alan and myself. Following editorial amendments, the final chapters were sent to SL so that he might craft a response and thus continue the conversation.

In this introduction we'd like to give you a bird's-eye view of the conversation and offer some guidelines that we hope will be helpful for your own weighing of the different assessments, as well as of SL's response to them.

As the table of contents indicates, the contributions divide generally into those that take a more methodological or contextual perspective on SL's proposal and those that view it from their religious tradition. But we suspect that it will be more helpful if we introduce here the chapters according to the verdicts they give on SL's proposal. So after a summary of SL's overview of his proposal, we group the responses in three categories: (1) those that *affirm* and show the potential of SL's proposal, (2) those that *correct* what they believe are inaccuracies in his criticisms of other viewpoints, and (3) those that suggest how possibly debilitating inadequacies can be fixed.

SETTING THE STAGE

SL sets the stage and context for this book's conversation by offering a compact synopsis of the second part of his Gifford Lectures dealing with interreligious theology, with a focus on his fractal interpretation of religious diversity. After illustrating how Mandelbrot's "fractal geometry of nature" is reflected in cultures and religions, SL unpacks—or perhaps, "unleashes"—the lethal implications of a fractal perspective for some of the sacred cows of the postmodern academy. If a fractal perspective is correct in showing that the differences between the religions are similar to the differences within each of them, and that "religions are neither all the same nor totally different," then three planks of the postmodern platform become wobbly: the religions of the world are *not* incommensurable; the notion of "religion" is *not* an academic concoction but, rather, a meaningful concept; and "mutual illumination" between the religions and thus interreligious theology *are* possible. SL concludes his overview with a substantiating example of the kind of mutual illumination that can result from an interreligious theological exploration of three very different, but fractally relatable, images from Buddhism, Christianity, and Islam: the Awakened One, the Son, and the Prophet.

AFFIRMING

Alan Race and *Kenneth Rose* both make strong but different cases that SL's fractal interpretation of religious diversity (FIRD) offers phenomenological backing for both a pluralist theology of religions and for an interreligious theology.

Confirming pluralism. As is generally known amid the trio of theologies of religions, exclusivism and inclusivism oppose pluralism in claiming that one religion exceeds all others in being either the *only* or the *superior* transmitter of transforming truth. Pluralism holds that such truth resides in multiple religions, with no one of them owning a superior or final version of such truth.

Rose and Race both argue that FIRD makes it clear that the claims of the exclusivists and inclusivists stand in harsh contradiction to the phenomenological evidence of fractal reflections. If correct, SL's fractal theory makes it abundantly clear that no one religion contains a unique discovery or truth that does not exist somewhere else. Whatever is claimed to be a superior or final truth shows up, in different packing or ranking, in some other religion. There is no such thing as absolute uniqueness. Rather, as Rose puts it, there are "universal types or patterns in all religions." Race even goes so far as to claim that FIRD provides the empirical or phenomenological data to move the pluralist theology of religions from its present status as a "hypothesis" to that of a "theory."

Confirming interreligious theology. For Rose, FIRD "uncovers the hidden relatedness" of all religions. It makes evident that they are all about the same project of religious discovery as "channels, sacraments, or bearers . . . of the full plenitude of being." So if all religions bear a hidden relatedness in their efforts to encounter and grasp the Mystery that grounds reality, they evidently have much to learn from their differences. What is different within some religions will most likely offer to other religions something to learn about the plenitude that no religion can ever exhaust.

Hans Gustafson, in another of his publications,[3] has developed his pansac-

---

[3]Finding *All Things in God: Pansacramentalism and Doing Theology Interreligiously* (Eugene, OR: Pickwick Publications, 2015).

ramental view of humankind's religious history. Simply stated, all of finite reality, insofar as it is sustained and infused by the Holy or the Real, can be a sacrament of the Holy. Gustafson suggests that such pansacramentalism and SL's proposal dovetail in that pansacramentalism can provide the theological, even metaphysical, grounding for the phenomenological data gathered by FIRD. The unity of the sacred and the finite that pansacramentalism affirms serves as the explanatory source for the recurring unity, or relatability and resonance, between the similar differences that the fractal perspective identifies.

John Makransky provides a kind of case study in how clues of the fractal nature of religious diversity can become spontaneously evident—indeed, as it were, smack one in the face—when one engages in a detailed exploration of examples of diversity within a particular religious tradition. He leads us into the intricacies of a big disagreement within Tibetan Buddhism. Tsong-khapa and Longchenpa had deep-reaching differences in their understandings of ultimate reality, how humans are related to this reality, and how they can achieve an awareness of it. Any Christian scholar—and I would add, mutatis mutandis, also Jewish or Muslim scholar—who accompanies Makransky on this tour of Tibetan Buddhist debates will immediately hear echoes of similar disagreements within their own tradition: Are we saved by faith alone or by good works? What is the relation between "nature" and "grace"? Are they distinct or coinciding? Is the human condition held in an original sin or in an original blessing?

Makransky makes clear that such similarities are not just a matter of interesting or striking likenesses; to explore such fractal reflections, and to understand how and why they appear in another tradition, can open up new opportunities in reassessing and repossessing one's own religious beliefs and practices. Again, if fractals are real, then some form of interreligious learning and theology is possible, even necessary.

Rong Wang takes us on an excursion through both the religious history of China and the current conversation in the Chinese academy of religion in order to make her case that only if Christianity embraces some kind of a pluralist view of other religions, as proposed by SL, will it really be able to become Chinese. Christianity is being called to be integrated, she points out, into China's long history of *Sanjiao Heyi*—the idealized harmony between the three traditions of Confucianism, Taoism, and Buddhism. She suggests that the harmony of Sanjiao Heyi is reflected in FIRD and at the same time "offers fertile ground in which the kind of religious pluralism proposed by Schmidt-Leukel can grow and perhaps find new forms." If Christianity is to become a Chinese religion, it will have to "harmonize" with other Chinese religions, which means that claims of supremacy or missionary efforts to replace or absorb Chinese religions will have to be abandoned.

She rather boldly hopes that SL's pluralist philosophy of religious diversity and his call for an interreligious theology will help not only Christianity but also Chinese religions themselves to harmonize. Indeed, she wonders whether SL's fractal grounding for a truly pluralist relationship among religions might well be a "harbinger of a transformation of Chinese religions and religious studies."

CORRECTING

Francis Clooney, SJ, has offered perhaps the feistiest of our contributions. In his dialogue with SL, Clooney is both defensive and constructive.

He organizes his *defense* mainly around the relationship between theology of religions (which seeks to clarify what value one sees in other religions) and comparative theology (which wants to explore what one can learn from other religions). In resistance to what he sees as SL's efforts to make comparative theology "an entirely dependent subfield of the theology of religions," Clooney insists that while the two fields are certainly related, they can be pursued independently of each other. And when SL warns Clooney that his avowed inclusivist theology will cause trouble for his work as a comparative theologian insofar as it necessarily subordinates other religions to Christianity, Clooney calmly clarifies that he is not an "inclusivist" but an "includer." He doesn't want to subordinate other religions; he just wants to include them in his work as a theologian who is seeking the truth about God. When SL presses his case and warns him that his inclusivist theology logically requires him to judge Hinduism to be false or inferior whenever it disagrees with Christian truth, Clooney, disregarding the logic, declares that he has never looked upon Hinduism as inferior.

But Clooney also responds *constructively* when he turns the tables on SL by pointing out that his fractal approach to religious diversity is much more supportive of Clooney's grassroots comparative work than it is of SL's theoretical pursuits as a theologian of religions. Engaging the particular fractal connections between and within religions is more akin to the comparativist's preference for concrete opportunities to learn rather than to grand theorizing. Comparative theologians delight in the messiness of fractality, while, according to Clooney, theologians of religions like SL want to clean it up in theory.

Ayon Maharaj, similar to Clooney, offers a twofold response to SL's proposal—both a correction and an admonition. His *correction* is pinpointed: SL seriously misunderstands the teachings of Vivikananda when he, like so many Western and some Indian commentators, identifies him as appearing sometimes as a pluralist and sometimes as an inclusivist. Maharaj counters with a subtle and tight case that Vivekananda, as well as his teacher Rama-krishna, have both "championed a full-blown doctrine of religious plural-ism."

His *admonition* to SL is more complex. He urges SL to make use of a distinction that SL's mentor John Hick made and to seek "mutual illumina-tion" only between differing religious teachings that are "soteriologically vital" (that is, those that deal with the nature of ultimate reality and salva-tion); religious teachings and practices that are "soteriologically nonvital" should be allowed to thrive in their differences. This, Maharaj adds, will offset a danger that he identifies in SL's understanding of interreligious theology: "that his emphasis on doctrinal integration and synthesis might come at the cost of neglecting the equally important aim of *honoring reli-gious difference.*"

FIXING

Ephraim Meier, from his Jewish perspective, finds SL's fractal theory and his way of doing interreligious theology to be too heady—too "logocen-tric." For Jews, he tells us, "mending the world is the task of religions. . . . Religions are a legitimate undertaking insofar as they improve the human condition." And so he suggests, indeed urges, that SL's "logocentric fractal interpretation of religious plurality be complemented by an existential, moral, deed-centered approach to religions." This will require a sweeping revision of where interreligious theology should start and finish—not with "sophisticated theological thinking" but "ethics as a common basis for all religions."

Jerusha Tanner Rhodes, as a Muslim comparative feminist theologian, takes up Meier's insistence on ethics rather than doctrine and offers more specificity. She speaks as an "outsider within" her own tradition—one of the many women who have been excluded or diminished within her own community. She therefore wants not just to interpret and connect religious communities; she wants to reform them. "Transformation, transgression, reconstruction" are her objectives.

She fears that SL's call to an interreligious theology shored up by FIRD can, contrary to its intentions, serve to "reinscribe and further reify an-drocentrism, patriarchy, or both." After all, the three fractal images that SL explores in his case study of interreligious theology—Son, Prophet, Buddha—"center on male figures and orthodox doctrines that are primary sites of female exclusion." So for her, the primary way in which comparative feminist theology can enrich fractal interpretation is to call SL and others to be attentive to power dynamics and political implications in their work.

FIRD should seek not just to understand and relate fractal patterns but to criticize and transform them.

Maria Dakake is in fundamental agreement with SL's fractal perspective and the way he makes use of it to suggest resonances between Jesus as incarnate Son and Muhammad as prophet. To understand Jesus as God's symbol correlates well with the Qur'anic conception of Jesus as "sign" and of Muhammad as "*dhikr* Allah" or the "remembrance/reminder of God." But she also chides SL for perhaps going too far in trying to persuade Muslims that they can accept the Christian affirmation of Jesus as God's Son if they only recognize that "Son" and "incarnation" are symbols that affirm divine revelation in human form. She fears that an interpretation of divine sonship along those lines might be regarded as too little by many Christians and as still too much by many Muslims given "the Qur'an's emphatic rejection of the attribution of filial relationships to God in any form."

More broadly, Dakake sounds a warning about SL's understanding of interreligious theology as a "world theology" or as "a constructive theology built outside the confessional confines of the individual traditions." Such an understanding contradicts or endangers what she understands to be the "liminal and temporary" nature of interreligious engagements in which "one meets the other for relatively fleeting moments of mutual or reciprocal illumination and theological exchange." She invokes the Muslim notion of *barzakh*—well-confined meeting points similar to the meeting of a freshwater river and the salty sea: "their mingling is limited to this liminal space, and is never allowed to compromise the integrity of the two bodies of water themselves." She is worried that in SL's notion of interreligious theology, founded in fractal similarities, religious traditions might well lose their "integrity."

SCHMIDT-LEUKEL'S RESPONSE

Responding to his critics, SL makes it clear that he considers his proposal for a fractal interpretation of religious diversity and for a multifaith theology of religions very much a work in progress and so welcomes this critical conversation about his proposals. His response to this conversation is both grateful and accepting as well as critical and insistent. We list here some of the pivotal questions that SL answers and that readers will want to try to answer for themselves.

Does the fractal perspective call for a pluralistic theology of religions? Here SL clarifies any misunderstanding that may arise from Race's and Rose's support for FIRD by stating that "the discernment of fractal structures does not in itself conclude the debate between exclusivists, inclusivists, and pluralists. . . . It does not demonstrate religious pluralism"—although, he immediately adds, FIRD "works best" with a full-fledged pluralist theology of religions. But it is a different story in regard to FIRD's support of an interreligious theology. For SL, if inter- and intrafractals are a reality among the religions, then the "mutual illumination" of interfaith theology is not only a possibility but a necessity.

Are there some differences between religions that eschew a fractal embrace? Are there some teachings or characteristics that are unique to only one religion and so incommensurable with others? To such questions posed by Meier, Maharaj, Dakake, and Clooney, SL gives a qualified response. What appear clearly to be incommensurable contradictions between two religions may turn out, in the fractal perspective, to be contradictions somehow held *within* each religion. If they are compatible within, they can be so without. Even the apparent contradictions that Makransky points out between Tsongkhapa and Longchenpa, SL argues, are able to speak to and learn from each other. Opposing differences turn out to be complementary differences. SL suggests that what makes unique particularities contradictory and incommensurable is when they are absolutized and claimed to be exclusive or superior over all others.

Is the fractical interpretation of religious diversity lacking an ethical basis and moral compass? SL responds to such concerns of Tanner Rhodes and Meier by recognizing and affirming the vital bonds between religion and morality, metaphysics and ethics. But he also firmly warns against reducing religion to morality. To do so, he holds, would run the risk of making doctrinal claims that are ethically meaningful but metaphysically silly. To Tanner Rhodes's fears that fractal theory might turn out to be an unawares shill for patriarchy, he responds that such might be the case only if fractal theory is divorced from interreligious theology. Fractals provide the data for resonances between religious teachings; theologians weigh the data for their coherence and ethical implications. Moreover, he adds that there are no sound theological or philosophical reasons why buddhahood, incarnation, and prophethood must be limited to males.

Has SL misrepresented the views of others in advancing his fractal interpretation? To Maharaj, SL appreciatively accepts his defense of Ramakrishna and Vivikananda as more soundly pluralist theologians than SL had deemed. But to Dakake's uneasiness that SL is asking too much of Muslims in calling them to recognize the fractal resonances between sonship and prophethood, he suggests that it is through such uneasiness that interreligious theologians can break through to new, but still faithful, learnings. Toward Clooney, SL first reassures him that in no way does he want to subordinate comparative theology to the theology of religions. Still, however Clooney understands the difference between being an "inclusivist" and being an "includer," SL persists in his warning that unless comparative theologians explicitly engage the complex issues of a theology of religions, they run the risk of becoming comparative religion scholars rather than comparative theologians.

ON TO SOMETHING?

Our hope as editors is that this introduction serves as an invitation to the conversations contained in this book as well as a sort of guide to assessing some of their main questions and controversies.

To further this hope, we note, first of all, that amid all the "affirming, correcting, and fixing" responses from the collection's contributors, all of them recognize the basic value and promise of Schmidt-Leukel's fractal interpretation of religious diversity. Given this general endorsement, we offer three summarizing reasons why we believe that with this proposal, SL is indeed on to something. With it he mounts staunch counterclaims to three widespread viewpoints and positions within the academy of religious and theological studies. Doing so, he also opens up new paths for an animated interreligious theology:

- *To the "exclusivists and inclusivists" who hold that one religion excels over all the others:* Besides making his theological case that a "pluralist" view of other religions can be found growing in the gardens of all religions, he also offers his phenomenological fractal interpretation of religious diversity in which there is no such thing as a unique religion that has something that no other religion has. Here Rose and Race may well be right in pointing out to SL that he underestimates the way his FIRD supports, even requires, a multi-religious pluralistic theology. At the very least, it places the *onus probandi* on the critics of pluralism to explain how, in the light of fractal resonances throughout the religious world, they can persist with not endorsing a pluralist position.
- *To the "particularists" who hold that the teachings of each religion are so socioculturally constructed as to be impermeable to and incommensurable with the teachings of other religious cultures:* FIRD indicates that all these social constructions, despite their geographic or historical separations, show similar patterns amid their differences, which call for, not incommensurability, but commensurability. Such similar differences evoke, naturally, comparison and relationship—that is, mutual illumination.
- *To the "postmodernists" who denounce all universal truth claims*

and "metanarratives" as concealed power-plays: FIRD indicates that there are truths identifiable within *multiple* religions and so *universal* in multiple religions. Thus, the job of the theologian (or spiritual seeker) can be carried out adequately only if carried out interreligiously. To be a theologian—whether Christian, Muslim, Hindu, and so on—is to be an interreligious theologian.

Are such claims of being "on to something" accurate and promising? That will be determined through more of the kind of scholarly and practical conversation that we hope this book stimulates.

December 2018

PART ONE

SETTING THE STAGE

A Fractal Interpretation
of Religious Diversity

An Overview

_____

Perry Schmidt-Leukel

In this chapter I would like to briefly introduce a new theory on religious diversity. I call it a "fractal interpretation" because the theory claims that religious diversity displays a fractal structure. Like so many other "new" theories, this one too is not entirely new. It has been, as I explain shortly, anticipated in the phenomenology of religions, in intercultural philosophy, and even, to some extent, in the religions themselves. As far as my own intellectual development is concerned, I now realize that I was "pregnant" with it for something like three decades—an unusually long pregnancy, I have to admit. It was only in 2015, when I was preparing my Gifford Lectures,[1] that the theory was born. In the middle of the night, round about 3 a.m. or so, labor set in. I woke up, went to my desk, and sketched on one or two sheets of paper how religious diversity might be best understood along the lines of fractal structures. The nucleus of the theory is that the diversity that we observe *among* the religions globally is mirrored in the diversity that we find *within* each of the major religious traditions. And that we can also discern some patterns of this diversity—or elements thereof—*within the religious orientation of individual persons*. In other words, religious diversity is neither chaotic nor entirely random. It rather follows to a significant extent a fractal structure. Thus, what I suggest is a fairly simple idea, but one that has some far-reaching implications and consequences if it turns out to be correct.

_____

[1]Perry Schmidt-Leukel, *Religious Pluralism and Interreligious Theology: The Gifford Lectures—An Extended Edition* (Maryknoll, NY: Orbis Books, 2017).

THE "FRACTAL GEOMETRY OF NATURE"
AND THE MICRO-MACRO-COSMOS SCHEME
IN TRADITIONAL RELIGIOUS METAPHYSICS

In 1975 Benoît Mandelbrot (1924–2010) introduced the term "fractals" for such patterns, structures, or forms that display either a rough or strict self-similarity across various scales. That is, a component of the pattern or structure constitutes either a strictly identical or roughly similar copy of the whole. Recursiveness and (rough) scale invariance are thus the two key features of fractals. Strict self-identity is typical for abstract geometrical figures such as the so-called Sierpinski triangle.[2] Here we also find the feature of infinity, that is, recursiveness across different scales stretches infinitely to ever larger and ever smaller units. This is not the case with those phenomena that we can find in inorganic and organic nature that also

bear a fractal structure but one that is marked by rough instead of strict scale invariance and stretches not over an infinite but a limited number of scales. Particularly well-known organic examples are fern leaves, cauliflower, or trees. A fern leaf is composed of smaller leaves showing the same pattern as the larger leaf. Similarly the pattern of the whole cauliflower is replicated in the structure of each of its florets. And for various trees it is true that the structure of the whole tree is mirrored in its branches and side branches. Typical examples from inorganic nature are certain ice crystals, rock formations, or coastlines. A fringed coastline is composed of spits, fjords, and bays, etc. But if you zoom into it, you find that a fjord has also its small spits and bays, or a bay its small fjords and spits, and so on. In a

---

[2]https://commons.wikimedia.org/wiki/File:Sierpinski_triangle.svg.

number of cases the fractal analysis shows that what appear to be rather chaotic phenomena are actually underpinned by fractal patterns. Regarding the seemingly chaotic nature of "white horses," this is neatly illustrated by the fractal resolution of Hokusai's famous artwork *The Great Wave*.[3] Fractal structures are actually so widespread in nature that Mandelbrot concluded, "There is a fractal face to the geometry of nature."[4] As I point out below, this apparently also applies to cultural and religious diversity.

It seems that various religions already had some awareness of the pervasiveness of fractal structures in our world. This is indicated by the wide prevalence of the micro-macro-cosmos scheme. I do not want to go into too much detail here but will proceed with just some brief examples.[5]

In Sufism there is the common saying, "The universe is a big man and man a little universe."[6] In other words, macrocosmic structures replicate on the microcosmic level, especially on the level of human existence, so that larger structures replicate at smaller scales. The conviction of a micro-macro-cosmic parallelism is also widely disseminated in Hinduism. It has found a remarkable expression in the so-called *Śrī Yantra* or *Śrī Chakra*, which embraces the human and the nonhuman sphere.[7] The nine intersecting triangles are of a multilayered symbolic meaning, representing, for example, earth, air, and sun as mirrored in body, breath, and the inner light of consciousness paralleled with further sets of threes.[8] The irregular but nevertheless clearly fractal structure of the *Śrī Yantra* is evident.

---

[3]http://www.delimited.io/blog/2014/2/24/fractals-in-d3-dragon-curves.

[4]Benoît B. Mandelbrot, *The Fractal Geometry of Nature*, updated and augmented ed. (New York: W. H. Freeman, 1983), 3.

[5]For numerous examples of ideas in the world religions that come close to fractal concepts of reality, see William J. Jackson, *Heaven's Fractal Net: Retrieving Lost Visions in the Humanities* (Bloomington: Indiana University Press, 2004), 28–59, 72–112.

[6]Titus Burckhardt, *Introduction to Sufi Doctrine* (Bloomington, IN: World Wisdom, 2008), 65.

[7]https://upload.wikimedia.org/wikipedia/commons/a/a2/Sri_Yantra_256bw.gif.

[8]See Subash Kak, "The Great Goddess Lalitā and the Śrī Cakra," *Brahmavidyā: The Adyar Library Bulletin*, 72–73 (2008–9): 155–72; http://ikashmir.net/subhashkak/docs/SriChakra.pdf.

A further, somewhat similar, example is the Buddhist idea of the world as "Indra's Net," which we find in the *Avataṃsaka Sūtra*. Indra's Net consists of an infinite number of crystal pearls, all woven into a celestial net, such that the whole net of empty pearls is mirrored or replicated in each single pearl. A fractal structure can also be recognized in the famous Chinese symbol of yin and yang (*taijitu*): an element of the dark principle, *yin*, is contained in the bright principle, *yang*, and vice versa. The fractal structure is particularly evident in those depictions that show not only the mutual implication of yin and yang but also replicate the dynamic shape as in the version ascribed to Zhao Huiqian (fourteenth century).[9]

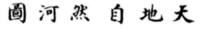

---

[9]https://en.wikipedia.org/wiki/Taijitu#/media/File:Bagua_Zhao_Huiqian.jpg.

My final example is taken from the *Bible moralisée*, a medieval picture Bible from the early thirteenth century.[10] The frontispiece depicts the creation of the world in a way that is somewhat reminiscent of the micro-macro-cosmos scheme. The image is often called "God as the architect of the world," yet this is inaccurate. From the cross in the halo it is evident that the depicted "architect" is not God the Father but Christ. This is in line with the ancient Christian and Platonic idea that God created the world through the Logos, that is, through the eternal Word or Mind of God, which at some point in time assumed human form in Jesus. This conception involves three interconnected levels: first, God as the ultimate source of everything; second, the Logos as the Mind or Word of God; and third, the world as created in and through the Logos. The image from the *Bible moralisée* shows this relationship by giving the same color to Christ's halo as to the orbit of the world. Another fractal touch is added by the fringes of the nocturnal sky, which exhibit a fractal pattern of the wave or coastline type.

The micro-macro-cosmos scheme as we find it in traditional religious metaphysics refers to the recursiveness of general structures in the mental and nonmental aspects of the universe. Hence it implies what Mandelbrot

---

[10]https://commons.wikimedia.org/wiki/File:God_the_Geometer.jpg.

called the "fractal face . . . of nature." Traditionally, it did not, as far as I am aware, refer to religious diversity. Yet to the extent that we understand the diversity of cultural and religious life as an integral part of the universe, especially of its mental dimension, the idea of a fractal structure of religious diversity is not only compatible with the micro-macro-cosmos scheme but the latter could even be viewed as an anticipation, or implicit awareness, of the former. The widespread dissemination of the micro-macro-cosmos scheme may therefore help the religions to accept that the same scheme is also applicable to the phenomenon of religious diversity, that is, to acknowledge the fractal nature of such diversity.

THE DISCOVERY OF FRACTAL PATTERNS
IN CULTURE AND RELIGION

As I have pointed out elsewhere, contemporary intercultural philosophy can be understood as the search for a middle way between, on the one hand, the thesis of a radical incommensurability of different human cultures and, on the other hand, the belief in their essential sameness or identity.[11] Those who find both extremes unpersuasive prefer to speak of various forms of "overlapping" (Ram Adhar Mall) or "intersection" (Bernhard Waldenfels) between cultures. That is, some elements or features of the alien culture are recognized in one's own culture, and some aspects familiar from one's own culture can be discerned in the alien one. This observation points toward a fractal interpretation of cultural diversity according to which the differences between cultures reappear, to some extent, within each one of the different cultures. The Swiss intercultural philosopher Elmar Holenstein has most clearly advanced such an understanding. Holenstein, who taught at Bochum, Zürich, Tokyo, and Hong Kong, spent much of his work in comparing Western with Far Eastern cultures. According to his findings,

The same oppositions that are thought to be ascertainable between two cultures (*interculturally*) can often be detected in the same kind and degree within one and the same culture (*intraculturally*), even within one and the same person (*intrasubjectively*) depending on age, surroundings, task or just on mood and humour.[12]

---

[11]See Schmidt-Leukel, *Religious Pluralism and Interreligious Theology*, 225–27.

[12]Elmar Holenstein, "A Dozen Rules of Thumb for Avoiding Intercultural Misunderstandings," *polylog: Forum for Intercultural Philosophy* 4 (2003): 1–61, 46; https://them.polylog.org/4/ahe-en.htm.

This is evidently a fractal pattern—even if Holenstein himself does not use this terminology. In the quotation above, he identifies three levels or scales across which the patterns of cultural diversity replicate: (1) the *intercultural level* of global cultural diversity, (2) the *intracultural level* of regional or culture-specific diversity, and (3) the *intrasubjective level* of different patterns of behavior, attitudes, sentiments, views, values, and so on, as they are found within the mental cosmos of one particular individual either more or less simultaneously or intermittently or successively within the course of a person's lifetime. I suggest that Holenstein's analysis also applies to religious diversity across the same three levels.

Employing Holenstein's architecture of cultural diversity, a fractal interpretation of religious diversity distinguishes at least[13] the following three levels or scales: (1) the level of *interreligious* diversity, that is, religious diversity at the global scale; (2) the level of *intrareligious* diversity, that is, the diversity within the major religious traditions; and (3) the *intrasubjective* level of religious diversity, that is, common but diverse predispositions of the human mind and psyche as they may manifest either simultaneously in the form of hybrid religious identities or successively as transitions of religious orientation in the course of individual religious biographies. The key assumption is that the patterns and distinguishing features that demarcate religious diversity at the first level of global religious diversity reappear at the second and third level. From a comparative perspective this implies that religions are neither all the same nor totally different. Instead they resemble each other in their internal diversity and give space to different forms and expressions of religiousness at the individual or subjective level.

This theory may be illustrated by the following example: Julia Ching and Hans Küng expanded Friedrich Heiler's widespread typological distinction between prophetic and mystic religions[14] into the tripartite scheme of prophetic, mystic, and sapiential religions (the latter being the indigenous traditions of China). In so doing, they observed that prophetic religions also contain elements and features of mystical and sapiential religions, mystical religions those of prophetic and sapiential religions, and sapiential religions those of prophetic and mystical ones.[15] That is, the structuring of religious diversity at the interreligious level into three different types of religions replicates itself at the intrareligious level, although in different forms and with different emphases. Moreover, corresponding spiritualities can be discerned not merely among individual members of those traditions

---

[13]I say "at least" because the level of "intrareligious diversity" may be further divided by introducing sublevels of diversity within major sections or strands of large religious traditions.

[14]A distinction going back to Nathan Söderblom.

[15]Hans Küng and Julia Ching, *Christianity and Chinese Religions* (New York: Doubleday, 1989), xv–xvi.

but also as simultaneous or successive components in the religious identity formation of particular individuals. This is just one, rather coarse example of a fractal pattern. My theory does not hinge on this particular typology. Instead I suggest that whatever kind of categories we use in describing and analyzing religious diversity, we will, presumably, be able to discern fractal, that is, scaling patterns. Thus, I propose a fractal interpretation of religious diversity with a strong pragmatic or heuristic connotation: whenever we develop conceptual instruments by which we distinguish, differentiate, contrast, contrapose, or counterpoise religions by their beliefs, attitudes, practices, institutions, and so on, we should attentively see if we can discern fractal patterns.

Comparative religion, especially as practiced within the phenomenology of religion, was about to discover the fractality of religious diversity before this important line of research came to a premature end due to the heavy resistance emerging from the postmodernist and poststructuralist aversion to any comparative perspective. Initially, phenomenologists of religion had aimed at establishing a typology of religions. They were seeking a better understanding of religious diversity by distinguishing and characterizing different types of religion. In addition, they also classified distinct elements (e.g., sacred places, times, objects, animals, humans; sacred institutions, authorities, rituals, regulations, precepts, practices; sacred myths, narratives, scriptures, doctrines; specific emotions, experiences, values, attitudes, etc.) within the different religious traditions. The obvious expectation was to establish a strong correspondence between the actual religions, on the one hand, and on the other, both the different types of religions as well as their characteristic elements. Yet it increasingly turned out that at the level of elements there were far too many parallels among the actual religions and far too many parallel differences within each of them than a clear-cut typology would permit. As Friedrich Heiler had already noticed, the actual religions often display a mixture and a merger of elements of the prophetic and mystical type.[16] The individual religions never fit tidily into the various typological frames. In 1960 Brede Kristensen even concluded that almost everything found in one religion seems to reappear in some way or another in other religions as well: "Seen more deeply, therefore, everything is held in common."[17]

Such insights became significant in as much as they paved the way for what can now be regarded as more or less generally accepted: none of the

---

[16]Friedrich Heiler, *Das Gebet: Eine religionsgeschichtliche und religionspsychologische Untersuchung*, 3rd ed. (1919; Munich: Verlag Ernst Reinhart, 1921), 233–34.

[17]W. Brede Kristensen, *The Meaning of Religion: Lectures in the Phenomenology of Religion* (The Hague: Martinus Nijhoff, 1960), 9.

major religious traditions is a homogeneous or unchanging entity; they are *internally diverse*, even heterogeneous, hybrid, syncretistic, and shaped by influences of other religious or nonreligious factors, and are subject to continuous further diversification, transformation, and development. This is an important presupposition for the discovery of fractal structures. But a fractal interpretation of religious diversity goes beyond the mere observation of intrareligious diversity in that it discerns significant parallels between intrareligious and interreligious diversity. It identifies patterns that replicate over both levels and are also found at the smallest level of the religious subject. In a sense, the different types of religions that the phenomenologists were trying to discern reappear at the level of elements and even at the level of individual believers within each of the different religious traditions.

A significant move toward such a fractal perspective can already be seen in the work of phenomenologist Hilko Wiardo Schomerus (1879–1945). Drawing on traditional Hindu classifications,[18] Schomerus distinguishes four major types of religions: (1) religions of the law, (2) magical-sacramental religions, (3) gnostic religions, and (4) devotional religions.[19] As prime examples he mentions Judaism (type 1), Indian mysticism (type 2), Greek gnosis and Buddhism (type 3) and Hindu *bhakti* traditions and Mahāyāna Buddhism (type 4). But he immediately adds the important remark that such typological distinctions only apply to dominant strands within the specific religions while many of the individual religions actually include several or even all of the four types. The dividing lines, says Schomerus, may not only be drawn vertically but also horizontally.[20] How close Schomerus gets to a fractal interpretation of religious diversity is obvious when he states: "Religion as such is hypostasized in a few major types, which persistently recur and unfold everywhere in similar ways, bringing about in all places kindred forms and formations."[21] Again, the point is not the specific typology that Schomerus prefers but his insight that the typological distinctions pertain both to the interreligious and the intrareligious level.

Regarding the *intrasubjective* level, William James and Rudolf Otto may be seen as forerunners of a fractal perspective. In his *Varieties of Religious Experience*, James states right from the start that religious life on earth is so diverse that it evades any coverage by one precise definition of "religion."[22]

---

[18]The "way of works" (*karmamārga*), the "way of meditation" (*yogamārga*), the "way of knowledge" (*jñānamārga*), the "way of devotion" (*bhaktimārga*).

[19]Hilko Wiardo Schomerus, *Parallelen zum Christentum als religionsgeschichtliches und theologisches Problem* (Gütersloh: Bertelsmann, 1932), 22.

[20]Ibid.

[21]Ibid., 26 (my translation).

[22]William James, *The Varieties of Religious Experience* (1902; New York: Vintage Books, 1990), 32–33.

But this diversity is structured. James suggests a "relativity of different types of religion to different types of [psychological] need,"[23] so that "different functions in the organism of humanity [are] allotted to different types of man."[24] To James, "the existence of so many religious types and sects and creeds" reflects the diversity of psychological dispositions and attitudes in individual human subjects.[25] "The divine can mean no single quality, it must mean a group of qualities, by being champions of which in alternation, different men may all find worthy missions."[26] In other words, there is a clear correspondence between, on the one hand, religious diversity at the inter- and intrareligious levels and, on the other hand, different psychological profiles at the intrasubjective level.

From a psychological perspective, religious diversity at the subjective level may not only be related to different types of personalities, as in James's pioneering work. Different types of religious attitudes and beliefs can also be traversed by a single individual successively in the course of one's life,[27] or may be present simultaneously as in the case of hybrid religious or multireligious identity. Especially the latter has currently attracted more attention in as much as it is a growing phenomenon in the West. In one of the best studies in this field, Rose Drew describes Buddhist-Christian dual belongers as individuals who often oscillate between two perspectives, derived from two religious traditions, and can therefore be seen as conducting an internalized spiritual dialogue. Thereby, as Drew notes, they "become microcosms of the dialogue as a whole."[28]

Another approach relevant to the subjective level comes from Rudolf Otto. Here the focus is not on the psychological dispositions but on the inbuilt structures of the human mind. According to Otto, both the different elements out of which the actual religions are composed and the parallel configurations of such elements as they can be observed in a huge number of different religions should best be explained by the "underlying congruent and common predisposition of humanity in general,"[29] which Otto understands as a disposition of the human mind in the sense of Kant's *transcendental* analysis. In his main work, *The Idea of the Holy*, Otto analyzes this transcendental disposition, the a priori cognition of the Holy, as a composition

---

[23]Ibid., 128. I have added the bracketed word.
[24]Ibid., 304–5.
[25]Ibid., 436–37.
[26]Ibid., 437.
[27]As researched by scholars including Lawrence Kohlberg, James Fowler, and Erik Erikson.
[28]Rose Drew, *Buddhist and Christian? An Exploration of Dual Belonging* (London: Routledge, 2011), 226.
[29]Rudolf Otto, *Vischnu-Nārāyana. Texte zur indischen Gottesmystik* (Jena: Eugen Diederichs, 1923), 217 (my translation).

of two main sets of components, rational and nonrational ones. According to Otto, the nonrational features are dominated by the two categories of the *tremendum* and the *fascinans*—that is, the repelling and the attracting aspects that the numinous assumes in religious experience—while the rational features comprise the two main ideas of absoluteness or perfection and of the moral good. The actual history of religions, with its vast diversity and its striking parallels, can then be understood as the gradual merger (*Ineinandertreten*) of these components—and all their subforms and side aspects—in ever-new combinations and varieties.[30] Thus, similar to James, who interpreted religious diversity as rooted in the psychological disposition of the human subject, Otto assumed that this diversity is, in its essential features, based in the transcendental structures of the human mind. Both approaches can be seen as complementary, and each of them assumes in its own way a correspondence of key structural patterns across the three levels of religious diversity as the fractal interpretation suggests.

In more recent years, Gerhard Oberhammer has taken up the project of a transcendental interpretation of religious diversity, which is also now currently pursued by Bernhard Nitsche.[31] Nitsche explores correspondences between theistic, monistic, and panentheistic concepts of transcendence and three fundamental modes of thinking or consciousness: I-Thou (sociomorph-theistic), I-It (cosmomorph-monistic), and I-Me (noomorph-panentheistic). As a working hypothesis, he suggests that "these basic dimensions of relating to transcendence are present in all large and complex religious systems, of course with different emphases and combinations of dominant and subdominant as well as with different priorities and interferences."[32] Again, this hypothesis indicates a fractal structure of religious diversity involving all three levels.

Finally, the exploration of the psychological and transcendental conditions giving room to both the diversity and fundamental patterns of religious life may be complemented by neurological research into religious experience. As Kenneth Rose and others have convincingly argued, there is no need to interpret the identification of neurological correlates of mental

---

[30]See Rudolf Otto, *The Idea of the Holy*, John W. Harvey, trans. (Oxford: Oxford University Press, 1936), esp. 116–20, 140–49. See also Fabian Völker, "On All-Embracing Mental Structures: Towards a Transcendental Hermeneutics of Religion," in *Interreligious Comparisons in Religious Studies and Theology. Comparison Revisited*, Perry Schmidt-Leukel and Andreas Nehring, eds. (London: Bloomsbury Academic, 2016), 142–60.

[31]Gerhard Oberhammer, *Versuch einer transzendentalen Hermeneutik religiöser Vielfalt* (Vienna: Publications of the De Nobili Research Library, 1987); Bernhard Nitsche, "Formen des menschlichen Transzendenzbezuges (1. Teil): Hypothese," in *Gott—jenseits von Monismus und Theismus?*, Bernhard Nitsche, Klaus von Stosch, and Muna Tatari, eds. (Paderborn: Schöningh, 2017), 25–61.

[32]Bernhard Nitsche, "God or the Divine" (unpublished working paper, 2016).

events as evidence for the illusory nature of all religious experience.[33] But, as one can learn from Rose's comparative research in different contemplative traditions, neuroscience can help to understand the interplay between cultural diversity and the nomothetic interest in universal conformity.[34] Such concern is well served by a fractal interpretation of religious diversity.

THE ANALYTIC AND METHODOLOGICAL VALUE OF A FRACTAL PERSPECTIVE

As indicated above, I understand a fractal perspective on religious diversity as a heuristic tool of significant analytic and methodological value.

1. *The cross-relationship between interreligious and intrareligious manifestations of religious diversity can only be analyzed by means of comparison.* A fractal interpretation therefore encourages *interreligious comparison* as indispensable in our academic efforts at understanding religious diversity.[35] It is thus directed against the various claims of a supposedly cultural and religious incommensurability. If incommensurability implies, as it usually does, the incomparability of radically distinct and closed homogeneous entities, a fractal interpretation of religious diversity assumes that religions are actually comparable precisely in—and because of—their internal diversity. Religions are internally so diverse that the other religion always contains some familiar features or elements. The other religion is therefore always different but, to quote Jerusha Tanner Lamptey, "never wholly other."[36] There can be partial or limited incommensurabilities, but they can only be identified on the basis of an overarching interreligious understanding as becomes possible by comparison and hence commensurability.

Yet what about the poststructuralist and postmodernist claim that any comparison inevitably violates the specific character of the individual phenomenon? An early and typical example of such criticism is Roland Barthes's mockery at the beginning of his famous essay "S/Z" (first published in 1970). He compares the structuralist agenda to the attempt at seeing a whole landscape in a bean by means of some obscure ascetic practice. The structuralist's efforts, the accusation goes, inevitably miss the unmistakable

---

[33]Kenneth Rose, *Yoga, Meditation, and Mysticism: Contemplative Universals and Meditative Landmarks* (London: Bloomsbury Academic, 2016); John Hick, *The New Frontier of Religion and Science: Religious Experience, Neuroscience, and the Transcendent* (Basingstoke: Palgrave Macmillan, 2006).

[34]See especially Rose, *Yoga*, 46–48.

[35]See Perry Schmidt-Leukel and Andres Nehring, eds., *Interreligious Comparisons in Religious Studies and Theology: Comparison Revisited* (London: Bloomsbury Academic, 2016).

[36]Jerusha Tanner Lamptey, *Never Wholly Other: A Muslima Theology of Religious Pluralism* (Oxford: Oxford University Press, 2014).

uniqueness of the particular.[37] But what if there are fractal structures? Then the idea of recognizing "a whole landscape in a bean" would no longer appear entirely absurd. The whole cauliflower can indeed be seen in the small floret, and the structure of the tall tree can be recognized in a little branch. A fractal view—especially if it merely presupposes a rough instead of strict self-similarity of the elements across the scales—is not forced to deny the specific nature of the individual phenomena, but it will put such specificity into the right perspective. We always need some similarity in order to identify what is different, and we need a fractal perspective in order to discern similar differences. The suggestion to look for fractal patterns in religious diversity is therefore also an encouragement to reestablish a structuralist research program although in a refined manner.

2. *A fractal interpretation of religious diversity rehabilitates the use of "religion" as a meaningful concept.* The extensive debates about "religion" as an analytic category[38] have revealed a dilemma between the concept's cognitive meaning and its applicability: The more the concept "religion" is loaded with particular meaning, the narrower is the range of its applicability; that is, if the concept is content-rich, it will fit only very few, culture- and epoch-specific phenomena. The broader its applicability across different cultures and epochs, however, the more the concept will become content-poor up to the point of becoming an empty shell.[39] This dilemma is avoided if "religion" is understood as a cluster concept comprising several components that appear across various cultures and epochs as part of similar patterns but in different forms, different combinations, and with different emphases,[40] as the fractal interpretation implies. Referring to some phenomena of a different culture as "religion" or "religious" expresses therefore the legitimate and meaningful expectation of finding a significant, though not strict, similarity to the diversity of phenomena—and their constellation—in one's "home religion."

3. *A fractal interpretation of religious diversity is of significant hermeneutical value* inasmuch as the discernment of specific fractal patterns will not only enhance the understanding of religious diversity as such but

---

[37]Roland Barthes, *S/Z* (Oxford: Blackwell), 3.

[38]See, e.g. Timothy Fitzgerald, *The Ideology of Religious Studies* (New York: Oxford University Press, 2000); Tomoko Masuzawa, *The Invention of World Religions: Or, How European Universalism Was Preserved in the Language of Pluralism* (Chicago: University of Chicago Press, 2005).

[39]Gregory Alles, "After the Naming Explosion: Joachim Wach's Unfinished Project," in *Hermeneutics, Politics, and the History of Religions: The Contested Legacies of Joachim Wach and Mircea Eliade*, Christian Wedemeyer and Wendy Doniger, eds. (Oxford: Oxford University Press, 2010), 51–78.

[40]Frank Whaling, *Christian Theology and World Religions: A Global Approach* (Basingstoke: Marshall Pickering, 1986); Ninian Smart, *Dimensions of the Sacred: An Anatomy of the World's Beliefs* (Berkeley: University of California Press, 1998).

also that of individual religious traditions. Building on the hermeneutically important insight that no religious tradition is homogeneous, a fractal
perspective moves further in suggesting that this internal diversity can be
better understood in the light of interreligious diversity and vice versa.
This point can be illustrated by the following two famous statements. In
1870 Max Müller, the well-known pioneer of comparative religion, noted,
"Whoever knows one [religion] knows none."[41] About three decades later,
German theologian Adolf von Harnack replied with the words, "Whoever
knows this religion [Christianity] knows them all."[42] While these two
statements appear to be, at first sight, irreconcilable, a fractal interpretation of religious diversity shows that, in a sense, both of them are correct.
The fractal structures that we can discern in religious diversity equal the
irregular forms of self-similarity as seen in coastlines. Some religions
are like large bays, others like fjords, and still others like spits. But if we
look at them more closely, we find that each comprises elements of all
three. The irregularity is one in terms of different emphases, different ar-
rangements, and different contexts. Thus Müller was right in arguing that
one needs to learn about many different religions in order to get a better
understanding of each one of them. And Harnack was also right in seeing
that what is found in other religions is also present, though in different
ways, in one's own religion, although he was wrong in assuming that this
is only true for Christianity.

   Taken together, the insights of Müller and Harnack demarcate the space
for what can be called "reciprocal illumination" between religions.[43] On
both sides—that is, in one's own and in the other religion—one may realize some correspondence between the otherness of the other religion and
the otherness of the other within one's own religious tradition who may
be neglected, suppressed, rejected, combated, and perhaps (often or at
times), insufficiently understood. Any religious or "theological" effort to
better understand and appreciate the diversity within one's own tradition
will then have an immediate impact on the attempt to make positive sense
of, and endorse, interreligious diversity—and, again, vice versa. From
a fractal perspective, the relationship between ecumenical theology and
interreligious theology is one of continuity, not discontinuity. This carries
the important promise of understanding that at least some contradictions

---

[41]Max Müller, *Einleitung in die vergleichende Religionswissenschaft* (Strassburg: Verlag von
Karl Trübner, 1874), 14.
   [42]Adolf von Harnack, "Die Aufgabe der theologischen Fakultäten und die allgemeine Reli-
gionsgeschichte (1901)," in Harnack, *Reden und Aufsätze*, vol. 2 (Gießen: Töppelmann, 1904),
159–87, 168.
   [43]Arvind Sharma, *Religious Studies and Comparative Methodology: The Case for Reciprocal
Illumination* (Albany: State University of New York Press, 2005).

within and between religions, which appear to be irreconcilable, may turn out as compatible and even enriching.

FRACTAL PATTERNS AND NORMATIVE PERSPECTIVES

The last thought necessitates a few remarks on the relationship between a fractal interpretation of religious diversity as a purely descriptive and analytic tool and its role within a *normative* religious or nonreligious *assessment* of religious diversity. In itself, the discernment of fractal patterns among religious diversity implies neither a religious nor a nonreligious stance. An atheist or naturalist who regards all religion as basically deceptive can view the fractal structures as patterns inherent to human illusion or fraud. But how may the discovery of fractal structures in religious diversity affect a religious interpretation of religious diversity?

To the religious exclusivist the discernment of fractal patterns in religious diversity constitutes a challenge regarding the recognition of parallels.[44] If such parallels relate to those features that the exclusivist assumes to be evidence of the unique possession of salvific truth in his tradition or subtradition, the exclusivist will have to deny the validity or genuineness of such parallels. Yet this challenge pertains to any significant parallels, regardless of whether they belong to fractal patterns or not.[45] Given that exclusivism tends to tie the knowledge or revelation of salvific truth not only to something unique but also to a narrowly defined complex of religious phenomena, exclusivists are generally not in favor of attesting religious value to religious diversity. In their case, the discernment of fractal patterns will not make any positive sense but can be regarded—as in the case of atheists—as part of human delusion. Yet it may perhaps puzzle the exclusivist that such exclusivist stances are themselves part of a fractal pattern, as has been neatly expressed by Wilfred Cantwell Smith when he remarked, "A claim to uniqueness is not unique."[46]

Inclusivists usually have no difficulties with the recognition of interreligious parallels, but they can accept religious diversity at best in a degraded sense. On inclusivist premises, the superior knowledge or revelation of

---

[44]See Alan Race, *Thinking about Religious Pluralism: Shaping Theology of Religions for Our Times* (Minneapolis: Fortress Press, 2015). On my own interpretation of the terms "exclusivism," "inclusivism," and "pluralism," see Perry Schmidt-Leukel, *God beyond Boundaries: A Christian and Pluralist Theology of Religions* (Muenster York: Waxman, 2017), 58–87.

[45]See on this Schmidt-Leukel, *God beyond Boundaries*, 111–15.

[46]Wilfred Cantwell Smith, "Idolatry in Comparative Perspective," in *The Myth of Christian Uniqueness: Toward a Pluralistic Theology of Religions*, John Hick and Paul F. Knitter, eds. (Maryknoll, NY: Orbis Books, 1987), 53–68, 64.

salvific truth is given only in a unique manifestation; otherwise inclusivism would turn into pluralism, which tries to combine difference/diversity
with equal validity.⁴⁷ Given that fractal patterns imply parallel forms of
diversity, inclusivists will tend to read these hierarchically: either in that
the diversity is regarded as composed of true and false elements, so that the
superior religion is strongest in the true and good components, or—if the
fractal pattern is seen as composed of only true and good components—the
inclusivist may assume that the most adequate or most balanced constellation of such elements is only found in one's own religion. This, by the way,
was the position of Rudolf Otto. He explicitly pondered the possibility that
different "types" of religions might be equally valid in terms of their truth
and salvific impact on the individual. But then he decided for the view that
in the end one religion, his own, would be superior to all others such as
"the firstborn to his brothers."⁴⁸

A religious pluralist will welcome religious diversity as the fertile ground
on which that kind of multireligious and interreligious discourse may flourish, which is the natural home of what I call "interreligious theology."⁴⁹
The discovery of fractal patterns offers a significant help to the project of
interreligious theology in that it provides a better understanding of the inner logic of religious diversity. This, however, does not imply that fractal
patterns would extend only to what may be regarded as true, good, and holy
among the religions. No one denies that the religions also contain what is
false, evil, and demonic—and this too may presumably appear in, or as
part of, fractal patterns.

But how do we account for the existence of fractal structures in religious
diversity? In general, they can be explained as the result of those anthropological conditions, including not only psychological, transcendental, or
neurophysiological aspects, but also all relevant sociocultural factors that
are operative in the formation of religious beliefs, values, institutions, and
practices. If there is a "fractal face" not only to nature but also to culture it
is not surprising to find that in religion as well. This explanation does not
exclude the possibility that such anthropological conditions shape, but also
permit, human insight into ultimate reality or the manifestation of the Ultimate in and through such insight. To what extent fractal structures within the
diversity of human religious experience may also reflect a diversity within
the Ultimate itself is open to discussion. John Cobb and Mark Heim—although in different ways—have argued in favor of such a possibility. But

⁴⁷See Schmidt-Leukel, *God beyond Boundaries*, 58–87; Schmidt-Leukel, *Religious Pluralism and Interreligious Theology*, 1–13.

⁴⁸Otto, *Vischnu-Nārāyana*, 222–23.

⁴⁹Schmidt-Leukel, *Religious Pluralism and Interreligious Theology*, 130–46.

one may also regard the informative value of the fractal patterns as confined to the diversity in the impact that the Ultimate has on human life instead of reading the latter as a mirror image of the divine reality itself.[50]

In sum, the sheer fact of fractal structures in religious diversity does not provide any conclusive evidence for one particular normative interpretation of religious diversity but is rather open to a wide range of normative reflection and assessment. Yet the fractal view is probably most illuminating within the context of interreligious theology, that is, within a theological development that can be regarded as the natural outcome of a pluralist position in the various religions' assessment of religious diversity.[51] Let me therefore conclude this overview by briefly sketching two examples of how the discernment of fractal patterns may serve as a basis for the constructive dimension of interreligious theological efforts.[52] The first example relates to Buddhist-Christian dialogue[53] and the second to Muslim-Christian-Buddhist trialogue.[54]

INTERRELIGIOUS THEOLOGY AND THE FRACTAL VIEW OF RELIGIOUS DIVERSITY: TWO EXAMPLES

Comparative studies have often described the difference between Buddhism and Christianity using categories such as *world-affirming* versus *world-renouncing spirituality*, *theistic* versus *nontheistic understanding* of ultimate reality, and the *estimation of the person* versus the *abnegation of the self*.[55] From a fractal perspective it can be shown without much difficulty that all three contrasts are also applicable to different manifestations within both traditions. Another contrast, which is related to the last of these three contradistinctions, characterizes Christianity as a religion of salvation by grace and Buddhism as a religion of salvation by one's own effort. Or, as has been stated fairly recently by Robert Magliola, "The irreducible difference between Buddhism and Catholic Christianity, as I see it, is that Buddhism is ultimately a 'self-help' (or 'self-power' or 'self-effort') religion and Catholic Christianity is ultimately an 'other-help' (or 'other-power') religion."[56]

---

[50]Ibid., 128–29, 144–46, 237–43.

[51]For pluralist approaches in the different religious traditions see ibid., 17–106.

[52]On the four methodological dimensions of interreligious theology (perspectival, imaginative, comparative, and constructive), see ibid., 139–46.

[53]A more detailed treatment will be found in Perry Schmidt-Leukel, *Buddhism and Christianity: A Fractal Interpretation of Their Relationship* (forthcoming).

[54]For a far more comprehensive treatment, see Schmidt-Leukel, *Religious Pluralism and Interreligious Theology*, 147–203.

[55]See also Schmidt-Leukel, *God beyond Boundaries*, 383–421.

[56]Robert Magliola, *Facing Up to Real Doctrinal Difference* (Kettering, OH: Angelico Press,

Again, it would be easy to show that both traditions include subtraditions that affirm the other half of the respective contrast. In Buddhism we find moderate and extreme forms of "other-help" teachings as much as there are moderate and extreme teachings of "self-help" within Christianity and also within "Catholic Christianity." Within the context of Buddhist-Christian interreligious theology the identification of this fractal pattern raises the questions of why both aspects are affirmed in both traditions and whether there might be a truth that gives legitimacy to both aspects, seeing them as pointing toward a more synthetic view.

A possible answer may be found in the view that the individual self needs to be liberated precisely from self-centeredness. Thus, on the one hand, it is oneself who needs liberation and therefore liberation has to be appropriated by oneself in order to materialize. This is the truth of "self-help." The truth of "other-help" is that the self is itself the central part of the problem. In order to prevent the necessary "self-help" from generating an even stronger affirmation of self-centeredness, the self needs to be liberated from itself. The dialectical tension between self-help and other-help leads to a para-doxical situation. "If you want to protect the self, you must not protect the self," as we read in the *Bodhicaryāvatāra* (8.173). Or as it is said in the Gospel of John (12:25), "Those who love their life lose it, and those who hate their life in this world will keep it for eternal life."

This paradoxical tension pushes toward a *synthesis*. This consists in introducing the concept of the *true* or *new self*, in which self-help and other-help both coalesce. That is, the true or new self participates in the ultimate reality, in the other-help from which the salvation or liberation of the ego-self originates, while at the same time the true or new self shares in the function of the ego-self inasmuch as it involves and engages the individual person who is in need of liberation. In Buddhism this synthesis is found in the concept of the originally pure or luminous mind and in its further development as the concept of Buddha-Nature. In Christianity an analogous synthesis can be seen in Paul's understanding of the Spirit (*pneuma*) or "Christ in us," so that Paul can say, "I died . . . so that I might live to God. I have been crucified with Christ; and it is no longer I who live, but it is Christ who lives in me" (Gal. 2:20). In both cases, the Christian and the Buddhist synthesis, the tension between self-help and other-help is retained and transcended.[57] The discovery of a fractal pattern—that is, the reappearance of the difference between self-help and other-help within

2014), 36.

[57]See also on this Paul Knitter, *Without Buddha I Could Not Be a Christian* (Oxford: Oneworld, 2009), 92–130; Paul Knitter and Roger Haight, *Jesus and Buddha: Friends in Conversation* (Maryknoll, NY: Orbis Books, 2015), 117–34.

both traditions—may thus foster a better and constructive understanding of this aspect of intra- and interreligious diversity.

A similar form of fractal coalescence can be observed in my second example. The three crucial religious epithets of the "Buddha"—the "Awakened One," the "Incarnate Son of God," and the "Prophet"—all contain elements of the other corresponding two.

- Gautama, under the Bodhi-Tree, *awakens* to the ultimate refuge from suffering, Nirvāṇa, and, out of compassion, *proclaims* the way he has found, thereby *embodying* Nirvāṇa and Dharma.
- Jesus, in his baptism in the waters of the Jordan and his subsequent retreat to the desert, *awakens* to the ultimate source of life, the Father, and experiences himself as commissioned by the Father to *proclaim* the good news of God's coming reign, to reflect and imitate the Father's mercy through his own life, and thereby *embodies* the eternal word of God.
- Muhammad, in the wilderness of the mountain, *awakens* to the ultimate unity of true reality, and out of divine commission *proclaims* God's oneness, justice, and mercy, thereby *embodying* both the eternal word of God in his message and the submission to God as the essence of all reality.

Becoming aware of this reciprocal inclusion of central doctrinal elements—and thus of a fractal structure in the relation between the three crucial categories of awakening, incarnation, and prophethood—allows and invites processes of mutual learning and reciprocal illumination. Through comparative or interreligious theology, Muslims may not only discover that, but also how and why, prophethood involves features of incarnation and of awakening. The prophet is someone in whom the word of God assumes an earthly incarnation in the form of the prophet's divine message. And even more so, a human being can become a divine prophet—without ceasing to be human—only if the potential or seed of being a prophet is somehow part of the human nature to which a human being awakens. The concept of a prophet-reality or "Muhammad-reality" in every human being, as we find it in some parts of the Muslim theological tradition, thus carries strong analogies to the understanding of "Buddha-Nature," as found in some parts of the Buddhist tradition.[58] Conversely, Buddhists might become better aware that buddhahood—and the proclamation of the Dharma—also includes the

---

[58]See Toshihiko Izutsu, *The Structure of Oriental Philosophy: Collected Papers of the Eranos Conference*, vol. 2 (Tokyo: Keio University Press, 2008), 170–71; Reza Shah-Kazemi, *Common Ground between Islam and Buddhism* (Louisville, KY: Fons Vitae, 2010), 59–60, 72.

quality of a prophetic voice and that the incarnational dimension of bud-dhahood may legitimately lead to personal expressions of the Ultimate as it actually often did in parts of the Buddhist tradition. Christians can recognize and appreciate the incarnational dimension of awakening and rediscover that, and how incarnational thinking is rooted in prophetic teaching and proclamation. Jesus can thus be seen as the one in whom the divine word assumed not just the form of a message but that of a whole life that itself became the message.

As much as self-help and other-help may turn out to be understood as different but legitimate aspects in the human attempt to understand the self's liberation from itself, the categories by which Buddhists confess Gautama as the Awakened One; Christians, Jesus as the Incarnate Son of God; and Muslims, Muhammad as the Prophet may turn out to be seen as different but legitimate aspects in the human attempt to understand the presence and mediation of ultimate reality in and through exemplary and formative figures of humankind's religious history. A fractal perspective on religious diversity fosters an interreligious theological inquiry that tries to make sense of the differences between and within the religions. It invites constructive reflection on the possibly complementary and hence legitimate nature of at least some such differences. It thereby carries the promise of shedding new light on significant facets of religious diversity as such.

PART TWO

METHODOLOGICAL/CONTEXTUAL PERSPECTIVES

Perry Schmidt-Leukel's Incarnated Prophets and Awakeners

Beyond Stalemates in the Theology of Religions and Comparative Theology

---

Kenneth Rose

TOWARD A PLURALIST, COMPARATIVE, AND SCIENTIFIC PHILOSOPHY AND THEOLOGY OF RELIGIONS

The lineage of contemporary pluralist theologians can be traced directly to influential comparativist Wilfred Cantwell Smith. John Hick, the leading pluralist theologian and philosopher of religions in the twentieth century, explicitly dated his own pluralist awakening to his reading of Smith's iconic text *The Meaning and End of Religion*,[1] which appeared in 1962. This pluralist awakening likely deepened when Hick heard the Cadbury Lectures that Smith gave at Hick's invitation in Birmingham in 1971. Hick then ignited the pluralist revolution with his epochal lecture "A Copernican Revolution in Theology," which was one of the public lectures delivered at the Carrs Lane Church Centre in Birmingham, England, in February and March 1972.[2] Hick issued a summons that banished the Barthian missiology of Hendrik Kraemer, whose exclusivist view of the world's religions, expressed forcefully and influentially at the International Missionary Council conference at Tambaram in 1938, still cast a long, if fading, shadow over theology.

The pluralist revolution spread into the mainstream of theology in 1987

---

[1] In *God Has Many Names* (Philadelphia: Westminster Press, 1982), 18, John Hick recounts that reading Smith's *Meaning and End of Religion* led him to question the idea that there is one true religion.

[2] Published in John Hick, *God and the Universe of Faiths* (New York: Macmillan, 1973), 120–32.

when Hick and Paul Knitter published conference papers under the startling title *The Myth of Christian Uniqueness: Toward a Pluralistic Theology of Religions* (Orbis Books, 1987). The "Rubicon Conference," as this conference was known in the then nascent field of the theology of religions, both challenged and shocked Christian theologians around the globe because, apparently for the first time in the history of Christianity, leading theologians pushed across the metaphorical Rubicon of Christian theology by proclaiming that the religions of the world should no longer be seen as revolving around Christianity. Although Hick articulated a comprehensive philosophical basis for religious pluralism in his Gifford Lectures of 1986–1987 (which appeared as *An Interpretation of Religion: Human Responses to the Transcendent*, Yale University Press, 1989), the pushback against pluralism became so intense among many theologians of religions in the coming decade that inclusivist theologies became standard for many theologians of religions by the late 1990s. But in the last few years, pluralism has begun once again to rise. This can be seen in recent publications from prominent pluralists such as Paul Knitter, Alan Race, Leonard Swidler, and Roger Haight, and in my *Pluralism: The Future of Religion* (Bloomsbury, 2013). And now, with German theologian Perry Schmidt-Leukel's 2015 Gifford Lectures, pluralism has once again begun to emerge as an unavoidable standpoint from which to evaluate the diverse heritage of human religiosity and spirituality.[3]

Alongside the revolutionary pluralist response to global religious diversity, there has been in recent years a remarkable—and, from the perspective of the old religious studies paradigm, unanticipated—revival of comparative theology. Since its last great efflorescence in the heady times of the Edinburgh World Missionary Conference in 1910 and after the fatal blow dealt it by Kraemer at Tambaram in 1938, comparative theology—even as carried on through Kraemer's understanding of the missionary as a religious artist who creatively uses the data of other religions to find points of contact between them and Christianity's exclusively true and saving Christian gospel[4]—had gone silent in Christian theology, while it never appeared on the agenda of religious studies. Although this revival was foreshadowed in David Tracy's 1987 essay on comparative theology in the *Encyclopedia of Religion*,[5] the resurrection of this long-moribund field can be traced, without

---

[3]In *Religious Pluralism and Interreligious Theology: The Gifford Lectures—An Extended Version* (Maryknoll, NY: Orbis Books, 2017), 19, Perry Schmidt-Leukel names many of the recent Christian pluralist theologians, virtually all of whom began their careers as exclusivists or inclusivists.

[4]Hendrik Kraemer, *The Christian Message in a Non-Christian World*, 2nd ed. (New York: International Missionary Council, 1947), 139–40; see also Kenneth Rose, *Pluralism: The Future of Religion* (New York: Bloomsbury, 2013), 67.

[5]David Tracy, "Theology: Comparative Theology," *Encyclopedia of Religion*, vol. 14, Mircea

controversy I think, to Francis X. Clooney's 1993 paradigm-shifting *Theology after Vedānta* (SUNY, 1993).[6] This revival was fortified by Clooney's 1995 essay "Comparative Theology,"[7] which Paul Hedges claims marks "the emergence of the contemporary discipline and practice of comparative theology onto the academic stage."[8] And then, in Hedges's view, "[a] further step was taken in 2006 when Clooney introduced the Comparative Theology Group at the American Academy of Religion, while the *Oxford Handbook of Systematic Theology* includes [Clooney's] chapter on comparative theology marking its recognition in wider theological reflections."[9] Clooney's chapter can be seen as situating his own comparative theological efforts within a stream of missionary theologians that looks back to European colonies in early seventeenth-, eighteenth-, and twentieth-century India and discovers, as Clooney writes, "in missionary writings a glimpse of the pre-history of comparative theology."[10] Except for a mention of David B. Burrell's *Knowing the Unknowable God* (University of Notre Dame Press, 1986), the other contemporary forays into comparative theology that Clooney references postdate his own *Theology after Vedānta*, a fact that clearly underscores his role as the restorer of comparative theology.[11]

This new comparative theology marked a real advance over the old comparative theologies, which were heavily Christocentric and often verged on a now indefensible replacement theology. As practiced by Clooney, this new approach fruitfully stresses the genial activity of interreligious learning while bypassing the theology of religion's triadic typology of exclusivism, inclusivism, and pluralism. Yet, as the implicit inclusivism of many of

---

Eliade, ed. (New York: Macmillan, 1987), 446–55.

[6]Tracy's essay falls within the outlook of the "old" comparative theology that operates, implicitly at least, within the framework of the tripolar typology of the theology of religions proposed by Alan Race, *Christians and Religious Pluralism: Patterns in the Christian Theology of Religions* (Maryknoll, NY: Orbis Books, 1982), 7 and throughout, while Clooney's approach marks the beginning of the "new" comparative theology that does not sense the need to engage with this typology; see Rose, *Pluralism*, 10–11. See also Reid B. Locklin and Hugh Nicholson, "The Return of Comparative Theology," *Journal of the American Academy of Religion* 78 (2010): 477–514; see also Kristin Beise Kiblinger, "Relating Theology of Religions and Comparative Theology," in *The New Comparative Theology: Interreligious Insights from the Next Generation*, Francis X. Clooney, ed. (New York: T&T Clark, 2010), 21–42.

[7]Francis X. Clooney, "Comparative Theology: A Review of Recent Books (1989–1995)," *Theological Studies* 56 (1995): 521–50.

[8]Paul Hedges, *Comparative Theology: A Critical and Methodological Perspective* (Leiden: Brill, 2017), 2.

[9]Ibid.

[10]Clooney, "Comparative Theology," in *Oxford Handbook of Systematic Theology*, John Bainbridge Webster, John Webster, Kathryn Tanner, and Iain Torrance, eds. (Oxford: Oxford University Press, 2007), 656; see also Francis X. Clooney, review of *Synthesizing the Vedānta: The Theology of Pierre Johanns, S.J.*, in *Theological Studies* 68 (2007): 934–36.

[11]I briefly trace the modern history of comparative theology in Rose, *Pluralism*, 45–63.

the new comparative theological projects has become apparent, a new approach, known as *interreligious theology*, is emerging that is forthrightly and methodologically pluralistic. Perry Schmidt-Leukel, a leading proponent and practitioner of this new approach is thus, along with Hick, part of a lineage that can be traced back to Smith,[12] whose pluralist reflections on global theology in his *Towards a World Theology* were generations ahead of their time and are only now beginning to find a wider audience.[13]

Just as forward-looking as Smith's religious pluralism was his view that a new link needs to be forged between the comparative study of religion—which was soon to find itself under assault by the rise in the late 1970s of Katzian constructivism—and the lived practice of religion and spirituality.[14] Today, this is beginning to occur as a new comparative approach to religion takes flight in religious studies. Taking its first steps almost two decades ago in Kimberley C. Patton and Benjamin C. Ray's *A Magic Still Dwells: Comparative Religion in the Postmodern Age* (University of California Press, 2000), it has recently begun to reclaim the territory once dominated by religious studies scholars like Mircea Eliade, Joachim Wach, and Joseph Kitagawa, who also created an audience for religious studies well beyond the academy. We can see this revival extending itself in the essays gathered together in the recent volume edited by Perry Schmidt-Leukel and Andreas Nehring, *Interreligious Comparisons in Religious Studies and Theology: Comparison Revisited.*[15]

For the first time in generations, a new wave of scholars is seeking to find ways to reconnect the study of religion to comparative methodologies. These scholars are also beginning to assume the old vocation of the comparative religionist in daring to suggest that the religions contain teachings and practices that can contribute to the search for meaning, the cessation of religious conflicts, and the cultivation of personal and societal well-being. This is a move beyond the strict methodological boundaries of classical religious studies, and a return to territory occupied by theology. Yet comparative theology need not be allied with the inclusivist or exclusivistic stances of any religious tradition. In the sense foreshadowed by Smith, comparative theology can also be a global comparative theology, one that takes its data from, in principle at least, all religious traditions. Such a global comparative

---

[12]Schmidt-Leukel, *Religious Pluralism and Interreligious Theology*, 114–19.

[13]Wilfred Cantwell Smith, *Towards a World Theology: Faith and the Comparative History of Religion* (Philadelphia: Westminster, 1981). This book was based on Smith's 1971 Cadbury Lectures.

[14]Smith, *Towards a World Theology*, 124, 151.

[15]I also have a chapter in this volume: Kenneth Rose, "The Singular and the Shared: Making Amends with Eliade after the Dismissal of the Sacred," in *Interreligious Comparisons in Religious Studies and Theology: Comparison Revisited*, Perry Schmidt-Leukel and Andreas Nehring, eds. (London: Bloomsbury, 2016), 110–29.

theology will serve the project of human and planetary flourishing rather than exclusively subordinating itself to any particular religious tradition.

A hopeful sign that just such a global comparative theology is possible is the burgeoning Theology without Walls movement that is growing among leading religious thinkers and theologians from multiple religious traditions. This movement was inspired by Jerry Martin, an agnostic philosopher who experienced a theistic awakening, which led him to engage in a transreligious quest that looks for religious and theological truths wherever they are available instead of attempting to contain religious truth within the limiting walls of individual religious traditions.[16] This project gives practical and theoretical expression to Wilfred Cantwell Smith's early call for a world theology that takes its start from, in principle, all religious traditions.

But this is not all that is new and exciting in the worlds of the academic study of religion and theology. Comparative theology, interreligious theology, and intercultural philosophy are turning increasingly toward the new sciences of religion for insight and collaborators, as I outlined in my recent book *Yoga, Meditation, and Mysticism.*[17] The evolutionary cognitive science of religion (ECSR) and contemplative neurobiology are helping scholars to see religion as grounded in the cognitive and biological capacities of human beings. Spirituality is coming to be seen as just as much a biological trait as language.[18] As this new mood awakens in academic religious studies and theology, I am emboldened to look for theological and philosophical resources as much in the sciences and mathematics as in traditional fieldwork and language study. We also see this energetic and highly promising new tendency in the recent writings of Perry Schmidt-Leukel on interreligious theology, who, as we will see, has turned to science and mathematics for theoretical models and insights.

INTERRELIGIOUS PLURALISM
AND THE FRACTAL SON, PROPHET, AND BUDDHA

The key organizing principle of interreligious pluralist theologian Perry Schmidt-Leukel's recent Gifford Lectures is the claim, inspired by the fractal theory of Benoît Mandelbrot, that the central categories distinguish-

---

[16]See *Journal of Ecumenical Studies* 51 (2016), which is dedicated to the Theology without Walls movement, http://dialogueinstitute.org/jes-volume51/, and the special issue of *Open Theology* 2 (2016), which also is dedicated to this movement, http://www.degruyter.com/view/j/opth.2016.2.issue-1/issue-files/opth.2016.2.issue-1.xml.

[17]Kenneth Rose, *Yoga, Meditation, and Mysticism: Religious Universals and Contemplative Landmarks* (New York: Bloomsbury Academic, 2016).

[18]Ibid., 43.

ing one religion from another at higher levels of scale recur at lower levels of scale within each religion. Taking fractal theory as his starting point, Schmidt-Leukel explores the categories of "the Son," "the Prophet," and "the Buddha," which stand for the ideas of incarnation, prophetic ministry, and awakening, and notes that these ideas mutually recur in enriching and suggestive ways within each of the traditions that, on their own, focus, more or less exclusively, on one of these three distinctive categories. Through close cross-traditional, textual explorations and interreligious dialogical encounters, Schmidt-Leukel shows that the Son, the Prophet, and the Buddha occur not merely as the central metaphor or image of their respective traditions, but that each of these images recur within each tradition as well. Thus, the incarnated one is also fractally a prophet and an awakener, the prophet fractally incarnates the highest truth as a force for awakening, and the awakener fractally incarnates the truth that is proclaimed. By showing that the central metaphor or image of one's own tradition can be found as fractally present within other religions, "the religious stranger," suggests Schmidt-Leukel, "turns out to be less strange than initially assumed."[19]

Schmidt-Leukel has developed his fractal interpretation of religious diversity through extensive dialogue with the theologians of religions, pluralist theologians, and intercultural philosophers who, in the last half-century, have urged religious traditions to move beyond particularist (*particularism* is a general category that I use to include both the weak particularism of inclusivism and the strong particularism of exclusivism) ways of conceptualizing and protecting their home religious traditions. His fractal theory of religious diversity is a major constructive proposal that significantly furthers the pluralist project and leads me to see him as the natural heir to the great pluralist trajectory initiated by Wilfred Cantwell Smith, John Hick, and Paul Knitter.

BUT ISN'T PLURALISM RELATIVISTIC?

Schmidt-Leukel's fractal theory is a notable step forward for the theory of interreligious pluralism, which I take as the only ethically sound basis for the academic study of religion. Yet resistance to interreligious pluralism is likely to remain strong in religious studies and theology. One familiar charge against the interreligious pluralism of Schmidt-Leukel that is likely to be repeated by antipluralists is the familiar claim that merely making the pluralist claim turns the pluralist into an exclusivist because the pluralist claim—like any other claim—exclusivistically excludes its negation. The

---

[19]Schmidt-Leukel, *Religious Pluralism and Interreligious Theology*, 243.

point of this sterile logical ploy of suggesting that the pluralist is in fact a crypto-exclusivist is to nip the pluralist impulse in the bud with what seems to be a bit of derisive laughter. But we can easily turn this turnabout around once again by pointing out that making this exclusivist claim about pluralism makes the exclusivist an exclusivist twice over because it exclusivistically excludes its own negation!

Another serious charge against pluralism is that it leads inevitably to the relativistic claim that all religions are true, since it is generally assumed that the pluralist must simply accept all competing religious claims as true to avoid becoming once again an exclusivist or an inclusivist. The pluralist, apparently left with no principled place to stand, seems to be obliged to concede the equal truthfulness of all views, religious and antireligious, in order to avoid taking a stand that would lead to the error of crypto-exclusivism.

One way to unlink pluralism from relativism is for the pluralist to reject the claim that all religions are equally true. Schmidt-Leukel does this by calling upon the practice within Hinduism of "grading of the different paths [within Hinduism] according to different needs."[20] This move calls to mind John Hick's influential essay "On Grading Religions," where Hick observed that "if we think for a moment of the entire range of religious phenomena, no one is going to maintain that they are all on the same level of value or validity."[21] Because Hick wasn't confident of success in grading religions, at least from the human perspective, he concludes his essay by suggesting,

> whilst we can assess religious phenomena, we cannot assess and grade religious traditions as totalities. For each of these long traditions is so internally diverse, containing so many different kinds of both good and evil, that it is impossible for human judgement to weigh up and compare their merits as systems of salvation. It may be that one facilitates human liberation/salvation more than the others; but if so this is not evident to human vision. As far as we can tell, they are equally productive of that transition from self to Reality which we see in the saints of all traditions.[22]

But Schmidt-Leukel is less ambivalent than Hick on the usefulness of the grading-religions approach in leading pluralism out of the dead end of relativism.[23] Following up on suggestions made by Hindu religious philosophers such as V. Raghavan, Arvind Sharma, Wilhelm Halbfass, Anantanand

---

[20]Ibid., 4, 59–60.

[21]John Hick, "On Grading Religions," *Religious Studies* 17 (December 1981): 451; http://www.jstor.org/stable/20005778.

[22]Ibid., 467.

[23]Schmidt-Leukel, *Religious Pluralism and Interreligious Theology*, 70.

Rambachan, and Jeffery Long,[24] Schmidt-Leukel explores the Hindu idea of *adhikāra-bheda* (or "difference in the capacities"),[25] which views different religious traditions as expressing varying degrees of what Schmidt-Leukel sees as "spiritual maturation," expressed diversely "by different states of insight and accompanied by different levels of truths."[26] Rather than attempting the more difficult and perhaps even impossible task of grading whole religious traditions on a scale of maturity, he follows Long and Rambachan in what he calls their "new and constructive twist"[27] of applying the notion of *adhikāra-bheda* within the traditions.[28] Thus, where one religion displays maturity in one of its phases, another religious tradition displays maturity in a different phase. This fractal insight suggests that all of the goods of the various religions are available, at least implicitly and in varying degrees of development, in each religious tradition, waiting only for the challenge of interreligious interactions to stimulate them into actuality.

This original refutation of relativism turns upon Schmidt-Leukel's fractal insight that the characteristic religious patterns, as discerned by comparative religion and theology, are both *recursive*, because they repeat themselves over and over again in the world's religious traditions, and *scale invariant*, because they are enacted between the religions, within each religion, and in the life of each person who participates in any one of these traditions.[29] In other words, a basic and repetitive shape or form marks religions *as religion* wherever it is expressed, just as music can be identified as music despite the many forms that it has taken over time.[30] Or, as Schmidt-Leukel writes while exploring the fractal potential of the theories of Joachim Wach, Mircea Eliade, Friedrich Heiler, Gerardus van der Leeuw, W. Brede Kristensen, Julia Ching, and Elmar Holenstein, "It becomes increasingly clearer that almost no specific features or clusters of features are exclusively present in just one religion while being totally absent from another one."[31] And this: "Thus almost everything that is found in one of the major religious traditions seems to appear in some way or another in other religions as well."[32]

Here is where Schmidt-Leukel's fractal theory connects with comparative religion and comparative theology and also evades the charge of relativism. If religion has a typical form or shape, which comparative study aided

---

[24]Ibid., 60–64, 69–70.
[25]Ibid., 70.
[26]Ibid.
[27]Ibid.
[28]Ibid.
[29]Ibid., 223–45.
[30]Rose, *Yoga, Meditation, and Mysticism*, 39–46.
[31]Schmidt-Leukel, *Religious Pluralism and Interreligious Theology*, 229.
[32]Ibid.

by contemplative neuroscience uncovers, then we can accept as a religion any cultural formation that expresses this form or pattern. The presence of this form or pattern also clearly distinguishes religious from nonreligious cultural formations, such as governments, universities, corporations, and so on. And, by ranging over the whole expanse of religious experiences and practices, which appear in varying degrees of realization in the many religious traditions, we can develop a theory of what counts as *adhikāra-bheda* or religious maturity. This leaves the issue of who gets to determine what counts as *adhikāra-bheda* or religious maturity still to be resolved, but that is a different issue than the charge of relativism, with which we began.

Besides its usefulness in undercutting the claim that pluralism leads to relativism, this fractal outcome also has the advantage of suggesting that because the set of attributes explicit in one religious tradition will differ from the set of attributes explicit in another religious tradition, the encounter between two or more religions can awaken cross-religious attraction. This can, in turn, lead to the full-blown contemporary phenomenon of multiple religious belonging or, more modestly, to greater openness to religious and spiritual insights that expand or challenge one's original religious perspective. Expanding upon what Schmidt-Leukel calls "a thrilling insight"[33] of Jewish pluralist Ephraim Meir that "trans-difference creates an 'open' identity that has otherness in itself,"[34] Schmidt-Leukel takes this openness of human identity to the otherness of other religions as the ground of a relatedness that allows for interreligious learning and exchange.[35] So, instead of merely finding our own truths mirrored back to us in interreligious interactions, as does the inclusivist, or seeing other traditions as merely and only other, as does the exclusivist, we open ourselves to the exchange of meaning and practice between the openhearted and open-minded participants in such exchanges. Thus, Alon Goshen-Gottstein can discover in the religions of India a "vivid tradition of how to cultivate an awareness of God's presence."[36] Thich Nhat Hanh can find in Jesus a model of forgiveness.[37] Zalman Schacter-Shalomi can affirm that Buddhism helped him in his study and practice of Jewish texts.[38] And Bhikkhu Buddhadāsa could hold that even "the few pages of the Sermon on the Mount" are "far more than enough and complete for practice to attain emancipation," with the

---

[33]Ibid., 40.

[34]Ephraim Meir, *Dialogical Thought and Identity: Trans-Different Religiosity in Present-Day Societies* (Berlin: DeGruyter; Jerusalem: Magnes Press, 2015), 160, quoted in Schmidt-Leukel, *Religious Pluralism and Interreligious Theology*, 40.

[35]Ibid., 40–41.

[36]Ibid., 41.

[37]Ibid., 184.

[38]Ibid., 41.

result that, according to Schmidt-Leukel, "Buddhadāsa referred to Jesus as a Buddha."[39]

Thus, it seems that, metaphysically speaking, the full potential of religion *as religion* is present to all historically and culturally produced religious traditions, while on the human and social side, each tradition can express but a finite range of the available religious goods. And so, this allows for many religions to be true without relativism and allows for real learning to occur without endorsing claims of inferiority and superiority. Perhaps more so even than the perichoretic structure of religion theorized by Raimon Panikkar and mentioned by Schmidt-Leukel,[40] Schmidt-Leukel's fractal approach uncovers the hidden relatedness that secretly relates all religions as channels, sacraments, or bearers in their diverse ways of the full plenitude of being. Schmidt-Leukel's fractal interpretation of religious diversity is thus one of the most promising theoretical attempts to date to ground interreligious learning in a formative principle that can plausibly be seen as informing each of the religious traditions it seeks to understand. It thus deserves attention from all scholars and practitioners of religion who are inspired by the universal principles of philosophy and religion.

OVERCOMING NONENGAGEMENT: THE LAST OBSTACLE TO PLURALISM

When the charge that interreligious pluralism is relativistic has been turned aside as meritless, particularist resistance to pluralism takes a new tack in what I see as its last stand. This is the stance of firmly committed particularists who categorically reject Alan Race's tripolar typology of the theology of religions, which sorts the various responses to religious diversity into the three now standard categories of exclusivism, inclusivism, and pluralism, and which was expanded by Schmidt-Leukel with the fourth category of naturalism.[41] Although the typology is a logically elegant tool useful for measuring the interreligious stance of any religious tradition and secular ideology by applying four comprehensive options, some particularists oppose it as irrelevant or even pointless theorizing that has

---

[39]Ibid., 81.

[40]Ibid., 22.

[41]Naturalism is the fourth category added by Schmidt-Leukel, *Religious Pluralism and Interreligious Theology*, 3, to the classic tripolar typology proposed by Alan Race in *Christians and Religious Pluralism*, 7; see also Perry Schmidt-Leukel, "Exclusivism, Inclusivism, Pluralism: The Tripolar Typology—Clarified and Reaffirmed," in *The Myth of Religious Superiority: A Multifaith Exploration*, John Hick and Paul F. Knitter, eds. (Maryknoll, NY: Orbis Books, 2005), 13–27, where he cogently analyzes the logic of the classic typology.

nothing (the stance of the exclusivist) or little (the stance of the inclusivist) to do with religious practices and beliefs. Implicit in this opposition is the inalterable conviction of these particularists that their religious tradition is simply the ultimate or only standpoint from which to view these matters. No appeal against this finality and normativity from any other religious tradition or from the standpoint of interreligious theology or philosophy, whether couched rationally, dogmatically, or scripturally, has standing or force for these particularists. At the end of the day, they see themselves as standing on their immovable religious foundation, whose truth remains the case whether it can be justified or not. Schmidt-Leukel envisions such resistance to his theology of religions, which he sees as "a refusal to answer—or even to seriously deal with—the question that religious diversity inevitably poses."[42] I think that this policy of nonengagement lurks behind much of the deeply felt resistance to pluralism among theologians who steadfastly oppose the essential and unavoidable analytical work of the theology of religions.

There is, I think, a compelling counterargument to the policy of non-engagement: one might ask, given competing particularisms, which one among the many particularisms—if any—is the true particularism? While the particularist theologian adhering to a policy of nonengagement will not be moved by this counterargument, those committed to a search for truth and who are not merely looking for a reaffirmation of their predetermined theological commitments will see the flaw here. They will recognize that standing firm on the view that one's own tradition is the final or normative tradition is a possible move in *all* religious traditions. One can take one's stand for the ultimacy of any set of religious beliefs, which is a relativistic insight that should unsettle anyone who makes such a claim. Unless a particularist can also be certain of the finality of their position in face of the contradiction implied by the scandal of competing particularisms, they risk choosing the wrong particularism. At best, they will need to be good guessers if they are going to choose the right one. At worst, they will be thrown back upon the conflicting evidences and assurances offered by the various particularisms.

This latter course is not likely to yield a resolution, since the sorts of evidences and assurances that one particularist offers are oddly similar to the sort of evidences and assurances that another particularist offers—which is also a fractal insight that lends further support to Schmidt-Leukel's fractal interpretation of religious diversity. We have interior certitude; they have interior certitude. We have apologists; they have apologists. They have powerful saints; we have powerful saints. They have revealed or inspired truth; we have revealed or inspired truth. They have scripture; we have

---

[42]Schmidt-Leukel, *Religious Pluralism and Interreligious Theology*, 5.

scripture. Nothing like Pascal's wager can help us here, since the choice isn't between a spiritual and a materialistic view of life, but between divergent spiritualities that offer compelling but contrary evidences and assurances. Compelling as each one may be on its own, none of them offers the only path to overcoming the temporal limitations of human experience. None of them is able to stand outside of time and space offering the proverbial view from nowhere, where, standing with what is ultimate, it could directly prove that it is the one religion that, as seen from the divine side of reality, is in fact final and normative for all of humanity.

Whether one engages theology of religions or not is a personal choice, but some sort of ultimate state of affairs as ideally analyzed by theology of religions must in fact be the case—even if our grasp of that ultimate state of affairs is necessarily finite. We can live and think without having metaphysical views, but we cannot exist unless some metaphysical situation is in fact the case. So, whether we choose to engage in theology of religions or not, some option within a theoretically complete form of the theology of religions is in fact the case, whether we can determine what it is or not. Rather than a counsel of despair, confronting this aporia means that we can always retain the freedom to choose our path on these matters. We can take the path of naturalism, a stance that deeper engagement with the sciences of consciousness and the evolutionary cognitive science of religion may make more attractive for some. We can take the option of particularism, with its weaker expression as inclusivism and its stronger expression as exclusivism. We can also choose nonengagement, but with the unwanted result that we must inexorably leave behind any academic, theological, or scientific theorizing that does not repeat verbatim and without change the self-regarding claims of our tradition. (In my view, nonengagement, even more so than particularism in its weaker and stronger forms, leads to religious hostilities, if prolonged sufficiently beyond our polite academic settings.) Or we can move toward an interreligious pluralism that no longer responds to the religious other either as one speaking nothing of significance, as with the exclusivist, or as one speaking our own language imperfectly, as with the inclusivist. For me, at least, it seems that pluralism is the only ethical basis for the academic and theological study of religion, since it embraces the whole life of humanity in all its philosophical, theological, religious, and cultural diversity without intentionally privileging any perspective. It gladly takes insights and methods from all sides and it changes course just as soon as it sees that it has fallen into the primal failing of absolutizing one's own standpoint.

While it is unlikely that those who practice nonengagement will accept the philosophical implications of Schmidt-Leukel's fractal theory of religious diversity, this theory offers significant support for interreligious pluralism by providing evidence for the view that what makes a religion *religious* is not its confessional or cultural credentials, but that, insofar as it is *religious*, it is an expression in fractally similar forms in each religious tradition and in the experience of each religious person of the universal types or patterns of religion. This recognition of the identity of religious teachings and themes when fractally expressed in the world's religions provides sufficient warrant for my claim that the stance of interreligious pluralism is more adequate than any form of particularism in accounting for religious diversity in an ethical and philosophically adequate manner.

FRACTAL RELIGION IS PLURALISTIC RELIGION: TOWARD A FRACTAL WORLD THEOLOGY AND INTERCULTURAL PHILOSOPHY OF RELIGIONS

Besides creating a new area of study in interreligious scholarly study—fractal comparisons—Schmidt-Leukel's theory also moves boldly beyond the fields of the theology of religions, comparative theology, and comparative religion by pursuing a global interreligious and intercultural theology. This theology, informed by careful study and groundedness in the world's religious traditions, charts the contours of an intercultural theology and philosophy that is sensitive to the spiritual core of life and being. This sensitivity, which naturally calls forth pluralist responses such as Schmidt-Leukel's fractal interpretation of religions, cannot begin from the theological materials of just one or two religious traditions but must, as suggested over a generation ago by Wilfred Cantwell Smith in *Towards a World Theology*, range over many traditions in order to discern the theological and religious truths that inspire all theological and religious thought whenever it arises. This call is taken up once again boldly and confidently by Schmidt-Leukel:

> I dare to prognosticate that theology, instead of being an essentially denominational enterprise, will become increasingly interreligious. In the future it will also draw on other religions when reflecting on major questions of human life and will reconsider, and further develop, the answers that have been given in one's own tradition in a fresh comparative light. It will also reflect on one's own tradition in order to see what possible contribution might be made to the issues on the agenda of a global interreligious theological inquiry.[43]

A fractal interreligious theology and intercultural philosophy will thus move beyond the views of individual traditions in isolation from each

---

[43]Ibid., 8.

other in order to discover in their own individual and unique ways what Schmidt-Leukel sees as the "larger overarching religious reality, of which they represent equally valid components."[44] Thanks to Schmidt-Leukel, those of us who stand in the lineage of Wilfred Cantwell Smith and John Hick now have a new opportunity to reanimate the pluralistic quest in order to uncover the general conditions that sponsor the rise of religions in virtually all human cultures by pursuing the study of religion with a broadness of vision and methodological exploration that has escaped us in recent centuries. Were the fields of the academic study of religions and religion to be renewed along these lines, we would be able to bring together scholars and practitioners from multiple religious traditions and multiple humanistic and social-scientific disciplines as well as natural scientists committed to the comparative and scientific exploration of religion and spirituality.

Religious studies can become a thriving community where leading pluralist theologians, intercultural philosophers, contemplative neurobiologists, and comparative religionists might come together to generate the research and practice programs in which the comparative and pluralistic study of religions may once again make major contributions in the quest for religious peace on our globe, the replacement of the dominant hypercapitalist economic model with more humane ways of organizing our economic and social life, and the overcoming of the fateful but not inevitable split between the resources of human spirituality and the methods of the sciences.

In short, the time is coming when the comparative and scientific study of religion and theology may once again aid human beings in their quest for an integral view of life, one in which personal, social, aesthetic, ethical, psychological, philosophical, and spiritual meanings are discovered and applied to the enriching of our common life together as inhabitants of this planet. But for this we will need to reconceive the totality of human religiosity along pluralist lines. And for this, Perry Schmidt-Leukel's fractal interpretation of religious diversity can serve as a sturdy foundation.

---

[44]Ibid., 112.

Fractal Theory, Fractal Practice: Theology of Religions, Comparative Theology

Francis X. Clooney, SJ

Religious Pluralism and Interreligious Theology—lectures given in China in 2014, and the Gifford Lectures given in 2015—is a fine consolidation of Perry Schmidt-Leukel's broad and thoughtful thinking about pluralism over many decades, freshened up by insight into how fractals help us visualize the pluralism within which we live. Schmidt-Leukel, by his own admission somewhat belatedly, finds fractal theory friendly to his understanding of pluralism. As he states in his introduction for the present volume,

> In this chapter I would like to briefly introduce a new theory on reli-
> gious diversity. I call it a "fractal interpretation" because the theory
> claims that religious diversity displays a fractal structure. . . . As far
> as my own intellectual development is concerned, I now realize that
> I was "pregnant" with it for something like three decades—an unusu-
> ally long pregnancy, I have to admit. It was only in 2015, when I was
> preparing my Gifford Lectures, that the theory was born. In the middle
> of the night, round about 3 a.m. or so, labor set in. I woke up, went
> to my desk and sketched on one or two sheets of paper how religious
> diversity might be best understood along the lines of fractal structures.

That is, fractal theory and practice help us to see the mirroring of exterior and interior resemblances and differences: "The nucleus of the theory is that the diversity that we observe *among* the religions globally is mirrored in the diversity that we find *within* each of the major religious traditions." Schmidt-Leukel goes on, more tendentiously, to predict even the inner life of the believer: "And that we can also discern some patterns of this diver-sity—or elements thereof—*within the religious orientation of individual*

39

persons." Schmidt-Leukel finds in this resemblance a predictive power regarding the meaning and form of religious diversity: "In other words, religious diversity is neither chaotic nor entirely random. It rather follows to a significant extent a fractal structure. Thus, what I suggest is a fairly simple idea, but one that has some far-reaching implications and consequences if it turns out to be correct." He uses fractals to buttress his long-established and long-held theology of pluralism.[1]

I have no substantive objections to Schmidt-Leukel's overall exposition of his pluralist position in the book, even if I do not find the pluralist position satisfactory or necessary. I respect Schmidt-Leukel's erudite articulation of it, and his fidelity to his long-held opinions. Of more interest to me is his use of fractal theory and imagery, in the final and most innovative part of the book. The turn to fractals is not an explicit theme throughout, but nicely supplements the bulk of the lectures and indicates ways that Schmidt-Leukel might consolidate his work in the future.

Unfortunately, here I must take an unexpected detour that in the long run leads us back into the world of fractals. I find it necessary to disagree strongly with a seemingly minor theme that appears early in the book: Schmidt-Leukel's critique of comparative theology, or at least of some forms of it, as timid and yet implicitly bonded to an odious form of the inclusivist theology of religion, and as likely to die out soon. While most readers may simply pass over the several pages devoted to demolishing much of comparative theology, I took notice, because it is nothing less than an explicit and severe criticism of my own work. In the first chapter, "Pluralist Awakenings in Christianity," Schmidt-Leukel defends his favored pluralistic position. There he goes out of his way to comment on my practice of comparative theology, seemingly a rival to be removed from the scene early in the book.[2] He worries about the connection, or lack thereof, between his understanding of the theology of religions discipline and my comparative theology discipline, and holds that the latter cannot be whole or credible

---

[1] In fact, fractals are taken up only in chapter 14 of the book, which is based on the fifth and final Gifford Lecture.

[2] He also criticizes the work of James Fredericks, by a reference to his 1999 book, *Faith among Faiths: Christian Theology and Non-Christian Religions*, and does so in a way that does not adequately represent Fredericks's views and does not in any case refer to any particular section of it. I suggest that interested readers turn to the eighth and final chapter of *Faith among Faiths*, where Fredericks makes a strong positive case for more investment by the theological community in comparative theological work. While he does not here use the word "moratorium," Fredericks does write that given the current inadequacies of the exclusivist, inclusivist, and pluralist positions, "the quest for a theology of religions should be put aside for the time being." Prophetically, he continues, "Abandoning the quest for a theology of religions will seem outrageous to some. However, honesty to our historical situation requires that we look for new ways to respond to the diversity of religions today" (166). In this chapter, I respond to Schmidt-Leukel regarding my work alone.

as a theological field unless it conforms to his requirements for a particular form of the theology of religions. It seems to me that he is dismissing what I do because of what I do not do and, even less fortunately, on the basis of notions that are not mine, nowhere stated even in the several works of mine to which he refers. I devote the first part of this essay to my response. After dealing with these matters, more constructively in the second part of this essay I show how attention to fractal practice as well as fractal theory helps us to understand why both the theology of religions and comparative theology are valid fields, interrelated and improved by one another, but neither so dependent on the other as to be mortally deficient without the other.

IN DEFENSE OF MY COMPARATIVE THEOLOGY

According to Schmidt-Leukel, comparative theology has often been connected with a call for a moratorium on the theology of religions. Why would anyone call for a moratorium? Schmidt-Leukel thinks that this has to do with the Vatican's rejection of pluralism, and with the fact that Catholic theologians (of the less courageous sort) play it safe: "Given the explicit and sharp rejection of religious pluralism by the Roman Catholic Church, some (primarily Roman Catholic) theologians have suggested a moratorium for the theology of religions."[3] I gather he means that being a pluralist in the Catholic Church has been dangerous, and so some Catholic theologians, such as Clooney and Fredericks, have pulled back and stopped doing the theology of religions altogether. But while I agree that the theology of religions was a difficult field in the Catholic Church in the epoch of Joseph Ratzinger,[4] it is inaccurate to assign fear of being caught out as a pluralist as the motive for the moratorium. The point was rather to open a space for more direct study to be done, such as occurs in comparative theology. Indeed, Schmidt-Leukel then seems to concede as much, since in the very next sentence he mentions a second and more constructive reason: "Theology should focus on comparative studies before it would be fit to freshly address the issues of a theology of religions."[5] This latter goal of preparation, which has nothing to do with fear of reprisals, is far closer to how Fredericks and I have for decades seen the dynamic of comparative theology and the theology of religions.

---

[3]Perry Schmidt-Leukel, *Religious Pluralism and Interreligious Theology: The Gifford Lectures—An Extended Version* (Maryknoll, NY: Orbis Books, 2017), 29.

[4]For some reflection on the ecclesial factor at the start of my career in the 1980s, see "Afterword: Some Reflections in Response to Teaching Comparative Theology in the Millennial Classroom," in *Comparative Theology in the Millennial Classroom: Hybrid Identities, Negotiated Boundaries*, Mara Brecht and Reid B. Locklin, eds. (Abingdon, UK: Routledge, 2016), 219–33.

[5]Schmidt-Leukel, *Religious Pluralism and Interreligious Theology*, 29.

My own view of the notion of a moratorium, in the written record, is fairly mild. I put it this way in my 2010 *Comparative Theology*: "Given the distinct purposes of these disciplines, it is not wise to respond to religious diversity by concentrating solely on producing better theologies of religions, particularly when this amounts to (re)reading theologians who write on this topic in abstraction from religions in the particular."[6] Wanting to address the imbalance of theory over practice, I sympathized with the moratorium proposal: "Given the need for comparative theological work and the small number of people doing it, I can sympathize with calls for a moratorium on the theology of religions, if such a moratorium allows us to direct more energy to comparative theology, the less practiced discipline."[7]

But Schmidt-Leukel pushes on. Doing comparative theology without also doing the theology of religions makes it "increasingly evident," he says, that such a form of comparative theology does not deserve to be called theology at all: "For as is becoming increasingly evident, the consistent exclusion of the theology of religions discourse from comparative studies would deprive such studies of their theological nature."[8] This seems to mean that comparative "theology" cannot be theological unless it is additionally theologized in his theology of religions discipline.

But I have always been attentive to the interface between theology of religions and comparative theology, as in my 2010 book: "Conversely, insofar as a theology of religions is linked to basic truth claims—such as, for the Christian, a confession of the uniqueness of Christ and universality of salvation in Christ—we need also to consider how comparative theology might shed light on matters of such importance."[9] Nor is this a one-way street. Fifteen years earlier, in an essay noted by Schmidt-Leukel, I had already been on record as recommending against an absolute moratorium: "Neither can there be a moratorium on reflection on pluralism, since people inevitably raise these questions and need to reflect on them. Theologizing on religions, and theologizing in an interreligious conversation, can and should continue, even according to tradition-specific approaches, provided the price for balance and integration is paid."[10] This is hardly the language of a person wishing to wash his hands entirely of the theology of religions.

Ironically, I conclude the pertinent section of my 2010 book with words that seem very much in the spirit of what Schmidt-Leukel says. Indeed, I

[6]Francis X. Clooney, SJ, *Comparative Theology: Deep Learning across Religious Borders* (Oxford: Wiley-Blackwell, 2010), 15.

[7]Ibid.

[8]Schmidt-Leukel, *Religious Pluralism and Interreligious Theology*, 30.

[9]Clooney, *Comparative Theology*, 15.

[10]Francis X. Clooney, "Theology, Dialogue, and Religious Others: Some Recent Books in the Theology of Religions and Related Fields," *Religious Studies Review* 29 (2003): 319–27, 324.

rather clearly admit that comparative theology without theology of religions might end up as a nontheological mode of study, rather a kind of comparative religion: "Were a Christian comparative theology never to approach these truths pertaining to Christ and salvation, it could easily be counted a non-theological discipline, its engagement with religious particularities at best a resource for real theologians dealing with issues of faith. Comparative learning should pertain to issues of truth, and not detach itself from matters central to faith."[11] But Schmidt-Leukel seems to have overlooked this statement, or insists that the theology of religions is the narrow gate through which comparative theologians must pass.

Criticism of the moratorium and limiting access to true theology are not the end of Schmidt-Leukel's critique. He detects a deeper problem, namely, that comparative theology does indeed entail a theology of religions, but just the wrong one: "James Fredericks and Francis Clooney, who most explicitly asked for a moratorium and for eschewing theology of religions, have in fact disclosed their personal preference for Christian inclusivism."[12] I am a Roman Catholic inclusivist; that Schmidt-Leukel should point this out is not in itself a problem, since for more than twenty-five years I have been forthright in admitting that I am an inclusivist. Early on, I was happy to contribute "Reading the World in Christ: From Pluralism to Inclusivism" to *Christian Uniqueness Reconsidered* (1990), edited by Gavin D'Costa, a volume that served as a rejoinder to *The Myth of Christian Uniqueness* (1987), edited by John Hick and Paul Knitter. I also readily confess my inclusivist roots in *Comparative Theology* (2010): "My comparative theology is in harmony with those inclusivist theologies, in the great tradition of Karl Rahner, SJ, and Jacques Dupuis, SJ, that balance claims to Christian uniqueness with a necessary openness to learning from other religions." I interpret this strand of inclusivism in a practical way that reflects my practice then and now:

> I do not theorize inclusion so as to imagine that Christianity subsumes all else, but prefer instead the act of including. I bring what I learn into my reconsideration of Christian identity. This is an "including theology," not a theory about religions; it draws what we learn from another tradition back into the realm of our own, highlighting and not erasing the fact of this borrowed wisdom. Done honestly and with a certain detachment that chastens grand theories, such acts of including need not be seen as distorting what is learned or using it for purposes alien to its original context.[13]

---

[11]Clooney, *Comparative Theology*, 15.
[12]Schmidt-Leukel, *Religious Pluralism and Interreligious Theology*, 30.
[13]Clooney, *Comparative Theology*, 16.

I am a practical inclusivist—an includer, if you will—preferring to do the work, without writing much in the allied but quite different theology of religions discipline. I have preferred to hold back from discourses that seek out improved models in the theology of religions, spending my time, limited as it must be, in engaging particularities. I have actually expressed a preference for helping construct a richer, more concrete theology of religions: "Whatever the merits such models [in the theology of religions] may have, they are almost always essentially abstract designs, developed without reference to any particular religious tradition other than the Christian. To be taken seriously in a comparative context, each will have to be rewritten with a far greater commitment to detail and examples."[14]

Luckily, says Schmidt-Leukel, this form of comparative theology is dying out even as he writes, "Perhaps it would be even more true to say that [the brand of comparative theology that excludes theology of religions] does not represent one of its types but *one of its rather short-lived phases.*"[15] Of course, none of us can predict the endurance of our disciplines, and Schmidt-Leukel is entitled to his predictions. But it seems unjustifiable to make comparative theology an entirely dependent subfield of the theology of religions—as if a feeder discipline—just as interreligious dialogue cannot proceed credibly if it is made into an entirely dependent subfield of evangelization.[16]

But we are not done, since it turns out that inclusivism is a very bad thing indeed. In Schmidt-Leukel's view, it is just as well that this comparative theology is short-lived, because deep down it relies on a very bad theology of religions, the rather nasty enterprise known as inclusivism:

> According to religious inclusivism other religions are not entirely false, but they are inferior or insufficient *to the extent* that they differ from one's own religion. If one's own religion or denomination is seen as the highest expression of religious truth, others can be true only inasmuch as they resemble one's own faith, and they are false to the extent that they differ. *So according to both, exclusivism and inclusivism, religious difference or diversity is perceived as ultimately negative. It indicates either falsity or at least inferiority.*[17]

[14]Francis X. Clooney, SJ, *Theology after Vedanta: An Experiment in Comparative Theology* (State University of New York Press: 1993), 194.
[15]Schmidt-Leukel, *Religious Pluralism and Interreligious Theology*, 29–30 (emphasis added).
[16]On the careful balance that is required between the language of dialogue and the language of evangelization, lest either be short-circuited by the other, see Jacques Dupuis, *Christianity and the Religions: From Confrontation to Dialogue* (Maryknoll, NY: Orbis Books, 2002), 218–35.
[17]Schmidt-Leukel, *Religious Pluralism and Interreligious Theology*, 6 (emphasis added).

Schmidt-Leukel fiercely critiques inclusivism, reducing it to one particularly noxious version, perhaps because he is intent on defending and promoting his own pluralist position: "Only religious pluralism seeks to combine religious difference with equal validity. It is therefore the only option that allows for a positive assessment of religious diversity."[18]

My work is fruitful, I have hoped, because I embrace not so much a theoretical inclusivism as a theologically informed practice of including, learning the other reverentially, and seeing what happens after this Catholic comparativist has done this with some particular text for one or three or five years or more. This I explained already in my 1993 *Theology after Vedanta*:

> The inclusivist position, thus revised, becomes the practice of including; this, in turn, is a major revision of the theology of religions as such, a shift from a theoretical enterprise to a set of strategies of practical and reflective engagement in a religious tradition other than one's own, particularly by way of reading. The required rewriting of inclusivism and its alternatives is yet another important task which confronts the comparative theologians of the next generation.[19]

My reasons for advocating this include reluctance to think about religions in general terms—which risks indulging in a conversation among theorists of "religion" talking to themselves—and my preference for the work of particular acts of including. Here is what I added in 2010, in defending the distinctiveness of comparative theology: "I have made the preceding comments on comparative theology, its truth, and its relation to the theology of religions, in resistance to the notion that comparative theology has identical goals with the theology of religions, or is at best a handmaid to more systematic theorizing."[20] But I still go out of my way to commend theology of religions: "But I do not entirely disown the wisdom of the theology of religions discipline."[21] Or to make the point in another way: the reader may wish to look at my studies in comparative learning: *Theology after Vedanta, Seeing through Texts, Beyond Compare, His Hiding Place Is Darkness*, and so on. I find it hard to imagine anyone reading any of my books and articles over the past forty years and coming to the conclusion that I think that the traditions of Hinduism are "inferior or insufficient to the extent that they differ from [my] own religion," or that they are false because they are dif-

---

[18]Ibid.
[19]Clooney, *Theology after Vedanta*, 195–96.
[20]Clooney, *Comparative Theology*, 16.
[21]Ibid.

ferent from my Catholicism.[22] But my books do abound in tensions, double claims, and efforts to hold differing positions in the balance.

Attentive readers will see that I work not from theory down, nor from books straight to theory, but from the intellectual and spiritual practice of close reading, up into theological insights that are never detached from the texts themselves. This comparative theology manifests a certain kind of persistent delight in the text. Even if this is not to everyone's liking, it is not to be condemned as an inclusivist theology of the harsher sort. I never say, nor think, that the Hindu texts I study are false or inferior. No one who reads my work with even some attention should be able to say this. Or to put it another way: I am an includer—and not, if we must observe the ordinary usages, an inclusivist.

FRACTAL THEORY, FRACTAL PRACTICE: HOW WE CAN LEARN DIFFERENTLY

I have just now spent a number of pages clearing up these unfortunate and unnecessary complications regarding *Religious Pluralism and Interreligious Theology*, a book that never mentions me or my work again after the offensive in chapter 1, except in passing in several footnotes. In turn, in the pages that follow I have little to say about Schmidt-Leukel's pluralistic theology. Rather, I am interested in clarifying the relationship between comparative theology and the theology of religions by paying more attention to fractal practice, a resource that Schmidt-Leukel has indeed helpfully put before us. I am particularly interested in the legitimacy of exploratory practices that can be shown to be obviously fruitful even when not rushing to support a preferred theory of fractals. I have in mind particular instances of learning that proceed by intuition, with a certain freedom toward whatever might result. These may be valued as fruitful, even if not woven in with robust theoretical moves.[23]

I wish to show how Schmidt-Leukel and I can both make positive use of fractals, yet to different effect, without positing a zero-sum game in which, as Schmidt-Leukel would have it, comparative theology without a (pluralist) theology of religions is no theology at all. Fractalists come in all kinds, from experimentalists to theorists, and they seem to live in peace with the fact that others work differently. A certain generosity toward differences

---

[22]It is true, however, that a few others have critiqued my work as secretly dismissive of Hinduism. See my self-defense against just such a criticism: "A Response to S. N. Balagangadhara's 'Translation, Interpretation and Culture,'" *Canadian Social Science* 12 (2016): 107–12.

[23]For an excellent introduction to fractals, see Kenneth Falconer, *Fractals: A Very Short Introduction* (Oxford: Oxford University Press, 2013).

seems to characterize the fractal community. This matters here, since some of the good work done with the general frame of fractals is closer to the practicality of comparative theology as I do it than to the theorizing of a theology of religions cherished by Schmidt-Leukel. It is a commendation, not criticism, that I often do not understand even the titles of essays gathered in volumes collecting fractal studies inspired by Benoît Mandelbrot, the founding figure in the field.

Such work is experimental, the math often outstripping any possible overall visualizations of it. It relies on certain practices and experiments; the field yields much of its value simply in the field-specific research done by experts, rather than in popularized versions of the same. The experimentalists and mathematicians seem content to leave to a few figures, most importantly Mandelbrot himself, the work of generalizing the field and of making it accessible, particularly visually, for a wider audience. Finding fractal resonances in different fields may indeed bear fruit in a certain kind of theorizing and literally big-picture payoff, but generous scholars such as Mandelbrot—expert *and* generalizer—still respect the attentive, imaginative work of colleagues whose experimentation may or may not be heavy in justifications and theoretical payouts. Though comparative theology can be defended as a certain manner of inclusive—including—theology in practice, it is not bound to theorizing—or theologizing—about religions even by inclusivist theory. We do our work, and the steadfast reader judges whether it is fruitful or not in itself.

If a certain professional generosity is important, so too is a certain intuitive curiosity. Donald A. MacKenzie has observed[24] the vital curiosity that inspired Mandelbrot to reach out in all directions, intuitively and by instinct, finding connections others thought did not exist, even in ways he could not justify in advance. Mathematicians can be impatient with anomalies, exceptions, and "monsters" that do not fit current theories, but by contrast Mandelbrot stubbornly preferred precisely those things that didn't easily fit into anywhere. As Mandelbrot put it, "I'm always ready to look at anything curious and bizarre." MacKenzie explains, "For example, Mandelbrot became interested in linguistics after reading a review that his uncle had thrown into his wastepaper basket. The review alerted him to Zipf's law, a regularity in word frequencies that holds across languages. It was apparently a mere curiosity from a field in which Mandelbrot had no training, and others might have disregarded it, but Mandelbrot did not. It was part of the circuitous route that took him to finance."[25] Yet Mandelbrot was under no

---

[24]Donald A. MacKenzie, *An Engine, Not a Camera: How Financial Models Shape Markets* (Cambridge, MA: MIT Press, 2006).
[25]Ibid., 107.

obligation to study comparative linguistics or the latest theoretical work in the field of finance; he visited, borrowed, often brilliantly, but stayed close to what he himself, the mathematician, did well.

By analogy, I have found that those inclined to theory can be impatient with the work of studying classic texts in depth and at length, wherever that study might lead: rigorists leave little room for curiosity, irregular as it may be, and use even their own reading in religious traditions to prove theoretical points about religion per se. I concede that a comparativist can be bothersome. In more staid theological circles, what we learn from the great texts of other traditions can indeed seem as curious, bizarre, irregular, "monsters" (in Mandelbrot's sense), finding no place in established theoretical frames. Comparative theology often enough zeroes in on the odd never-translated text, the obscure citation that takes many hours to retrieve, the subcommentary to a commentary, and nongeneralizable argument with and to which theologians of a more ordered and systematic sort become impatient or even hostile. As I am always ready to admit, my comparisons are intuitive, most often arising from personal insights, justified by their completion and in their completeness. The reading of a Hindu text, in Sanskrit or Tamil, prompts me to root about in the cluttered files of my Catholic memory in order to find the right text that provides the right chemistry, so as to bring to life this Catholic's reading of this or that Hindu text. If it works, it can be wonderful. Nevertheless, some systematicians, perhaps including Schmidt-Leukel, are nonetheless irritated by the lack of (the right kind of) theory in my work.

MacKenzie comments too on Mandelbrot's success in traveling a maverick path that does not rely on membership in an established guild of scholars: "Mandelbrot's self-perceived and self-chosen social situation is precisely that in which [the sociologist of knowledge David] Bloor predicts the dialectical, monster-embracing method will flourish: one in which both group identities and hierarchies are weak." Is it not the comparative theologian, and not the pluralist theologian of religions, who is often the marginal person, barely noticed by the mainstream? Mandelbrot confesses, "For many years, every group I knew viewed me as a stranger, who (for reasons unknown) was wandering in and out."[26] Some systematicians may think this of the comparativist who refuses to make her work respectable by proffering a theology of religions.

Neither, MacKenzie reports, was Mandelbrot ashamed of the role of randomness in his research, the resistance of "more organized" figures notwithstanding:

---

[26]Ibid., 108.

In my interview with him, Mandelbrot commented: ". . . very often people tell me 'How come you attract more randomness than anyone else?' In fact, I don't think I do. But most people lead a more organized life. They know where their power can be exerted, who has this power over them. They know their place in society. Also, randomness perturbs, and institutions don't like it, hence correct for random inputs very rapidly. . . . Many of the events which I describe would have been simply dismissed by almost everybody. People would say . . . "this doesn't belong to my field, I must first finish writing some papers."[27]

While I will not go so far as to put all theologians of religions among those wanting to lead "a more organized life," a point here is worth considering. Good comparativists are experimentalists, tolerant of ambiguities and loose ends, and likely to do work—I have experienced this myself—that some theologians of religions bypass in their quest for a better theology of religions. I have no problem with comparativists who choose to work at making explicit their theology of religions. I admire theologians of religions who do their work very well—I think here of a Jacques Dupuis or an S. Mark Heim—but there has to be a reciprocal respect—such as Dupuis and Heim show—for those who do not choose to translate comparative learning into theology of religions categories. It would be sad if, in his enthusiasm for his new fractal frame, Schmidt-Leukel were to push aside those of us who do not love systems as much as he does.

Disciplinary generosity and intuitive creativity meld well with patience with detailed work that may or may not work out. While Mandelbrot himself valued generalization and indeed is famous for generalizing the field, even some of his ostensibly popular essays are in fact very particular, even unreadable by the amateur. He knows that most of the work that needs to be done relies not on writing about fractals but rather on experts working simply with case after case after case, reporting their results without showcasing predictive theory. Mandelbrot himself recommends the "casebook" approach, which gathers cases and lets the reader learn from them: "Physicians and lawyers use 'casebook' to denote a compilation concerning actual cases linked by a common theme. This term has no counterpart in science, and I suggest we appropriate it. The major cases require repeated attention, but less important cases also deserve comment."[28]

---

[27]Ibid.

[28]From the introduction to the *Fractal Geometry of Nature*, updated ed. (San Francisco: W. H. Freeman, 1983), 2. Sensitive to the difficulty of the cases contained in his book, Mandelbrot is therefore refreshingly candid about options before the reader: "Nevertheless, this work pursues neither abstraction nor generality for its own sake, and is neither a textbook nor a treatise in mathematics. Despite its length, I describe it as a scientific Essay because it is written from a personal

Much of what is hardest and to me most interesting in my books lies in the work of the close reading of texts, the labor of love undertaken for its own sake. How often have I conceded, though, that this close reading may be politely skipped over even by benevolent readers hoping to pick up and carry away the gist of my insights just by examining the first and last chapters. There would be a certain irony if it turns out that Schmidt-Leukel's insightful drawing of fractals into the realm of the theological study of religions inadvertently ends up providing a space for a comparative theology that thrives despite its "mess of unproven assertions and loose ends," despite not being a co-traveler with theological pluralism, and so forth.

At the end of "Mathematical Analysis While in the Wilderness" Mandelbrot himself illumines his own maverick path by referring to the work and experience of his uncle, Szolem Mandelbrojt, who was always ready to defend messy particularities in the face of a thirst for generality. He quotes Mandelbrojt in cautioning against getting caught in a "formal world":

> Generality is a great virtue in mathematics, and some scorn is directed to particular cases. But I cannot view generality as a god . . . Generality is beautiful when it explains . . . There is an optimum to generality . . . To generalize merely because of an attraction to generality or abstraction risks entering a formal world . . . I would not like to live in the world of formal logic envisioned by some of my colleagues . . . No divine law that I know forces us to abandon a being I view as complete for one that has the same virtues but is drier and more formal.[29]

Making connections and putting things together coherently is important, but there must also be room for a turn to things in themselves, intuitively enjoyed: "It is said that the goal of mathematics is to study the relation between things and not the things themselves. I approve, but [as] I see it, a mathematician lives a double life: . . . in a world of intuitive ideas and . . . a world of difficulties that bring so many joys and without which his life would be too vague or too easy."[30]

Even in theology, the enduring presence of the particular can be an affront to the guardians of generality. And yet particularity, seized first, held

---

point of view and without attempting completeness. Also, like many Essays, it tends to digressions and interruptions. This informality should help the reader avoid the portions lying outside his interest or beyond his competence. There are many mathematically 'easy' portions throughout, especially toward the very end. Browse and skip, at least at first and second reading" (ibid.).

[29]From Mandelbrot's "Mathematical Analysis While in the Wilderness," in *Fractals and Chaos: The Mandelbrot Set and Beyond* (New York: Springer 2004), 278–79. The ellipses are in Mandelbrot's rendering of the passage.

[30]Ibid., 279.

dearest and last, is often at the heart of what really matters. Is Jesus Christ not an irreducible particularity, a scandal, and a stumbling block?

After quoting his uncle, Mandelbrot himself pushes back against impatience with the particular. Here he alludes to the often-paired hypotheses of mathematicians Gaston Julia and Pierre Fatou,[31] and comments on their uneven reception: "During the 1950s and 1960s, the Fatou-Julia theory was utterly unfashionable, in the wilderness, because it consisted of many special examples and few 'great modern theorems.' The terms 'dried leaves,' 'isolated,' 'interesting individual,' or 'particular case' fitted it perfectly. This is the reason why it fell altogether outside of the mathematical main-stream and was, for all practical purposes, abandoned."[32] But, in the long run, it turned out that Fatou-Julia was to be generative of fruitful fractal learning. This seems to favor Poincaré, the messy experimentalist, over Bourbaki, the grand theorist:

> Do not forget that for Bourbaki, [Jules Henri] Poincaré was the devil incarnate, who had left behind a mess of unproven assertions and loose ends. They boasted that they had cleaned up that mess. Of course, Poincaré has long been a source of concern to French mathematicians. In the 1880s, Hermite kept writing to Mittag-Leffler to complain that young Poincaré never completed a proof.[33]

By contrast, Mandelbrot adds with mild irony, "For students of chaos and fractals, Poincaré is, of course, God on Earth."[34] There is a certain consolation here for the "messy comparativist."

It seems to me that we can draw an analogy that points to a fair compromise between the Schmidt-Leukel and Clooney dispositions. Perhaps

---

[31]Kenneth Falconer gives this succinct background on the very technical Julia-Fatou hypotheses: "In 1915, the Académie des Sciences in Paris declared that the topic for its 1918 Grand Prix was to be the global properties of iteration of functions. The War was raging, and whilst serving with the French army, the mathematician Gaston Julia (1893–1978) received serious facial injuries. Nevertheless, he managed to continue his mathematical work in his hospital bed, and in December 1918 was awarded the Prize. At the same time, another French mathematician Pierre Fatou (1878–1929) was working along similar lines, although he did not enter the competition. Thus in 1919, Julia and Fatou independently published major papers on the iteration of functions on the plane, including those of the form $z \rightarrow z2 + c$. These papers contain the definitions of what are now known as Julia sets and the Mandelbrot set as well as including the Fundamental Theorem above. . . . However, Julia and Fatou had little idea what these sets looked like, or even that they possessed any form or fine structure. There was no reason to suspect that the sets were particularly unusual; in any case with the calculating machines of the day it was not feasible to check the many iterates of the functions from many starting points that would be needed to observe fractality" (Falconer, *Fractals*, 82–83).

[32]Mandelbrot, "Mathematical Analysis," 280.

[33]Ibid.

[34]Ibid.

he and I have sympathies paralleled in the world where Mandelbrot found himself and made his brilliant interventions. Schmidt-Leukel is more like Bourbaki, stubbornly determined to tie up loose ends; I am more like Poincaré, stubbornly insistent on dwelling with loose ends that do not fit neatly into ordered explanatory frames. It may be the case that the determination to clean up the field of interreligious learning, swept clean by the broom of pluralist theory, is a Bourbakian–Schmidt-Leukelian move. The insistence on protecting the undertheorized work of comparative theology as a practical "including" theology is a Poincarian–Clooneyan move. If so, then there is plenty of room for those who theorize the fractal perspective in an effort to bring order to religious diversity (Schmidt-Leukel) and those who keep experimenting, finding, and simply enjoying ever new cases of religious learning that do not quickly fit into any desired theoretical frames (Clooney).

A SATISFACTORILY UNTIDY CONCLUSION

It is smart of Schmidt-Leukel to link fractals and theology, a positive and difficult venture, that profitably links the intra- and interreligious forms and dispositions of religions. Fractal pictures are, after all, amazingly communicative, and we can intuitively approve of what Schmidt-Leukel is suggesting. But the language of fractals does not translate into ordinary language. We see in all the wonderful computer-generated images only a tiny portion of what is intelligently at stake, and we are soon faced with equations too difficult for the novice. Even if we grasp the point of fractals rather easily, it is difficult for us ever to have a sufficient command of what we are discussing. Mandelbrot was wise in his advice, already quoted above: the informality of the "fractal casebook" "should help the reader avoid the portions lying outside his interest or beyond his competence. There are many mathematically 'easy' portions throughout, especially toward the very end. Browse and skip, at least at first and second reading." Thus, the hope of the comparativist too: read my books once for the general idea, then read them again, pondering all those cited texts that give the books their substance and vitality.

Many of us love to think that the latest science is on our side, so that the best methodology and the best theory show that my way of doing things finally gets it all right. But we are not there yet. Hard math, historical and contemporary scientific insights, impetuous intuitions, and undertheorized creativity are all parts of a complex collaboration that very few of us will master, but in the end the fractals are beautiful to those with eyes to see. Multiple approaches need to be welcomed in theology too, from the most general to the most grammatical and philological, from the most swiftly theorized to painstaking work that is in no rush but will take a century or two to become mature enough to be clearly seen. In the meantime, we need to welcome "the stranger who (for reasons unknown) was wandering in and out." There is no value in declaring that someone else's approach is really not theological, or mean-spiritedly theological, or on the edge of extinction because it refuses to cloak itself in a respectable theology of religions. And all this is even before we get to contemplating the mystery of a God who is never in the grasp of the concepts and words that theologians expertly use. Complexity and mystery both warn us not to let fractal geometry—complicated, otherworldly, beautiful—be co-opted by any particular version of the theology of religions or even of comparative theology. We need to welcome the energetic theorizers, but also those who still have time to find God in the particular, each time, over and over, "in ten thousand places."

Feminist Fractals?

Perry Schmidt-Leukel's Fractal Interpretation of Religious Diversity and Comparative Feminist Theology

Jerusha Tanner Rhodes

In his book *Religious Pluralism and Interreligious Theology*, Perry Schmidt-Leukel introduces a "fractal" interpretation of religious diversity. This interpretation highlights the way in which *inter*religious diversity is similarly manifest *intra*religiously and *intra*subjectively.[1] Differences that occur interreligiously are in some ways also present in the other two realms. This observation is grounded in the view that "each religion comprises characteristic features of other religions."[2] Thus interreligious diversity is not the result of holistic difference or incommensurability; diversity is rather a matter of scaling, variation, location, and integration of recurring fractal elements.[3] Schmidt-Leukel's fractal interpretation of religious diversity recognizes the complexity and integrity of religions yet refuses to draw hard and fast boundaries among them. Schmidt-Leukel argues that this approach has both hermeneutical and theological value in interreligious and comparative theology. Hermeneutically, it shifts emphasis away from both common ground and strict particularity. Theologically, it highlights a continuity between ecumenical theology and interreligious theology, and thereby cultivates an "appreciative attitude, a view that understands and assesses religious diversity as complementary."[4]

In this chapter I place Schmidt-Leukel's proposal of a fractal approach

---

[1] Perry Schmidt-Leukel, *Religious Pluralism and Interreligious Theology* (Maryknoll, NY: Orbis Books, 2017), 233.
[2] Ibid.
[3] Ibid., 233, 235.
[4] Ibid., 237.

in conversation with comparative feminist theology. My goal in doing so is to explore the ways in which the fractal theory aligns with, is challenged by, and potentially enriches interreligious feminist theological exchange. I begin by introducing the nascent yet growing field of comparative feminist theology. I then explore some convergences and divergences between the fractal interpretation and feminist theologies concerned with religious diversity, pluralism, and interreligious engagement. I conclude by proposing ways in which the two approaches can potentially enrich each other.

COMPARATIVE FEMINIST THEOLOGY

Comparative feminist theology is a specialized form of comparative theology. Thus, it is helpful to begin with a very brief overview of comparative theology itself. Francis X. Clooney, SJ, offers one standard definition of *comparative theology*: "acts of faith seeking understanding which are rooted in a particular faith tradition but which venture into learning from one or more other faith traditions . . . for the sake of fresh theological insights."[5] This definition underscores that comparative theology is simultaneously comparative and theological. It also emphasizes that this mode of theological exploration is impelled by and made possible through deep commitment and knowledge. Comparative theology is not possible on the basis of shallow commitment and understanding of one's own tradition(s) or of other traditions. It is a double process of venturing out of one's tradition(s) to learn deeply about and from other traditions and returning to one's own tradition(s) with new insights, questions, and perspectives.

The process of comparative theology initially consists of deep learning about other traditions. Such learning requires openness, humility, and development of competency in another tradition. Learning about and from others is described as learning about them on their "own terms," that is, as listening to and taking seriously what people in the other tradition say about themselves and their tradition.[6] This type of leaning is not superficial, and therefore requires time and thorough study. Competency is vitally important as a way to maintain respect and responsibility. By learning deeply about another tradition, the comparative theologian develops and expresses respect for its integrity, theological infrastructure, and internal concerns. Comparative theologians strive for a dual accountability in this regard; they strive to

---

[5]Francis X. Clooney, SJ, *Comparative Theology: Deep Learning across Religious Borders* (Malden, MA: Wiley Blackwell, 2010), 10.

[6]James Fredericks, *Buddhists and Christians: Through Comparative Theology to Solidarity* (Maryknoll, NY: Orbis Books, 2004), xii; Fredericks, *Faith among Faiths: Christian Theology and Non-Christian Religions* (Mahwah, NJ: Paulist, 1999), 164.

present their own and the other tradition in a way that is recognizable and meaningful to members of the respective communities.[7]

On the basis of competency, the next step in the process is to place knowledge of the other tradition in conversation with one's own tradition(s) through limited acts of comparison. This frequently involves side-by-side reading of authoritative texts from the two traditions. However, the focus of comparative explorations is beginning to broaden.[8] The process cultivates a refined sensitivity to similarities as well as differences between the traditions; it identifies substantial but incomplete instances of resonance.[9] Overlaps and ruptures thus awaken new theological considerations—and this is the central objective of comparative theology: production of new theological insights, questions, and approaches. We come to understand ourselves in new ways in the "light" of the other.[10] This does not mean that the objective is appropriation, direct cooptation, or abandonment of one's own tradition(s),[11] It is an assertion that we see new facets of ourselves, our traditions, our sources, and our practices when they are illuminated by comparative engagement. We ask new questions of our traditions and "discover patterns hidden beneath the grooves of well-worn narratives."[12]

Comparative feminist theology follows this basic approach and process with a few central modifications. First, it places in the center what Michelle Voss Roberts calls the "outsider within" traditions, rather than "insider" orthodoxies, by focusing on feminist discourses, texts, and practices.[13] Voss

---

[7]Clooney, *Comparative Theology*, 13.

[8]Michelle Voss Roberts, *Tastes of the Divine: Hindu and Christian Theologies of Emotion* (New York: Fordham, 2014); Jeannine Hill Fletcher, "What Counts as 'Catholic'? What Constitutes 'Comparative'?" and "Response to Daria Schnipkoweit," *Studies in Interreligious Dialogue* 24, no. 1 (2014): 78–85, 91–93.

[9]Zayn Kassam, "Response to Daniel Madigan," in *Catholicism and Interreligious Dialogue*, James L. Heft, SM, ed. (New York: Oxford University Press, 2012), 75–77, 75; Francis X. Clooney, SJ, ed., *The New Comparative Theology: Interreligious Insights from the Next Generation* (London: T&T Clark, 2010), 199; Clooney, *Comparative Theology*, 16–19.

[10]Clooney, *Comparative Theology*, 16; Voss Roberts, *Tastes of the Divine*, xxii; Reid B. Locklin and Hugh Nicholson, "The Return of Comparative Theology," *Journal of the American Academy of Religion* 78 (2010): 477–514, 499.

[11]Fredericks, *Faith among Faiths*, 178; Peter Phan, "From Soteriology to Comparative Theology and Back: A Response to S. Mark Heim," in *Understanding Religious Pluralism: Perspectives from Religious Studies and Theology*, Peter Phan and Jonathan Ray, eds. (Eugene, OR: Pickwick, 2014), 260–64, 262; John J. Thatamanil, *The Immanent Divine* (Minneapolis: Fortress, 2006), 23–24; Tracy Sayuki Tiemeier, "Comparative Theology as a Theology of Liberation," in *The New Comparative Theology: Interreligious Insights from the Next Generation*, Francis X. Clooney, SJ, ed. (London: T&T Clark, 2010), 129–50, 139.

[12]Michelle Voss Roberts, *Dualities: A Theology of Difference* (Louisville, KY: Westminster John Knox, 2010), 18.

[13]Michelle Voss Roberts, "Gendering Comparative Theology," in *The New Comparative Theology: Interreligious Insights from the Next Generation*, Francis X. Clooney, SJ, ed. (London: T&T Clark, 2010), 109–28, 114–15; Voss Roberts, *Dualities*, 4–5.

Roberts contends that this focus destabilizes generalizations, moves beyond texts, and offers new sites of comparison in comparative theology.[14] Comparative theology, with its emphases on deep learning about and accurate representation of traditions, has the unfortunate side effect of excluding voices and perspectives that are not part of the authoritative canon of traditions. Women feature and have historically featured prominently in this category. They are often excluded in texts, scriptures, and interpretations, and as competent scholars of their own traditions. Comparative theology is typically focused on "insider" to "insider" engagements, but comparative feminist theology seeks to contest the "traditional enough" standard and bring outsiders into the conversation.[15]

Second, comparative feminist theology revisits the way in which the "fruits"—the fresh insights—of comparative theological engagement are received by and resonate with the original tradition. A substantial connection to one's own community is a vital component of comparative theology in general.[16] This claim, though, is further specified in comparative feminist theology. Since the outsiders within are centered, the expectation of communal resonance and accountability is unavoidably different. Feminist outsiders within already challenge the structures of authority within their respective communities; they do not desire to uphold the structures as they are. While feminist theologians aim to resonate with their tradition and religious communities in pursuit of change, history demonstrates that reception of their ideas will be a combination of resonance and disregard, if not outright resistance. Therefore, the idea of communal reception must be reconfigured. Communal resonance is important, but feminist theologies are more interested in *provocative* communal resonance—that is, in stirring people to embark upon difficult yet imperative and tradition-rooted conversations.

Third, comparative feminist theology is especially attentive to hegemonic expectations of parity in concerns, methods, and theologies. Comparative feminist theology is a means to conscientiously and critically engage other feminist theologies without glossing important differences or universalizing a particular feminist theological perspective. Comparative feminist theology enables this by requiring deep knowledge and attentiveness to particularities. It is not premised upon—nor capable of being undertaken on the basis of—caricatures or thin understanding. It necessitates learning about the other tradition on its own terms, learning about the central concerns, vari-

---

[14]Voss Roberts, "Gendering Comparative Theology," 114–15; Voss Roberts, *Dualities*, 4–5.

[15]Voss Roberts, *Dualities*, 12; Voss Roberts, "Gendering Comparative Theology," 116.

[16]Catherine Cornille, "The Confessional Nature of Comparative Theology," *Studies in Interreligious Dialogue* 24 (2014): 9–15, 13–15.

ous responses to those concerns, and authority structures of the tradition. Comparative feminist theology—while unpredictable and dynamic—ironically provides a more stable and safe structure for interreligious feminist engagement, which is too often characterized by power, stereotypical or superficial depictions, and limited knowledge.[17]

Finally, comparative feminist theology does not avoid all "grand narratives," as early comparative theologians often assert. Avoidance of grand narratives and theories is clearly laudable in terms of fostering real engagement with and learning about other traditions. It is a valid qualification on the approach of comparative theology, but it is a qualification that needs to be qualified again in light of comparative feminist theology. Comparative theology aims to foster new theological insights and to create "bonds of solidarity."[18] Comparative feminist theology, though, aims to use theological insights and solidarity to create change. It does more than seek out and reflect upon ideas that might be interesting or theologically enhancing; the ultimate goals are change, equality, and liberation.

The goals of comparative feminist theology therefore are transformation, transgression, and imaginative theological reconstruction within and in conversation with the tradition(s) of the comparative theologian.[19] At the same time, comparative feminist theology provides a way to learn with other traditions, and to gain new and indispensable insights related to egalitarianism and liberation. Interrogations of power, attentiveness to on-the-ground realities, and a thrust toward liberation become empowering aspects of comparative feminist theology. Engagement among traditions becomes a theologically sound, theologically rich, and practically effective means of change. It reveals new resources crucial to our own struggles.

CONVERGENCES AND DIVERGENCES

Schmidt-Leukel's fractal interpretation and comparative feminist theology align and diverge in a variety of ways. Exploration of these areas of alignment and divergence further illuminates the distinctiveness of each and also lays a foundation on which to propose mutual enrichments.

---

[17]Aysha Hidayatullah, "The Qur'anic Rib-ectomy: Scriptural Purity, Imperial Dangers, and Other Obstacles to the Interfaith Engagement of Feminist Qur'anic Interpretation," in *Women in Interreligious Dialogue*, Catherine Cornille and Jillian Maxey, eds. (Eugene, OR: Cascade, 2013), 150–67, 150–51.

[18]James L. Fredericks, "Off the Map: The Catholic Church and Its Dialogue with Buddhists," in *Catholicism and Interreligious Dialogue*, James L. Heft, SM, ed. (New York: Oxford University Press, 2012), 127–44, 143.

[19]Locklin and Nicholson, "Return of Comparative Theology," 493.

One central area of alignment between fractal interpretation and comparative feminist theology is the depiction of religions as complex and hybrid entities that are never wholly distinct from each other. There is no absolute incommensurability, nor is there absolute sameness. In articulating his theory and providing concrete examples of interreligious theology based on the theological notions of the Prophet, the Son, and the Buddha, Schmidt-Leukel demonstrates that traditions are neither internally homogeneous nor monolithic. While they do contain dominant strands and points of emphasis, they also contain other components and aspects that, while more marginal or less emphasized, are nonetheless organic to the traditions themselves. He contends, moreover, that that which is less emphasized in one tradition may be dominant in another, and vice versa. This is the fractal replication that creates similarity through varied emphasis and scaling, creates crossovers between intra- and interreligious theology, and creates the very possibility of interreligious and comparative theology. Schmidt-Leukel's constructive grappling with the Prophet, Son, and Buddha provides an example of the latter possibility.

Comparative feminist theology also challenges the presentation of traditions as discrete, distinct, and internally homogeneous. One way it does so is through the centering of "outsiders within" in the constructive theological process. "Outsiders within" in their very existence challenge the presentation of traditions as internally homogeneous. They identify with the tradition, while simultaneously contesting dominant formulations of theology, dogmas, interpretations, and practices. They also reclaim nondominant formulations and introduce new formulations in conversation with feminist theologians and scholars in other traditions. This conversation is validated by the comparative feminist theological observation that concerns—such as androcentrism, patriarchy, and misogyny—cut across religious traditions. These concerns manifest diversely according to traditional structures of authority and practice, but the concerns are nevertheless present across the boundaries of traditions. In addition, comparative feminist theologians draw critical attention to the way religious boundaries are often invoked to bolster claims to a single orthodox or legitimate interpretation of a tradition; a tradition is depicted as being distinct from—often superior to—all others due to its wholly particular and monolithic teachings. This stance both silences "outsiders within" and squelches interreligious conversation. Similar to fractal interpretation, this critique highlights a convergence in the intra- and interreligious, albeit here in a less than fruitful manner.

Another significant area of alignment is openness to mutual enrichment or transformation that arises from interreligious exchange and learning. Schmidt-Leukel argues that the fractal interpretation tends toward religious pluralism and moves beyond "the idea that diversity is always an expression of either falsity or inferiority, as is presupposed by exclusivism and inclusivism."[20] Religious pluralism here denotes not just the fact of diversity but the positive valuation of religious diversity. If truth is not confined to one tradition alone and fractal patterns replicate across the dynamic and porous boundaries of traditions and within religious traditions, then "reciprocal illumination" and "mutual transformation" are possible and invaluable.[21]

In comparative feminist theology, a similar openness is evident. The very motivation for comparative feminist theological engagement is the idea that there is something valuable and potent to be learned, and that such learning is possible and perhaps even necessary. Critical, comparative engagement can prompt us to imagine new legitimate and rooted options beyond the dominant forms of theology, interpretation, and practice within our traditions.[22] The comparative lens assists in penetrating the "unthought" and the "unthinkable," meaning those aspects of and possibilities within our *own* traditions that are obscured or rendered invisible by prevailing formulations of orthodoxy and interpretations of texts and practices.[23] While comparative theology does not barter in absolute parity or an evolutionary view of feminist theological discourse—that is, the hegemonic view that feminists in diverse traditions are at various developmental points on the same, singular path with the same ultimate goals—there are profound areas of overlap. In charting courses toward liberation and egalitarianism, comparative feminist theologians benefit from familiarity with these areas of overlap and openness to the possibility of learning from and with other scholars and theologians. As noted earlier, engagement among traditions thus becomes a theologically sound, theologically rich, and practically effective means of change that reveals new resources crucial to our own struggles. Rather than a side project or illegitimate means of formulating theological reflection, comparative feminist theology recasts interreligious engagement as an invaluable resource for practical and theological reflection *and* action.

Convergences between fractal interpretation and comparative feminist theology also occur in relation to the foci of comparative and interreligious theology. Early comparative theology tended—even with its validation of hybridity and mutual transformation—to focus primarily on comparative engagement of texts and exegeses. This focus, evident for example in the

---

[20]Schmidt-Leukel, *Religious Pluralism and Interreligious Theology*, 237.

[21]Ibid., 143–46.

[22]Voss Roberts, *Tastes of the Divine*, xxii; Francis X. Clooney, SJ, "Afterword: Some Reflections in Response to Teaching Comparative Theology in the Millennial Classroom," in *Comparative Theology in the Millennial Classroom*, Mara Brecht and Reid B. Locklin, eds. (New York: Routledge, 2016), 219–34, 227.

[23]Mohammed Arkoun, *The Unthought in Contemporary Islamic Thought* (London: Saqi Books, 2002).

work of Clooney, places authoritative texts and interpretations into conversation. Both fractal interpretation and comparative feminist theology seek to expand this initial focus. Schmidt-Leukel does not discount a textual focus outright, yet his own engagement focuses on theological models or categories (Son, Buddha, Prophet). He also indicates that interreligious engagement need not be limited to these areas but could also expand into other concerns and even the "darker aspects" of religions.[24]

Expansion beyond textual comparative theology is one of the main expansions of comparative feminist theology. This expansion occurs for a few notable reasons. First is the recognition that the "authoritative" canon and "authoritative" body of exegesis surrounding that canon often—if not always—exclude the participation and voices of the outsider within. Therefore, this cannot be the primary basis of comparative feminist engagement. Moreover, even the skill set required to engage in textual comparative study (including but not limited to linguistic skills) excludes many outsiders within. Many outsiders within are barred within traditional religious structures not only from participation in canonization and exegesis but also from gaining access to theological and other education that would enable them to engage in this process. On this basis, comparative feminist theologians expand the foci of interreligious engagement by including new texts and new interpretations of texts, and also by shifting to oral texts and histories, feminist theological concerns, embodied ritual performance and practice, and even aesthetic and emotive representations.[25] As with fractal interpretation, it is the diverse, yet simultaneously overlapping, manifestations in all these areas that make them legitimate areas of comparative theological consideration.

While these substantial areas of alignment exist, there are also some notable and provocative divergences between Schmidt-Leukel's fractal interpretation and comparative feminist theology.

One clear divergence relates to the specific examples that Schmidt-Leukel explores in his constructive interreligious theology. While he acknowledges the plausibility of a multitude of other foci for fractal analysis, the three confessional categories that he engages—the Son, the Prophet, and the Buddha—center on male figures and orthodox doctrines that are primary sites of female exclusion and critique by feminist theologians, including comparative feminist theologians.[26] These categories are historically and theologically gendered; they are thus at a minimum androcentric if not pa-

---

[24]Schmidt-Leukel, *Religious Pluralism and Interreligious Theology*, 237, 243–45.
[25]See, for example, Voss Roberts, *Tastes of the Divine*; Hill Fletcher, "What Counts as 'Catholic?'" and "Response to Daria Schnipkoweit."
[26]Schmidt-Leukel, *Religious Pluralism and Interreligious Theology*, 243.

triarchal. These categories and doctrines are also connected to theological anthropologies and ritual practices that enshrine androcentrism and patriarchy. This does not negate their comparative value in a general sense. However, it does mean that they would be unlikely candidates for *constructive* comparative feminist theological exploration, even while they are sites of deep *deconstructive* analysis. The comparative feminist theological concern with these categories is not only topical; it is not only about centering and selecting other categories or concerns. Comparative feminist theology also raises questions about whether interreligious theology—when focused on such categories and the fact that these categories occur with different emphasis and variation across many traditions—functions to reinscribe and further reify androcentrism, patriarchy, or both. These categories facilitate interreligious theology premised upon fractal interpretation. But do they do so at the expense of further naturalizing androcentrism and patriarchy by underscoring its fractal repetition?

This is an important concern and question that directly connects to another divergence between fractal interpretation and comparative feminist theology: the objective or goal of interreligious engagement. Schmidt-Leukel describes fractal theory as a hermeneutical approach that supports the goals of interreligious agreement and transformation.[27] He also argues that interreligious theology aims at discerning and identifying "theologically relevant *truth* as it may be testified to in other religious traditions."[28] This process is grounded in the assumption that all truth is compatible, and that a fundamental unity of reality exists. The goal, therefore, becomes transformation and mutual illumination that leads toward integration, synthesis, and better understanding of this ultimate reality.[29] Schmidt-Leukel describes this goal as ongoing and never finished, but this is the goal nonetheless.

In comparative feminist theologies, transformation is clearly also a goal. Interreligious engagement is legitimated and advocated for on the basis of its transformative potential. Comparative feminist theologians, however, do not typically invoke the ideas of synthesis, unity, and integration, partly because of the feminist sensitivity to the ways in which diversity is and has been co-opted under the rubric of a universal norm, reality, or truth. This is the enduring feminist theological concern with universal norms and assumptions of parity across diverse human groups; universal norms and assumptions of parity are often used to silence female voices and dampen agency. They are also often founded upon supposed "universal" criteria, but in fact are generalized norms of particular groups or communities. In

[27]Ibid., 232, 235, 134.
[28]Ibid., 243 (emphasis added).
[29]Ibid., 138–39, 141.

comparative feminist theologies, this concern surfaces in relation to both the presentation of women and the presentation of religious others. There is a deep sensitivity to and healthy suspicion toward claims that assert any universal norm. Comparative feminist theology is thus not premised upon, motivated by, justified through, or aimed at identifying agreement.

Having said that, comparative feminist theologies may actually be invoking another form of universalism. They clearly define the goal of interreligious engagement as the pursuit of and moving closer to liberation and equality. While not explicitly stated, equality could be the "ultimate truth" that they wish to uncover. Nonetheless, this does not result in an automatically positive evaluation of integration and synthesis as objectives. Also, it is notable that comparative feminist theologians assert this "truth" of equality up front even before engagement; it is not discovered through engagement, although it can be refined and further specified through interreligious engagement. This, of course, has implications for the broader comparative theological insistence on avoiding grand claims and determinate end points. Complete avoidance of grand claims and end points, however, presents a dilemma since comparative feminist theology retains the feminist theological commitment to positively impacting the lives of people on the ground and fostering what is often called *human flourishing*.[30]

The focus on liberation and equality hints at a final divergence. Connected to the divergence in categories and objectives of interreligious engagement, comparative feminist theology also diverges in that it is not solely interested in what currently exists in traditions, even if only in marginal form. In line with other feminist theologies, it does engage in deconstructive analysis, and it also seeks to reclaim and recenter aspects of traditions that may be minimized historically and theologically. But it does not confine itself only to reconfiguration of that which exists. It is also interested in the new: new ideas, new practices, new canons, and new possibilities that may not yet exist. Fractal interpretation is focused on scaling, emphasis, and configuration. The theory is premised upon the idea that certain patterns repeat, with variation, among all traditions. Comparative feminist theology would not debate this theory, but it does raise important questions: Can there ever be a wholly new pattern or fractal?

Part of comparative feminist theology is a shift in emphasis. Part is a provocative reclamation of tradition. Another part is a challenge to orthodox boundaries and interpretations. Yet still another piece is concerned with the not yet realized, the new. Fractals can produce new patterns, new variations, and new scales. Fractals can cross or blur boundaries. Fractals occur interreligiously, intrareligiously, and even intrasubjectively. Is fractal

---

[30]Voss Roberts, "Gendering Comparative Theology," 123–24.

theory open to and capable of accommodating the "new"? Can there ever be wholly original ideas, practices, and beliefs? Or does it remain only a matter of emphasis and configuration? Emphasis and configuration are certainly vital in describing and arguing for the possibility, necessity, and value of interreligious theology. Comparative and interreligious feminist theologies seek to deconstruct, deemphasize, reclaim, and introduce egalitarian configurations. However, they are not interested only in recognizing and learning from fractal configurations. They seek to *interrupt* and *modify* configurations toward the broad, yet specific, ends of liberation and justice.

MUTUAL ENRICHMENTS

By way of conclusion, I want to outline some potential mutual enrichments between fractal interpretation and comparative feminist theology. To begin, fractal theory can further justify the deconstructive and constructive work of comparative feminist theology. One of the mentioned convergences is a shared contestation of religious traditions as wholly discrete, distinct, and internally homogeneous. This is asserted by comparative feminist theologians and becomes the basis of intratradition critiques and intertradition engagements. The fractal interpretation, however, can underscore the legitimacy of intertradition engagements by providing another theoretical explanation of its value. If diversity is a matter of emphasis, scaling, and configuration of an array of fractal patterns, then comparative feminist theological efforts to learn from and with people in other traditions—to widen the "canon" interreligiously—are further legitimated.[31] Notably, such legitimation is vital in contesting dominant formulations of theology and practice—some of which hinge on excluding or demonizing interreligious engagement—and in articulating constructive alternatives. Legitimation is also vital to encouraging wider and deeper participation in comparative and interreligious feminist theology. A first-things-first approach can lead feminist theologians to focus intratraditionally alone, to argue that internal critique and change are the priority, and that resources and skills should be focused on this "fight" alone. Fractal theory assists in challenging this view and presenting interreligious feminist engagement as theoretically, theologically, and practically necessary.

Another way fractal theory deepens comparative and interreligious feminist theology is by underscoring the absolute necessity of informed and knowledgeable engagement. This approach is not particular to fractal theory, and it is a component in comparative feminist theology and comparative

---

[31]Schmidt-Leukel, *Religious Pluralism and Interreligious Theology*, 241.

theology. But lack of knowledge and overly simplified or caricatured perspectives have impeded some interreligious feminist engagements, prevent-
ing transformation and illumination.[32] The fractal theory further limits the
possibly of this outcome in two ways. It reiterates the requirement of deep,
complex, and nuanced knowledge of other traditions, and it advocates for
interreligious conversations that move beyond bilateral engagements.[33] The
push beyond bilateral comparisons mitigates against overly reductive and
oppositional caricatures. It also mitigates against normative terms, concepts,
and concerns being defined (even generally) by one dominant tradition.
Notably, the latter is a preeminent concern in feminist theology and comparative feminist theology. Multilateral interreligious engagement—based
on deep, complex knowledge—could be an additional strategic disruption
to universal norms and power differentials among and within traditions.

The topic of power brings us to the primary way in which comparative
feminist theology can enrich fractal interpretation. Comparative feminist
theology—as well as some newer formulations of comparative theology—strives to be attentive to power dynamics and political implications
of theologies, practices, and theories. In line with the emphasis on the
goals of liberation and equality, comparative feminist theology seeks not
only theological insights through interreligious engagement. Comparative
theology in general aims to foster new theological insights and to create
"bonds of solidarity."[34] Comparative feminist theology, though, aims to use
theological insights and solidarity to create change, equality, and liberation.
Comparative feminist theology thus offers a productive challenge to fractal
interpretation by asking about the political implications of this theory. The
response to this challenge cannot be that fractal theory is wholly apolitical
or simply phenomenological. It is not simply a neutral description. The
power-critical lens of comparative feminist theology forces us to consider
what is being reinscribed in a fractal theory, what fractals are identified and
why, and—back to the already stated divergence—can these fractals and
their diverse emphases ever be changed, especially when we acknowledge
their impact on human lives and bodies? Comparative feminist theology
contests the notion that *any* theology—even one aimed at uncovering
truth—is or can ever be apolitical. It thus invites examination of the latent
political assumptions of fractal interpretation and conscious and conscien-
tious articulation of theologies that employ fractal theory.

---

[32]Hidayatullah, "The Qur'anic Rib-ectomy," 150–51; Kassam, "Constructive Interreligious
Dialogue concerning Muslim Women," 127–49.

[33]Schmidt-Leukel, *Religious Pluralism and Interreligious Theology*, 140–46, 128, 138.

[34]Fredericks, "Off the Map," 143.

The Silent Witness of Intuition

Pansacramentality, Interreligious Encounter, and a Fractal Interpretation of Religious Diversity

—————

Hans Gustafson

In describing his awakening to a fractal interpretation of religious diversity in the introduction to this volume, Perry Schmidt-Leukel recounts that "in the middle of the night, round about 3 a.m. or so . . . I woke up, went to my desk, and sketched on one or two sheets of paper how religious diversity might be best understood along the lines of fractal structures." His theory was born after realizing he "was 'pregnant' with it for something like three decades." It arrived in a swift fit of insight, of intuition. Intuition is the key here. As Benoît Mandelbrot and Schmidt-Leukel point out, fractals appear everywhere, and are perhaps most obvious in nature (e.g., fern leaves, cauliflower, trees, coastlines). Malidoma Somé, well-known West African shaman, observes that "Nature is actually the silent witness of intuition. . . . Nature is interested in the inner eye, the inner ear, the inner capacity to make sense out of something which external consciousness might consider chaotic."[1] A fractal interpretation of religious diversity brings some order to the seemingly chaotic and exhausting complexity of religion in the world.

Schmidt-Leukel also states earlier in this book, "The nucleus of the theory is that the diversity we observe *among* the religions globally is mirrored in the diversity that we find *within* each of the major religious traditions. And that we can also discern some patterns of this diversity—or elements thereof—*within the religious orientation of individual persons*" (emphasis in original). Schmidt-Leukel's application of fractality to religious diversity has profound implications for those working in the area of encounter

---

[1] *Innsæi: The Power of Intuition*, Kristín Ólafsdóttir and Hrund Gunnsteinsdottir, dirs. (Iceland: KLIKK Productions, 2016), Netflix, minute 39–40.

between and within religions, so much so that it is not possible to reflect on it all here. Rather, in the interest of precision, this chapter focuses on the theory's applicability to a pansacramental worldview and its implications for fruitful interreligious engagement. First, I introduce the idea of pansacramentality by providing an overview of a panentheistic pansacramental worldview, its limitations, and two metaphors for understanding its conceptual architecture. Second, I explore the kinship between religious fractality and a pansacramental worldview. Finally I turn to Schmidt-Leukel's three levels of religious diversity and apply them to a useful framework for how people become involved with interreligious engagement and reflect on their own religious identity.

PANSACRAMENTALITY

In 2016 I published a book titled *Finding All Things in God*[2] that proposed "panentheistic pansacramentalism" as a model for understanding the relationship between the divine, world, and persons. This pansacramental view holds that all things can potentially serve as sacraments. What's more, all things are in the divine (and the divine is in all things), and thus all things can serve as mediators of the divine in the world. My book ventured rather deeply into the meaning of the term "sacrament," pansacramentalism's kinship with panentheism, and pansacramentalism's many philosophical and theological implications. The present chapter gives an overview of pansacramentality and its relation to a fractal interpretation of religious diversity. In this section I introduce the term "sacrament," identify its limitations, and conclude with an overview of panentheistic pansacramentality. The aim, as stated, is to articulate a pansacramental worldview for the purposes of correlating it with a fractal interpretation of religious diversity.

What Is a Sacrament?

The word *sacrament* often conjures up the image of a Roman Catholic priest dispensing a wafer with red wine to the faithful during the Mass. Although the term has come to be closely associated with the Christian tradition, and even for many Protestants it can sometimes sound very Catholic, it predates Christianity.[3] Regardless, because today it is almost exclusively

---

[2] Hans Gustafson, *Finding All Things in God: Pansacramentalism and Doing Theology Interreligiously* (Eugene, OR: Pickwick, 2016).

[3] Joseph Martos writes, "There were sacraments in the Greek and Roman religious world of early Christianity. There were the formal sacraments of the official state religion: oaths and offerings, oracles and auguries, public festivals and family devotions. There were also the sacraments

used in the Christian and Catholic context (which is a limitation), there may be sufficient cause to consider other terms instead, as I address below.

The understanding of sacrament proposed here relies on the fundamental assertion that sacraments function as symbols of religious or ultimate significance. Symbols function in a number of ways. One core function of a symbol is mediation between the particular and the universal. Sacraments, as symbols, make the universal particular and make the particular universal. Further, symbols can function as signs pointing to something beyond themselves. However, symbols are more powerful than signs. They make present, or concretize, that which they symbolize. Symbols also invite transformative participation by drawing in the subject and making demands on the subject to act. With this understanding of symbol in mind, a sacrament functions as a religious symbol. In short, a *sacrament* is a symbol of the sacred[4] or a religious symbol of ultimate significance. A sacrament expresses the sacred in the world in a symbolic way by making the sacred present.

As a religious symbol of ultimate significance . . .

- *A sacrament is not merely a sign.* It points beyond itself (as a sign), but also points inwardly by making the sacred present in the world. This upholds the classical theistic concern of maintaining divine immanence and transcendence by positing the sacred as made present by the sacrament, but also always transcending itself by pointing beyond (as a sign).

---

of the mystery religions: symbolic rituals that dramatized deeper religious meanings for those who sought them" (Joseph Martos, *Doors to the Sacred: A Historical Introduction to Sacraments in the Catholic Church*, rev. ed. [Liguori, MO: Liguori/Triumph, 2001], 23). "Sacrament" has roots in two pre-Christian-era terms: the Latin *sacramentum* and the Greek *mysterion*. Both words have rich histories, which are well beyond the scope of this chapter. For instance, *sacramentum* was first used to refer to a legal financial pledge made in a Roman temple and was later used to refer to the swearing of an oath in a legal, military, or religious context. Eventually, Tertullian used it to articulate the manner in which Christian rituals ought to be understood as sacred (e.g., baptism), and thus it took on a popular usage to refer to any sacred symbol or ceremony (Martos, *Doors to the Sacred*, 4; Gustafson, *Finding All Things in God*, 54). *Mysterion*, in the Christian tradition, comes from Paul in the New Testament in reference to baptism and the Lord's Supper. In the Greek context, *mysterion* often took its meaning from the gnostic mystery cults and referred to a ritual of sacred significance that symbolically revealed a hidden meaning. These rituals facilitated the instantaneous process of revealing a hidden mystery. *Mysteria* revealed the hidden depths of reality through rites and ritual. In short, the Christian understanding of sacrament that emerged effectively combined aspects from both words: from *sacramentum*, the communal aspect such as an oath made between persons, and from *mysterion*, the individual aspect, such as a momentary flash of personal insight into ultimate reality.

[4]"Sacred" is understood differently depending on one's tradition, language, and worldview. It may refer to the divine, God, Gods, Brahman, the transcendent, Great Spirit, Dao, Ultimate Concern, or the Real *an sich*. This is not a claim that these terms for "the sacred" are the same or similar, or that they refer to identical concepts or realities.

- *A sacrament concretizes by making the sacred present through corporeal elements.* The world's religions have many examples of robust rituals such as Christians partaking of the bread and wine in Holy Communion, Lakota experiences of pipe smoking and related ceremonies, Muslims reading the Holy Qur'an, and Jews gathering at the synagogue). These rituals employ earthly elements and relations to make present (concretize) the sacred in time and place. A pansacramental view proposes that all things can function in this manner because it begins with the presupposition that the sacred universally pervades the corporeal cosmos.[5] Therefore, the sacred can be experienced through particular manifestations in particular places at particular times and by particular people. A sacrament renders the sacred, which is universal, particular in these instances.
- *A sacrament is participatory by beckoning attention to itself and drawing people into its depths.* Not all sacraments invite participation to all people, especially explicitly recognized religious sacraments. Many of these sacraments are tradition-specific and only invite those who belong to that tradition to participate, while forbidding outsiders. Works of art, natural wonders, and other people are examples of potential sacraments demanding others to participate with them.[6] Sacraments call the person to experience ultimacy in a transformative way. Standing at the base of a mountain, sitting on the shore of the sea, listening to a powerful ballad, viewing a moving piece of art, or gazing into the depths of another's eyes are all potential sacramental moments that beckon a person inward to reflect on one's place in the world. In this manner, sacraments provoke action, foster self-reflection, and invite self-transformation.

Panentheistic Pansacramentality

A pansacramental worldview posits that all things, corporeal or otherwise, serve as potential mediators (symbols) of the sacred.[7] Panentheism refers

---

[5]This pansacramental worldview cascades out of a Christian context and can thusly be accused of Christian appropriation of non-Christian rituals. It is open to the charge of imposing the Christian category of sacramentality onto non-Christian traditions.

[6]A moving example of this is Henri Nouwen's reflection about seeing Rembrandt's *The Return of the Prodigal Son*, which forced Nouwen to question his vocation and place in life and, in Nouwen's words, "set in motion a long spiritual adventure that brought me to a new understanding of my vocation and offered me new strength to live it" (Nouwen, *The Return of the Prodigal Son: A Story of Homecoming* [New York: Doubleday, 1994], 3).

[7]Variations of this section were first presented in Gustafson, "Pansacramentality as a New Model for the God-World Relationship in Panentheism," paper presented at the Upper Midwest Regional Meeting of the American Academy of Religion, Luther Seminary, St. Paul, Minnesota,

to a worldview that posits that all things are in the divine (*theos*), yet the divine is more than all things. A primary task for panentheists is to explain how the sacred dwells in all things, and how all things dwell in the sacred. In other words, what does the "en" (in) in *pan-en-theism* mean? This section articulates a "panentheistic pansacramentality," a worldview for under-standing the relations between the sacred, the world, and persons. It rests on P³ (a "principle of panentheistic pansacramentality"), which holds that all things *sacramentally* exist in the sacred, and the sacred *sacramentally* exists in all things. In other words, P³ is an answer to the question of how all things exist in the sacred: they do so *sacramentally*. Panentheists often conceptualize the relationship between the sacred and the world through the image of the world as the body of the sacred (i.e., the world as God's body).[8] This metaphor remains a powerful way to describe the relationship between the world and the sacred. Consider the following two metaphors that further explain this relationship by highlighting the functionality of (pan)sacramentality: (1) the relation of builder to house (creator to creation), and more powerfully, (2) the relation of mother to child.

Builder-House. My grandfather and father were homebuilders, and now my brother is too. They've built hundreds of painstakingly artistic houses. Upon entering these houses, visitors not only experience the house but they meet my homebuilding forefathers (and brother). Their houses make them present in a concrete way. Over the years, visitors uttered, as we stood in the latest home, "Your father is in this house," even though my father was not literally there with us. The house bore the mark of the builder. What is going on here? Imagine a builder designs and builds a house. The builder is not the house and the house is not the builder. They stand in distinction to one another; however, according to P³, the builder is in the house and the house is in the builder, sacramentally. The house symbolically re-presents the builder. Though the house makes the builder present, the builder is still more than the house. Theists might say the builder is immanent to, yet transcends the house. The builder is not reduced to the house; he can build other houses. The metaphor can only go so far, since the analogy

April 6, 2013, and in Gustafson, *Finding All Things in God*, 288–93.

[8]Many panentheists find this approach appealing while others remain cautious. Michael W. Brierley identifies advocates as Philip Clayton, David Ray Griffin, Jay McDaniel, and Sallie McFague; those who remain cautious as John Macquarrie and David Pailin; and Arthur Peacock as one who outright rejects this model: see Michael W. Brierley, "Naming a Quiet Revolution: The Panentheistic Turn in Modern Theology," in *In Whom We Live and Move and Have Our Being: Panentheistic Reflections on God's Presence in a Scientific World*, Philip Clayton and Arthur Peacocke, eds. (Grand Rapids: Eerdmans, 2004), 136–38. The most accessible text on the metaphor of the world as God's body comes from Keith Ward, "The World as the Body of God: A Panentheistic Metaphor," in *In Whom We Live and Move and Have Our Being*, 62–72.

of the builder to the sacred (God) will eventually expose the limitations of the builder: the builder can only build the house; he cannot create the wood, stone, and steel needed to construct it. Nonetheless, the house will always be more than the sum of its parts. Visitors to the house come to see the house, not the materials as such. They not only experience the house as such (literally), but they experience the builder as well (symbolically). They meet the builder, for the house bears the marks of the builder. The builder is symbolically "in" all his houses through design, material, function, and feel, while all of the houses are intellectually "in" the builder, who is the source of their origination and actualization. The builder and his house dwell in one another; they mutually indwell.[9]

Mother-Child. You have heard, "You have your mother in you," "You are your father!" and "I see you in your mother." Clearly not meant literally, these figurative statements mean something quite definite. Of course, you *are not* your father, literally. However, it remains meaningful to say so. Most parents know this is not a one-way street. Others not only see us in our children, but they also see our children in us. For mothers, their child was quite *literally* in them. After birth, however, the child remains in the mother, *symbolically*. We are all familiar with this metaphor, which expresses the impressions the parent and child make upon each other. Mother and child are symbolically in each other, yet remain more than each other. Parent and child are both immanent to, and transcendent of, each other. The implications and promise of this metaphor extend significantly beyond most metaphors in articulating a pansacramental model of the sacred-world-person relationship.

A popular panentheist refrain states that all things are in the sacred and the sacred is in all things. The pansacramental version articulated in these metaphors declares that all houses are in the builder and the builder is in all his houses, and the mother is in all her children and all the children are in the mother. A strength of panentheistic pansacramentality, and the aforementioned metaphors, lies in demonstrating how all things as sacraments can mediate. In the builder-house relationship, the house as sacrament mediates between builder and nonbuilder (visitors). To deeply know the builder, the visitors must experience the house. The sacrament of the house is necessary. To deeply know a mother as a mother, we need to meet and know her child(ren). To know Shakespeare deeply, we need to read his work. Likewise, to know the sacred we can look to all things—and knowing the sacred can teach us about the nature of all things. For if the sacred

---

[9]This metaphor can be broadened to an *artist-art* relationship generally: poet to poetry, painter to paintings, musician to music, photographer to photos, and so on.

is sacramentally in all things and all things are in the sacred, in a similar manner to the metaphors above, then looking to all things as symbolic mediators of the sacred can yield insight about both. This is especially the case if we take seriously a fractal interpretation of religions themselves, and the diversity between and within religions.

PANSACRAMENTALITY AND RELIGIOUS FRACTALITY

Perry Schmidt-Leukel's fractal interpretation of religious diversity brings to life various implications of a pansacramental worldview. In particular, the two metaphors introduced above (builder-house and mother-child) demonstrate pansacramentality's kinship with religious fractality. Schmidt-Leukel's theory of fractal interpretation applied to religious diversity states in this book's introduction, "the diversity we observe *among* the religions globally is mirrored in the diversity that we find *within* each of the major religious traditions. And that we can also discern some patterns of this diversity—or elements thereof—*within the religious orientation of individual persons.*" The first clause of this assertion is the focus of this section, while the second clause—*"within the religious orientation of individual persons"*—is the focus of the next section.

Schmidt-Leukel keenly recognizes earlier in this volume the resonance and compatibility between a fractal structure of religious diversity and the micro-macro-cosmos scheme found in "traditional religious metaphysics, [which] refers to the recursiveness of general structures in the mental and nonmental aspects of the universe." A rather well-known example of this in contemporary Christian thought comes from Raimon Panikkar's "cosmotheandric" vision, of which one of its many implications is that "Man is a microcosm and divine icon. . . . What goes on in the universe at large has resonances in us. There is a universal correlation, a *perichōrēsis.* . . . The relation of all with all is one of inter-in-dependence."[10] Panikkar's cosmotheandric *perichōrēsis*, similar to a pansacramental worldview, is a proposal for how to understand the relations between persons (humanity), the sacred (divine), and world (cosmos). It is a micro-macro-cosmos scheme, which for Panikkar is one of Christian Trinitarian interpenetration (*perichōrēsis*).

I concur with Schmidt-Leukel who wonders earlier whether the micro-macro-cosmos scheme, in general, "could even be viewed as an anticipation,

---

[10]Raimon Panikkar, *The Rhythm of Being: The Gifford Lectures* (Maryknoll, NY: Orbis Books, 2010), 59, quoted in Perry Schmidt-Leukel, *Religious Pluralism and Interreligious Theology: The Gifford Lectures* (Maryknoll, NY: Orbis, 2017), 222.

or implicit awareness, of" a fractal structure of religious diversity. Indeed, the pansacramental relationship between person-God-world offers a robust micro-macro-cosmos scheme, and herein lies its most obvious kinship with fractality. In short, fractals provide a measure of reassurance, to some degree, that Panikkar's vision of coinherence is on to something. If this is the case, then the pansacramental worldview, as exemplified in the two metaphors, might serve as an effective forerunner for greater acknowledgment and acceptance of the fractal nature of religious diversity. The unity of the sacred and the finite that pansacramentalism affirms might serve as one way to explain the similar differences that the fractal perspective affirms; that is, similarity of diversities (fractals) are grounded in the omni/pan-presence of the sacred as understood in the manner Panikkar seems to have in mind with his coinherence vision of interpenetration.

A fractal interpretation applied to religious diversity affirms that the diversity observed between the different religions of the world is found within each particular tradition itself. Applied to a pansacramental worldview, the spirit of fractality yields an orientation searching for a deep interdependent and interpenetrating relationship between the sacred, world, and persons. Notice the fractal implications of the metaphors introduced above, both of which follow the panentheistic formula of stating that all Xs are sacramentally or symbolically in Y and Y is sacramentally or symbolically in all Xs. The builder is symbolically in all his houses, and all his houses are symbolically in the builder. All children are symbolically (and at one time literally) in their mothers, and all mothers are symbolically in all their children. The sacred is sacramentally in all things, and all things are sacramentally in the sacred. An implication that stems from the spirit of the fractal formula states that if X is in Y and Y is in X, then we can learn about the nature of X by examining Y and vice versa. In short, the nature of one tells us something about the nature of the other.

More to the point, the kinship between a fractal interpretation of religious diversity and a pansacramental worldview can be shown to reflect each other according to three parallel observations:

Fractal Interpretation of Religious Diversity:

1. We find religious diversity in the world as the reality of the many religious traditions (referred to as *interreligious* or *external* religious diversity).

2. We find such diversity within each particular religious tradition itself (referred to as *internal* or *intra*religious diversity).

3. We find such diversity within the individual person (referred to as *intrasubjective* religious diversity).

Pansacramental Worldview:

1. We find the sacred[11] in the world as the reality of all things claimed to be sacred (or potentially sacred) by the many and various religious people and communities of the world (referred to as *external* or *cosmic* sanctity).

2. We find the sacred in each particular thing itself (referred to as *internal* sanctity).

3. We find the sacred within the individual person in a way that mirrors the sacred itself and the sanctity of the cosmos (referred to as inner or *intrasubjective* sanctity).

If the sacred, world, and person mutually interpenetrate, what does one teach us about the other two, and how does such a scheme square with our religious traditions?

The builder-house and mother-child metaphors bring out various implications and questions about the pansacramental, micro-macro-cosmos scheme. If humans and the world suffer, then the sacred suffers as well. When children suffer, parents suffer alongside them (albeit it in a different manner). The popular question among philosophers of religion regarding divine and human freedom is relevant here too. Do the sacred and the human have equal freedom? Once built, a house is now "out there" and separate from the builder, like a child in the world away from her mother. Though on their own, the house remains a part of the builder and the child a part of her mother. However, the world freely impresses itself upon the house and child in a way beyond the control of the builder and mother. The world freely interprets, criticizes, praises, oppresses, and treats the house and child. Exposed to the realities and suffering of the world, they suffer, and the builder and mother suffer with them.

A pansacramental worldview, which posits all things *in* the sacred and the sacred *in* all things, can be qualified by defining the *in*, in the previous clause, to refer to "in solidarity with" ("solidarity" referring primarily to co-suffering). The mother suffers in solidarity with her child, the builder suffers in solidarity with his house, and the sacred suffers in solidarity with world and person. These metaphors provide a conceptual framework for thinking about the interrelations among the three entities. The next section turns to the particularity with which individuals encounter external, internal, and interior religious diversity.

---

[11] I am suggesting here that a pansacramental view can accommodate many ultimates. I've chosen to use the word "sacred" for ultimacy.

RECKONING WITH EXTERNAL, INTERNAL, AND INTRASUBJECTIVE RELIGIOUS DIVERSITY

Schmidt-Leukel, in his fractal interpretation of religious diversity, draws on the three levels of cultural diversity in Swiss philosopher Elmar Holenstein's "architecture of cultural diversity," (*intra-*, *inter-*, and *intrasubjective*) and applies them to religious diversity.[12] They are (1) *intrareligious*, (2) *interreligious*, and (3) *intrasubjective*. These three levels also provide a useful framework to think about how people come to the table of interreligious engagement; they are "gateways to engagement with religious diversity."[13] These gateways need not be understood as mutually exclusive, nor are they always explicitly "gateways." Rather, they can be levels of religious diversity (as Schmidt-Leukel proposes) but also modes of religious inquiry and facets of the architecture of religious diversity.

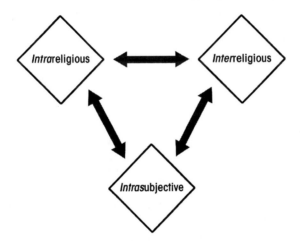

The level of *intrareligious* diversity refers to the diversity found within the various religious traditions, the level of *interreligious* diversity refers to the reality of the existence of various religious traditions on a global scale, and the level of *intrasubjective* religious diversity refers to "the diversity found within the mental cosmos of one particular individual" (Schmidt-Leukel, introduction to this volume). Schmidt-Leukel's fractal interpretation argues that features that distinguish religions from one another (*interreligious* di-

---

[12]Schmidt-Leukel, *Religious Pluralism and Interreligious Theology*, 226–27.

[13]This section is an expanded and revised version of Hans Gustafson, "Gateways to Engagement with Religious Diversity," State of Formation, May 7, 2018; http://www.stateofformation. org/2018/05/gateways-to-engagement-with-religious-diversity/.

versity) also appear again in the other two levels. In this section I draw on these three levels to explain how and why they function interdependently and can often serve as gateways to each other.

Intrareligious Encounter Leads to Interreligious Engagement

After recognizing the diversity that already exists within their own tradition, people commonly wade into the pool of intentional interreligious engagement. A Christian might reframe this by saying ecumenical dialogue often leads to interreligious dialogue. For instance, Leonard Swidler, well-known "pioneer and peacemaker"[14] in interfaith dialogue, reports first becoming interested in Protestant-Catholic dialogue as a graduate student at the University of Tübingen in the late 1950s.[15] Today Swidler remains one of the most well-known and prolific scholars and leaders in ecumenical and interreligious dialogue in the West, and his journey began with an interest in the internal diversity of his home religion of Christianity. This narrative plays out again and again with countless people in the many traditions. Someone who recognizes the important distinctions in her home tradition often realizes (1) not only must there also be important differences lurking within traditions other than her own but (2) these differences matter and (3) they are not often recognized by those outside the tradition.

Recognizing the internal diversity of religions is not only important for understanding our own religious traditions but also for understanding the traditions of others. A major obstacle to constructive interreligious engagement today lies in oversimplifying traditions other than our own, which is to say ignoring the vast diversity that exists in other religions. It is generally not accurate to claim that "all Muslims do X, all Jews believe Y, or all Christians forbid Z." This ignorance is not often born out of malice; rather, it arises simply out of a lack of basic religious literacy and exposure to religious diversity. Thus, elsewhere I have argued for the cultivation of "interreligious wherewithal"[16] and "(inter)religious literacy."[17]

---

[14]Harold Kasimow, "Leonard Swidler: Dialogue Pioneer and Peacemaker," *Journal of Ecumenical Studies* 50 (2015): 37–41.

[15]River Adams, *There Must Be You: Leonard Swidler's Journey to Faith and Dialogue* (Eugene, OR: Resource Publications, 2014), xxiv.

[16]Hans Gustafson, "Interreligious Wherewithal: Cultivating a Leadership Virtue," State of Formation, November 16, 2017; http://www.stateofformation.org/2017/11/interreligious-wherewithal-cultivating-a-leadership-virtue/.

[17]Hans Gustafson, "What Does It Mean to Be (Inter)Religiously Literate?" State of Formation, April 27, 2018; http://www.stateofformation.org/2018/04/what-does-it-mean-to-be-interreligiously-literate/.

Interreligious and Intrareligious Encounter Lead to Intrasubjective Reflection

Encountering the diversity that exists internally and externally in our own and other traditions often turns us inward to reflect on our own religious identity in a deeper manner. Not only is this part of the methodological spirit of comparative theology, as I understand it, but it also gets at what Raimon Panikkar had in mind when he wrote about the "intrareligious dialogue"— that conversation that takes place within oneself about one's own religious identity in the encounter with other religions.[18] His encounter with external traditions (interreligious encounter) led him to reflect on his own religious identity (intersubjective religious diversity). This is the interior reflection, or intrapersonal dialogue, that takes place when one recognizes that diversity is not simply something outside of oneself but also within oneself.

This dynamic process can often lead someone to not only (re)consider her religious identity in the context of her home tradition—that is, how she orients around the internal diversity of her own religion—but she also might consider how she religiously identifies vis-à-vis traditions outside her own. The process may cast her into deep reflection about the very heart of her own religious identity as such, regardless of her home tradition. Schmidt-Leukel recognizes earlier in this volume "a clear correspondence between, on the one hand, religious diversity at the inter- and intrareligious levels and, on the other hand, different psychological profiles at the intrasubjective level."

Diane M. Millis identifies three "conversations" always taking place in a gathering of people: (1) *external*, spoken words between people; (2) *internal*, dialogue in the head interpreting what is seen, heard, and so on in the exterior world; and 3) *interior*, the conversation "that happens in the deepest core of our being,"[19] which is akin to intrasubjective reflection. Millis teaches that silence is a key to cultivating this reflection; she writes, "When we get quiet—really quiet—we become more aware of all the noise

---

[18]Panikkar describes this as the "something [which] stirs within us; . . . the internal dialogue triggered by the thou who is not in-different to the I. Something stirs in the inmost recesses of our being. . . . It takes place in the core of our being . . . an internal dialogue in which one struggles with the angel, the *daimôn*, and oneself. . . . [It helps] us discover the 'other' in ourselves" (Panikkar, *The Intra-Religious Dialogue* [New York: Paulist Press, 1999], xvi–xix; see also William Grimes, "Raimon Panikkar, Roman Catholic Theologian, Is Dead at 91," September 4, 2010, http://www.nytimes.com/2010/09/05/us/05panikkar.html). Panikkar's language here is similar to, if not the same as, the intrasubjective level of religious diversity. Panikkar famously said about his own religious identity after returning from India to study Indian philosophy and religion, "I left Europe as a Christian, I discovered I was a Hindu and returned as a Buddhist without ever having ceased to be Christian" (*Intra-Religious Dialogue*, 42; Grimes, "Raimon Panikkar").

[19]Diane M. Millis, "Silence and the Art of Conversation," Faith and Leadership, November 18, 2013, https://www.faithandleadership.com/diane-m-millis-silence-and-art-conversation.

around us, between us, and within us."[20] Dwelling in such silence, one might begin to recognize the many different religious identities he potentially carries with him. He is not unique. For those who identify with a particular tradition, this deep reflection on their interior religious identity can push them into considering how they might also identify with multiple religious identities (MRI), whether it be via "multiple religious belonging" (MRB) or "multiple religious participation" (MRP).[21] For the growing number who identify as "nones" or "spiritual but not religious," this could mean reflecting on how, even though they may not identify with any particular tradition, they might still participate in one or more traditions. This might be "single religious participation" (SRP) or MRP, but not "single religious belonging" (SRB) or MRB.

Intrasubjective Reflection Leads to Intrareligious and Interreligious Encounter

Intrasubjective religious reflection also entails the possibility of leading one (back) to interreligious and intrareligious engagement. The conversation that takes place within one's self (one's own intrapersonal dialogue) can serve as a microcosm of the dialogue that takes place both within one's own religious tradition and between the religious traditions of the world. Schmidt-Leukel recognizes this connection and references scholars Rose Drew and Mira Niculescu and their studies of the MRB of "JuBus" (people with Jewish-Buddhist identity). He writes that Niculescu "describes the spiritual attitude of so-called 'JuBus' . . . as a 'perpetually ongoing inner dialogue,'" and that "Drew concludes that in this kind of internalized spiritual dialogue dual belongers 'become microcosms of the dialogue as a whole.'"[22]

This internal dialogue is not unique to those with multiple religious identities, but rather takes place within many people. It is conceivable that part of what it means to be human is to wrestle with this incessant internal conversation, which is perhaps the most important of the three levels here since it pushes some persons into the other two levels. The recent film

---

[20]Ibid.

[21]I distinguish between "multiple religious belonging" and "multiple religious participation," both employed here under the rubric of MRI. "Multiple religious belonging" refers to the complete simultaneous embracing of, and commitment to, two or more religions. See Gustafson, "Descandalizing Multiple Religious Identity with Help from Nicholas Black Elk and His Spirituality: An Exercise in Interreligious Learning," *Journal of Ecumenical Studies* 51 (2016): 83–84n.

[22]Schmidt-Leukel, *Religious Pluralism and Interreligious Theology*, 234, quoting Rose Drew, *Buddhist and Christian? An Exploration of Dual Belonging* (London: Routledge, 2011), 209; and Mira Niculescu, "I the Jew, I the Buddhist: Multi-Religious Belonging as Inner Dialogue," *Crosscurrents* 62, no. 3 (2012): 350–59.

Innsæi: The Power of Intuition showcases the Icelandic word *innsæi*, which means intuition or insight, but holds various deeper meanings in Iceland. It can mean "the sea within," "to see within," and "to see from the inside out." The film teaches,

> *The sea within* is the borderless nature of our inner world. It is constantly moving. It goes beyond words. It is a world of vision, feelings, and imagination. The sea within cannot be put into boxes because then it ceases to flow. . . . *To see within* is to know yourself; to know yourself well enough to be able to put yourself into other people's shoes, and to bring out the best in you. . . . *To see from the inside out* is to have a strong inner compass so you can navigate your way into our ever-changing world.[23]

Innsæi, in this deeper sense, captures the spirit of intrasubjective reflection by keeping sight of the capacity of internal reflection to push one back toward empathetic engagement with others ("to put yourself into other people's shoes"). By referring to the "borderless nature of our inner world," *innsæi* recognizes the inner fluidity of the subjective self. Finally, *innsæi* functions virtuously as a means for navigating a religiously complex and fluid world—a leadership virtue I have referred to elsewhere as "interreligious wherewithal."[24]

These three levels of religious diversity, or modes of religious inquiry, are most certainly interrelated and interdependent. Further, as gateways to encounter, they are not mutually exclusive, nor do they function independently of one another. Rather, they flow concurrently and harmoniously. As such, they have important practical implications for interfaith relations. Jeannine Hill Fletcher recognizes that a downside of the process of religious identification is the lingering concern of exclusivity in determining who is in and who is out (e.g., who gets to be a Christian?). She points out that this "logic of identity"[25] or "grouping of persons into the various categories of 'the religions' and the assumptions made on the basis of those groupings too easily erase[s] the diversity and difference within any one community."[26] This can dilute the rich internal diversity of a religion by

---

[23]*Innsæi: The Power of Intuition*, Kristín Ólafsdóttir and Hrund Gunnsteinsdottir, dirs. (Iceland: KLIKK Productions, 2016), Netflix 1:09:18–1:13:37 (emphasis added).

[24]"'Interreligious Wherewithal' is that virtue of being aware of a potential tension or opportunity in (inter)religiously complex situations and having the skill to do something constructive about it through thoughtful action, leadership, and motivation of others" (Gustafson, "Interreligious Wherewithal").

[25]A phrase Hill Fletcher borrows from political scientist Iris Marion Young.

[26]Jeannine Hill Fletcher, "Shifting Identity: The Contribution of Feminist Thought to Theolo-

lumping all Muslims together into one group (regardless of their identities as Sunni, Shia, etc.) or all Christians together into one group (regardless of denominational affiliation and creedal confession). It often erases "the diversity and difference"[27] within the traditions and reinforces one of the major obstacles to constructive interreligious encounter today: the oversimplification of the religious other. On the other hand, a positive consequence is that it sometimes brings together, or "forges solidarity"[28] among, those with different identities within a religious group (e.g., Protestants with Roman Catholics with Eastern Orthodox, etc.). Forging solidarity is good, but erasing the diversity and difference that exist within religious groups can strip individuals of aspects that make them different from one another.

LOOKING FORWARD

There are several promising avenues and applications of a fractal theory of religious diversity. This volume takes up the task of utilizing this theory to bring order to what seems to many to be the chaotic and confusing conversation about religious diversity. This is perhaps one of the theory's most promising attributes. For many scholars and teachers of religious studies, recognizing and affirming the vast internal diversity and dynamic nature of religious traditions and worldviews is paramount (i.e., countering essentialism and reductionism). However, in doing so, they also want to avoid the extreme of concluding that the traditions and worldviews are so different that they are incommensurable, thus rendering futile any effort of comparison. A fractal interpretation comes to the rescue in this dilemma by assuming, as Schmidt-Leukel points out, that "religions are actually comparable precisely in—and because of—their internal diversity. Religions are internally so diverse that the other religion always contains some familiar features or elements" (introduction, this volume).

Further, the dimensions of universality within the language of fractality offer a greater benefit than the same dimensions of universality within pansacramental language and categories. Fractal structures in the world (religion, culture, nature, etc.) offset claims of radical difference and instead affirm similarities while preserving difference. Pansacramental language is, well, "sacramental," a term that is associated primarily with Christian, especially Catholic, traditions. Adjusting the universal claims of pansacramentality to those of religious fractality may help to avoid the use of

---

gies of Religious Pluralism," *Journal of Feminist Studies in Religion* 19, no. 2 (2003): 14.
    [27]Ibid.
    [28]A phrase Hill Fletcher employs to refer to this phenomenon.

Christian-centric language. Perhaps other terms can take the place of the language of sacramentality—such as Eliade's "hierophany" or "theophany." In this case, pansacramentality might be better labeled as panhierophanism or pantheophanism. In fact, such language is more in keeping with the spirit of practicality, for Eliade used these terms to express his recognition of "wide-ranging structural similarities across all religions."[29] Eliade states, as quoted by Schmidt-Leukel, "we are faced with a manifestation, vastly different obviously, of the sacred in a fragment of the universe."[30]

The assessments of this "vastly different manifestation of the sacred" by a fractal theory of religious diversity on the one hand, and by pansacramentality on the other, are not the same. A fractal theory of religious diversity is a phenomenological observation or assertion about the differences between and within religions. Pansacramentalism is a theological perspective claiming that all things can serve as potential mediators of the divine. Trying to relate the two, one might say that the fractal theory of religious diversity provides a potential backdrop (foundation) for pansacramentality—as they both pursue their common quest of seeking to make sense of religious diversity.

This is perhaps an example of the phenomenological coming together with the theological, which is one of the six "fruitful perspectives" predicted by Schmidt-Leukel at the end of his book when he writes that "a fractal theory of religious diversity brings back the *phenomenology of religion* . . . [and] suggests that comparisons should be done . . . without phenomenology's former principle of excluding the scholar's own background from the sphere of research."[31]

At a broader level, this call to "bring back the phenomenology of religion" without abandoning the scholar's possible theological commitments will contribute to overcoming the tension (and often the anxiety that comes with it, in North America at least) between religious studies and theology. Overcoming such tension, one can assume, is one of the larger aims of Schmidt-Leukel's proposal for making "interreligious theology" a normative approach in theology. Interreligious theology strives to ease this tension by reaching beyond strict confessional lines and taking "religious truth claims seriously, those of one's own religious tradition and those of all others. Taking them seriously," he contends, "means to search for possible truth in all of the religious testimonies,"[32] including atheist and naturalist

---

[29]Schmidt-Leukel, *Religious Pluralism and Interreligious Theology*, 227.
[30]Mircea Eliade, *Patterns in Comparative Religion* (1949; Lincoln: University of Nebraska Press, 1996), 463; also quoted in Schmidt-Leukel, *Religious Pluralism and Interreligious Theology*, 227.
[31]Schmidt-Leukel, *Religious Pluralism and Interreligious Theology*, 244.
[32]Ibid., 13.

interpretations of religion.[33] Furthermore, a fractal theory invites several disciplinary approaches to analyze and compare religious diversity "from sociological, psychological, aesthetical, and philosophical perspectives."[34]

This chapter serves as but one example of bridging the phenomenological with the theological, which many may find refreshing and appealing while others may consider it scandalous, tiresome, or off-putting. Finally, and perhaps most importantly, this effort to relate the phenomenology of the fractal theory of religious diversity with the theology of pansacramentalism can provide, it is hoped, some help in dealing with the often seemingly unrelated complexity of our religiously diverse world. In today's geopolitical climate, few areas are more in need of "coming together" in order to "make sense of" than the many contexts in which people are confronting the need to enable "religious diversity" to become the context for "interreligious encounter and collaboration."

[33]Ibid., 245.
[34]Ibid., 227.

PART THREE

MULTIRELIGIOUS
PERSPECTIVES

Rethinking Religious Pluralism and Interreligious Theology in China

Rong Wang

Perry Schmidt-Leukel is a scholar who has been deeply involved in the field of religious pluralism and interreligious theology for a long time and has made significant contributions. His book *Religious Pluralism and Interreligious Theology*[1] is an important study using the perspective of religious pluralism (i.e., affirming the validity of many religions and the supremacy of none) in order to develop an interreligious theology. In making his case, Schmidt-Leukel refers positively to Chinese religious harmony and religious siniciza-tion. This question of sinicization—how a "foreign" religion can be integrated into Chinese reality—is a central issue that I address further in this essay.

The main issues that Schmidt-Leukel addresses in his book are: First, how have pluralist approaches been developed in Christianity, Judaism, Islam, Hinduism, Buddhism, and the Chinese religions? What are the characteristics of these developments? Second, what kind of theology is interreligious theology? What are its principles and methodologies, as well as its intended fruits? Finally, what does the fractal interpretation of religious diversity advocate for, and what are its positive fruits? This article reflects on these three issues contained in Schmidt-Leukel's exploration of religious pluralism and interreligious theology.

THE DEVELOPMENT OF RELIGIOUS PLURALISM IN VARIOUS RELIGIONS

At the very beginning of *Religious Pluralism*, Perry Schmidt-Leukel states that today people are far more aware of religious diversity than ever.

---

[1]Perry Schmidt-Leukel, *Religious Pluralism and Interreligious Theology* (Maryknoll, NY: Orbis Books, 2017).

The questions of how to interpret the fact of religious diversity and how to deal with it have become very challenging and controversial for many religious believers. Schmidt-Leukel points out that the "pluralist" perspective proposed in his book is not only a philosophical interpretation of religious diversity but also a religious interpretation that needs to be developed in each religious tradition.[2] The question to be asked, therefore, is: can each religious tradition provide such a pluralistic foundation?

According to Schmidt-Leukel, for an atheist or a naturalist, the religious understandings of reality are basically wrong. Religious diversity, as a problematic phenomenon, has been used by atheists and naturalists to support their viewpoints. Religious diversity also impels believers to question why their own religion is not the only one in the world. Why do so many other religions exist? Why do so many other people practice other beliefs? Schmidt-Leukel has discerned that many traditional religious thinkers hold that all religions, except their own, are wrong, and he points out that such assessments are no different from those of atheists or naturalists. Obviously, such negative interpretations of religious diversity seem to undermine the credibility of each religion.[3]

Schmidt-Leukel asks, "Is it inevitable for religions to take such a negative stance on religious diversity as they have often done in the past? Or are there any other options that they might choose?"[4] As we know, Alan Race provided a typology for the interpretation of religious diversity in 1983: exclusivism, inclusivism, and pluralism.[5] However, through a careful review of the ongoing disputes over this typology, Schmidt-Leukel concludes that because of the very different ways in which these types have been interpreted and used, a great deal of confusion has resulted. Many scholars have therefore questioned the typology's utility. However, Schmidt-Leukel has carefully analyzed the typology as a logically comprehensive scheme:

> The religious claims of teaching a path of salvation are either all false (naturalism) or they are not all false. If they are not all false, then either only one of them is true (exclusivism) or more than one is true. If more than one is true, then there is either one singular maximum of that truth (inclusivism) or there is no singular maximum, so that at least some are equally true (pluralism).[6]

---

[2]Ibid., 1.

[3]Ibid., 3.

[4]Ibid., 2.

[5]*Christians and Religious Pluralism: Patterns in the Christian Theology of Religions* (Maryknoll, NY: Orbis Books and London: SCM Press, 1983).

[6]Schmidt-Leukel, *Religious Pluralism and Interreligious Theology*, 4.

If we understand the classification in this way, we will find that it is logically comprehensive.

Schmidt-Leukel also points out that the model of "religious pluralism" is basically different from religious tolerance. Tolerance means that we tolerate something we don't like. Religious pluralism claims that religions can be not only tolerant of each other, they can also explore and develop a true mutual appreciation. Hence Schmidt-Leukel argues that pluralism is different from naturalism, exclusivism, and inclusivism, for it calls for a positive approach to religious diversity. He points out further that religious controversy is quite different from religious dialogue: controversy seeks to identify the weaknesses and shortcomings of the "religious other" in order to demonstrate the superiority of one's own faith, whereas in genuine dialogue one looks for the strengths of other religions and the insights contained in their tradition in order to learn from them.[7]

In the first part of his book (chapters 2–6), Schmidt-Leukel carefully examines the foundations for religious pluralism in Christianity, Judaism, Islam, Buddhism, and Chinese religions. In his opinion, although Christianity, Judaism, and Islam have often adopted a very strong attitude of exclusivism, they actually have the potential to affirm the validity of religious diversity. So-called Eastern religions also have their own history of claiming superiority, which remains a particular challenge to those who are eager to seek true pluralism.[8]

In Schmidt-Leukel's understanding, tendencies either to support or oppose religious pluralism are present in Hinduism. The history of the relationship between Hinduism and Islam, as well as between Hinduism and Christianity, is full of many disputes, tensions, and conflicts. Some past recognitions of mutual understanding and integration have taken place, but none have been very successful. Buddhism, throughout its history, has found it difficult to form a positive interpretation of religious pluralism due to its inherited sense of exclusive or inclusive superiority. Also, some Buddhists hold Buddhism to be doctrinally so different from other religions that it is difficult to correlate its teachings with those of other traditions.[9]

When talking about any pluralist orientation in Chinese religions, Schmidt-Leukel explores both Chinese history and contemporary context and notes that the long experience of religious diversity in China has involved intense confrontations and religious conflicts. Thus many contemporary Chinese scholars are looking for theological and philosophical avenues in order to promote religious harmony. In the contemporary dis-

---

[7]Ibid., 4–5.
[8]Ibid., 6.
[9]Ibid., 89.

course, China has become a huge laboratory for religious experiments. In recent years, the works of Christian pioneer theologians such as Wilfred Cantwell Smith, Raimon Panikkar, John Hick, and Paul Knitter have been translated into Chinese. However, Chinese theologians disagree intensely as to whether religious pluralism is able to foster the kind of sinicized theology they want to develop.[10]

In my estimation, Schmidt-Leukel has made a creative and constructive contribution to efforts to understand religious diversity by showing that within all the religious traditions there is the potential—though often untapped—of assuming a pluralistic view of other religions that recognizes their validity. He states accordingly,

> To every religious pluralist it is therefore, on one hand, essential to demonstrate some continuity between the pluralist approach and his or her own religious tradition. But, on the other hand, every pluralist will also have to be critical of those elements within one's own respective tradition that support its claims of an either exclusivist or inclusivist superiority. In this twofold sense of being faithful to and being critical of one's own tradition, pluralist approaches have to be tradition-specific through and through. . . . Pluralism can exist only as Christian pluralism, Jewish pluralism, Muslim pluralism, and so on.[11]

In other words, Schmidt-Leukel believes that resources can be gleaned from multiple religious traditions to form the foundations for interreligious theology.

However, before discussing whether Schmidt-Leukel's ideas of pluralism can contribute to how religion is understood in China today both academically and practically, I would like to offer some critical comments on the position of some Chinese scholars who are known as proponents of "religious ecology." Schmidt-Leukel states the challenge succinctly: "Christianity is perceived as a danger because of Christianity's intolerant and exclusivist nature, which threatens the harmonious 'ecological' balance between Chinese religions instead of integrating Christianity itself into it."[12]

I partly agree with the concerns of these proponents of religious ecology. And I would like to add that some scholars in China even take a view that precisely because of its intolerant and exclusivist nature, Christianity has expanded rapidly and aggressively in China. Obviously, there is a tension within Christian self-understanding in China. On the one hand are those who

---

[10]Ibid., 101–2.
[11]Ibid., 7–8.
[12]Ibid., 105.

advocate a Christian witness that is unique and exclusive, and on the other hand are theologians and others who would be content to hold Christian faith as one among many in a pluralist understanding, with the latter being more acceptable to the state's desire for "religious harmony."

Actually, the spread of Christianity in China always had its own problems. According to Chinese scholar Ming Xie, in the contemporary discourse of China the development of Christianity evinces three characteristics:

1. There is a problem with the education and qualifications of many Christian preachers. Instead of being trained pastors, most preachers are common people without any professional training. They spread Christianity among those people who are familiar to them, such as neighbors, friends, and colleagues. Although this approach helps make Christianity easily acceptable to its hearers, such preachers often interpret doctrines according to their own untrained understandings, which has caused many disputes among believers.

2. Christianity has only one route for spreading in China: interpersonal preaching. Apart from the Bible, most of the common Christian believers in mainland China, especially in the countryside, seldom obtain information through mass media such as newspapers, TV, or books.

3. The content of most preaching includes many distorted interpretations of Christian doctrines, which is harmful to the development of Christianity itself. Ming Xie argues that these characteristics of the way Christianity has spread in China make it harder for the government to regulate and manage religions.[13] Moreover, the spread of unsophisticated Christian doctrines and practices is not only injurious to Christianity itself but also contributes to undermining social stability.

From these observations, we can see that it is not only because of Christianity's intolerant and exclusivist nature that it is perceived as a danger in China. On the contrary, it is also because of the lack of critical and up-to-date theological thinking on the part of many Christian leaders and preachers that many are calling for the transformation of Christianity in China. This is a real challenge for Chinese Christianity today. To a great extent, because of this situation, many have proposed a Christian pluralistic theology in the hopes that it can contribute to a sinicized Christian theology that promotes religious harmony.

Zhicheng Wang's embrace of pluralism has been met with only partial approval; some Chinese theologians question whether religious pluralism will be a benefit to a sinicized Christianity theology. What they might also recognize, however, is that the development of religious pluralism in China

---

[13]See Ming Xie, *How Contemporary Christianity Is Spreading in China* (doctoral diss., Chinese Academy of Social Sciences, 2010), 111.

has had an evident impact on the development of contemporary Chinese religious studies. Zhicheng Wang and his colleagues have devoted themselves to the study of religious pluralism and religious dialogue for more than twenty years. As a result, religious pluralism and religious dialogue have been widely known in the Chinese academy.

During these last two decades, the works of many theologians from the West involved in the debates surrounding religious pluralism and religious dialogue have been translated into Chinese. Various theologians—including W. C. Smith, John Hick, Paul Knitter, John Cobb, Francis Clooney, Raimon Panikkar, Hans Küng, and Perry Schmidt-Leukel—have precipitated a debate between scholars of religious studies and proponents of religious pluralism in China. Out of this confrontation, one can hope, a clearer appreciation will arise for the contribution that a pluralistic theology can make to religious studies in China.

According to Zhicheng Wang, the development of religious pluralism in China shows the following characteristics:

1. The academic translation of non-Chinese thinkers has fostered the transplantation of new insights and perspectives. As we know, the Chinese people's understanding of Western philosophy depends to a large extent on the translation of Western philosophical works by Chinese scholars. Translation is a transplant of thought; today the Chinese understanding of religious pluralism and religious dialogue is dependent on the interpretation of translated texts. In the 1990s, Zhigang Zhang, a scholar from Peking University, began to discuss religious pluralism in his teaching and writing. Guanghu He, a scholar from Renmin University, was the first to translate John Hick's *Philosophy of Religion* into Chinese.[14] However, little serious discussion followed. Zhicheng Wang wrote his dissertation on John Hick's pluralistic proposal. After publication of Zhicheng Wang's dissertation and his translation and introduction of works and thoughts of other religious pluralists, religious pluralism and religious dialogue gradually became known to a larger community of Chinese scholars. As more and more related works of scholars like Hick, Knitter, and Panikkar were translated into Chinese, more and more scholars in the Chinese academy became familiar with religious pluralism, many of whom offered their own contribution to the broadening discussion of a pluralistic theology and philosophy.[15]

2. A defense of a pluralist perspective has been growing in the Chinese academy, the earliest defender being Zhicheng Wang. In his book *Interpre-*

---

[14]John Hick, *Philosophy of Religion*, Guanghu He, trans. (Beijing: SDX Joint Publishing Company, 1988).

[15]Zhicheng Wang, *A Study of Contemporary Religious Pluralism* (Beijing: Religious Culture Publishing House, 2013), 298.

tation and Salvation,[16] he argued that Hick's religious pluralism is much more reasonable than religious exclusivism and inclusivism for explaining religious diversity in the world. Another scholar, Qingxiong Zhang, from Fudan University, is also critical of religious exclusivism and is inclined to support religious pluralism. He said, "The reasonable standard of religious pluralism is acceptable because it advocates the freedom and tolerance of religions."[17] Finally, Lin Li, who focused on the thought of W. C. Smith, also has supported religious pluralism.[18]

3. Alongside such support for pluralism in China, there have been philosophical objections. Chin Ken Pa, a scholar from Taiwan, repudiates religious pluralism on the grounds of postmodernism and evangelism. Also, De Zhi Duan, from Wuhan University, studied pluralism carefully and, as a result, has repudiated Hick's pluralism and supported inclusivism.[19]

Apart from these critics, some scholars such as Yu Wang and Guoxiang Peng made use of religious pluralism to develop a new understanding of Chinese cultural traditions. And Sheng Kai and Weichi Zhou directly proposed a new theory of pluralism in Buddhism and Daoism.[20]

In conclusion, we could say that religious pluralism has become an integral part of religious studies in China. Given the ongoing disputes and confrontations about the merits of a pluralistic perspective, scholars, whether from the affirmative or negative side, have had to wrestle with issues surrounding religious pluralism. Further, in my understanding, such confrontations take place today not only in the academy but also in the daily interactions between Christians and Buddhists. Religious pluralism can help people change their attitude toward other religions, and it can aid them to move from confrontation to real religious dialogue. Only with an attitude of mutual respect can a true dialogue among religions proceed in China. Moreover, as Wuqing Peng, a scholar from Xinjiang Normal University, has argued, the sinicization of religions is an inevitable requirement for the development of religions in China.[21]

But just what is mean by "religious sinicization"? Primarily, it calls on all "foreign" religions to adapt themselves so that they do not conflict with the existing religions of China—Buddhism, Daoism, and Confucianism—but instead fit in with the harmony of religions.

---

[16]Zhicheng Wang, *Interpretation and Salvation* (Shanghai: Academia Press, 1996).

[17]Qingxiong Zhang, *Tao, Life, and Responsibility* (Beijing: SDX Joint Publishing Company, 2009), 100.

[18]Lin Li, *Inner Transcendence and Multi-Unification of Faith: On the Religious Studies of Wilfred Cantwell Smith* (Beijing: China Social Sciences Press, 2012), 407.

[19]Zhicheng Wang, *A Study*, 300–301.

[20]Ibid., 302–5.

[21]Wuqing Peng, "The Sinicization of Religions as an Inevitable Requirement for the Development of Religion in China," China National News, June 6, 2017.

However, to be honest, this topic is still under discussion and exploration in the Chinese academy. Zhigang Zhang holds a quite representative opinion. He argues that "religious sinicization" is not a brand-new ideal, even though it has only been advocated in China recently. He points out that "religious sinicization" is a longtime project or mission. As we know, Buddhism, Islam and Christianity are the religions that arrived in and spread through China in a process of cultural encounter and communication; hence these "foreign religions" have not only faced the difficult project of incultura-tion as they arrived, but they also have engaged in the task of adapting to the ongoing changes in Chinese culture and society. Zhang argues further that this mission also applied to native religions such as Daoism because, unless it kept pace with ongoing historical and cultural change, it would unavoidably face decline. So, religious sinicization is a task that any religion wishing to thrive in China has to embrace.[22]

According to Zhang, religious sinicization presents a threefold challenge: (1) religions in China must necessarily and expressly take up the task of integrating themselves into Chinese culture, the Chinese nation, and Chinese society; (2) the leaders and scholars of each religion must show how the religion's identity can take shape within the cultural, national, and social identity of China—a challenge that is much debated within the academy; and (3) and this means that religions that originated outside of China cannot simply be imported and copied; they have to be planted in and grow out of China's cultural, historical, and social soil.[23]

Obviously, Chinese religion scholars and believers have been challenged officially to develop some new styles of theology to meet the needs of Chinese society. In this sense, I think Schmidt-Leukel's exploration of inter-religious theology will become a valuable resource for Chinese theologians in developing a localized creative theology.

Let me now move to discuss Schmidt-Leukel's interreligious theology and how it might benefit Chinese scholars seeking to develop a construc-tive Sino-theology.

THE CONSTRUCTION OF INTERRELIGIOUS THEOLOGY

What Schmidt-Leukel envisions as interreligious theology is closely tied to his proposal for a pluralistic perspective for understanding religious diver-sity. He predicts that future theology will be more and more interreligious

---

[22]Zhigang Zhang, *Sinicization of Religions: A Theoretical Study* (Beijing: Religious Culture Publishing House, 2017), 3.

[23]Ibid., 3–5.

and to a great extent will take the form of interreligious theology. Based on that, he discusses the methodologies of interreligious theology, proposing that it will be carried out on the basis of four principles:

1. A *fundamental trust that there is more truth in many religions than there is in any one of them*—and that, therefore, something is to be learned in a dialogue with people of other traditions.
2. A *fundamental trust in the unity of reality*, because of which, whatever truth is found in one religion must, in some way, be compatible with the truth of other religions.
3. A *commitment to ongoing interreligious conversation* because, if there is truth in other religions that is compatible with mine, the only way to get at it is through open, sincere dialogue.
4. A *recognition that this dialogue will never be finished* and that it may lead us in surprising directions, to which we must always be open.[24]

After affirming these four basic principles, Schmidt-Leukel formulates the methodological characteristics of interreligious theology as follows:

*   *Perspectival.* It recognizes and works with the perspectives of diverse doctrines and teachings.
*   *Imaginative.* It seeks, as much as is possible, to imagine the world as the other tradition or believer sees the world and tries to recognize the truth of that vision.
*   *Comparative.* All those engaged in this conversation and exploration are seeking reciprocal illumination; there are new things to discover on the part of all.
*   *Constructive.* The new truths that are learned are truths that must be lived; thus, an interreligious theology seeks mutual transformation.

Schmidt-Leukel then moves into the substantive second part of his book, in which he shows how the methodology of interreligious theology might proceed in practice by creatively exploring how the three pivotal figures in Buddhism, Christianity, and Islam—Gautama, Jesus, and Muhammad—can relate to and enrich each other. After discussing the Muslim critique of Jesus as the "Son of God" and the Christian critique of Muhammad as the "final Prophet," Schmidt-Leukel suggests an interpretation of the concepts of "Son" and "Prophet" that creates a constructive relationship between them. In a similar way, he also deals with the reciprocal critique and constructive dialogue between Buddhism and Christianity, and between Buddhism and

---

[24]Schmidt-Leukel, *Religious Pluralism and Interreligious Theology*, 130–39.

Islam, and arrives at an understanding of "Son," "Prophet," and "Buddha" that elucidates the inherent interrelatedness of all three concepts within the context of a creative interreligious theology.[25]

In this creative example of an interreligious theology carried out in a conversation between Abrahamic and Eastern religions, Schmidt-Leukel makes clear that the differences between Buddhism, Christianity, and Islam reflect differences within each of them—and that an exploration of and conversation between these differences can lead to the mutual learning and transformation of all three traditions.

Such an example of interreligious theology is an invitation to all religions and all religious believers to rethink, construct, develop, and transform their own traditions through interaction with others and so for all of them to meet the needs of the wider world. On the one hand, each religion needs to absorb nutrition from other religions; on the other hand, each religion needs to maintain the distinctiveness of its own tradition as it deepens and expands it in dialogue with others. The fact that such a process of illumination and transformation through engagement with "the other" has occurred naturally throughout the history of religions is confirmation that it can occur consciously and energetically in our present globally connecting and clashing world.

Here I raise the explicit question: can Chinese religious believers and scholars accept the four principles and methodology of an interreligious theology? Given the pluralistic history of religions of China, I think that they could accept the vision of an interreligious theology as an acceptable basis for a new approach—even a new worldview—and an exciting opportunity for Chinese theologians as well as ordinary believers.

Historically, in my opinion, the developing process of *Sanjiao Heyi* ("the three teachings combine into one" or "harmony" of the three teachings) demonstrates that Chinese people accept pluralism in their own faith practice.

Xinchuan Huang, a scholar from the Chinese Academy of Social Sciences, argues that the reality of *Sanjiao Heyi* is grounded in deep-reaching sociopolitical and economic factors in Chinese history but that it also bears its own religious characteristics and dynamics. Ancient Chinese rulers regarded Confucianism, Buddhism, and Daoism as three indispensable pillars for maintaining their rule, in that these three religions had their own characteristics and played various social roles. Specifically, Confucianism could be used to rule the country, Buddhism could be utilized to heal the mind, and Daoism could be applied to body management.[26]

---

[25]Ibid., 147–203.

[26]Xinchuan Huang, "The Developing Process and Characteristics of *San Jiao He Yi* in China and its Influence on Neighbouring Countries," *Study of Philosophy* 8 (1998): 26.

Xinchuan Huang further points out that Confucianism was prominent before Buddhism spread throughout China. After Buddhism arrived in China, in order to fit into Chinese culture and especially mediate areas where it seemed to conflict with Confucianism and Daoism, Buddhism consistently drew on Confucian and Taoist teachings to demonstrate the consistency of all three religions. At the time of Wei, Jin, and the Northern and Southern Dynasties, the three religions were close to each other, even merging into each other, and yet this consistency and confluence could not hide abiding tensions and struggle among them.[27]

During the Sui and Tang Dynasties, Buddhism completed a process of sinicization. After the Song and Yuan Dynasties, the harmony among Confucianism, Buddhism, and Daoism grew much deeper, and the trend toward "unity" was recognized in mainstream Chinese academic thought.[28]

In the Song and Ming Dynasties, Confucianism underwent its second transformation and appeared mainly as *Neo*-Confucianism[29] and Lu and Wang Mind.[30] *Neo*-Confucianism still held to the ethical thought of Confucius and Mencius as its core, but it also both resisted and at the same time relied on Buddhism and Daoism. In a sense, Neo-Confucianism's attitude of "bringing Confucianism into Buddhism" and "integrating Confucianism into Daoism" ultimately introduced many characteristics of Buddhism, Zen, and Daoism into Confucian identity. As a result, divisions between these three religions narrowed, enabling them to merge into a unity of Chinese traditional culture.[31]

I believe that the long development of *Sanjiao Heyi* in ancient China makes clear that the development of religions in China has been toward integration, which has had political and theological implications. At different points in Chinese history, rulers have made use of religious integration to foster sociopolitical unity, but this integrating interplay between the three religions has also stimulated theological and philosophical insights for each of them.

Furthermore, *Sanjiao Heyi* in Chinese history also encourages contemporary Chinese scholars and believers to carry on this dynamic of Chinese religions to affirm and engage each other. The four principles and methodological characteristics that Schmidt-Leukel proposes for interreligious theology can be a valuable stimulus and guide for Chinese Christians in

---

[27]Ibid.

[28]Ibid., 27.

[29]Neo-Confucianism is also called the Teaching of *Cheng and Zhu*, originating from Chengjing and Chengyi in the Northern Song Dynasty, and from Zhu Xi in the Southern Song Dynasty.

[30]Lu and Wang Mind is also called the Teaching of *Lu and Wang*, containing the ideas of Lu Jiuyuan in the Northern Song Dynasty, and of Wang Yangming in the Ming Dynasty.

[31]Huang, "Developing Process," 28.

realizing an integrating dialogue with Confucianism, Buddhism, and Daoism and so enabling Christianity to become an integral, even indispensable,
part of Chinese culture.

In fact, Chinese Christian believers and scholars are presently actively
engaged in discussing how to promote a more adequate sinicization of
Christianity. For example, Feiya Tao urges that to realize a Christian sinicization, we need to draw on a wide variety of resources, including the
historical literature on indigenization from Hong Kong, Taiwan, Macao,
and the Chinese living abroad.[32] Ze Jin holds that Christian indigenization
is not a unique problem for China, but is indeed a widespread religious
phenomenon. Therefore we need to learn from the indigenization of other
religions in the world.[33] This will help respond to China's needs for what
Jin Guang Liu calls a harmonious, genuinely Chinese-Christian theology.[34]
Xinping Zhuo calls for a collaboration between the government, Christian
churches, and the Chinese academy in promoting Christian sinicization.[35]

We must also recognize, I believe, that for many believers, interreligious
discourse is a double-edged sword. To engage in a mutually transformative
dialogue with persons of other religions presents the complex challenge of
simultaneously maintaining commitment to one's own tradition and openness to another tradition. But genuine openness to another tradition requires
that all the religions meet on what we can call a "level playing field" on
which each religion is regarded as valued and important. But this has not
always been the case in Chinese history. According to Xinchuan Huang,
although Confucianism, Buddhism, and Daoism were all advocating *Sanjiao
Heyi*, each from its own perspective, the main contributor, as it were, in
this conversation was always Confucianism. Buddhism and Daoism played
supplemental roles.[36] In such circumstances, the subordinate religions
were always concerned whether their own voices and contributions were
adequately recognized. Dominant religions in a particular culture find it
difficult to be truly open to other religions.

So despite China's history of "religious harmony," the achievement of a
truly dialogical and collaborative engagement of all the present-day religious
traditions in China faces serious challenges: how to balance commitment
and openness, how to truly listen to another tradition that in the past has
been dominant over or subordinate to one's own, how to deal with the realities of political power and influence, and how to construct new theological
foundations for a truly effective dialogue. China's history offers both hope

[32]Shuang Wang, "The Problem, Route, and Significance of Christian Sinicization," *Chinese Social Science*, April 4, 2012, B01.
[33]Ibid.
[34]Ibid.
[35]Ibid.
[36]Xinchuan Huang, "Developing Process," 26.

and caution. The process of religious renewal and transformation calls for testing, exploration, and commitment.

A FRACTAL INTERPRETATION
OF RELIGIOUS DIVERSITY

In the last chapter of his book, Perry Schmidt-Leukel proposes a new way of understanding and engaging religious diversity and of doing theology: "Religious diversity can indeed be interpreted in a fractal way and . . . this understanding of religious diversity is highly significant for interreligious theology and perhaps for any future study of religious diversity."[37] In introducing his fractal interpretation of religious diversity, Schmidt-Leukel first shows how the fractal structure can be found both in the organic and inorganic natural world. Then he suggests how this fractal perspective applies also to the fields of culture and religions. After discussing some aspects of the fractal theory in religious diversity, he reviews how fractal structures have always been found in modern religious studies. Finally, based on his own study, he briefly points out the advantages of this theory and shares the results of his research.

According to Schmidt-Leukel's proposal, the fruitfulness of the fractal theory for religious diversity is evident in six different expressions:

1. The fractal interpretation is very helpful in showing the continuity between ecumenical theology and interreligious theology.
2. The fractal interpretation of religious diversity offers a meaningful alternative to theories of radical cultural and religious incommensurability that have become influential in the wake of postmodern philosophy.
3. The fractal perspective implies that "religion"—contrary to postmodern claims—is not an empty notion; fractals show that religions bear family traits that are both similar and different.
4. The fractal perspective is a restated invitation for scholars to engage in a phenomenological comparison of religions, always including, rather than suspending, one's own personal perspectives.
5. The fractal theory of religious diversity can be made use of by both religious believers and atheists or naturalists.
6. A fractal approach to religions can be adopted to interpret religious diversity not just theologically but also sociologically, psychologically, and aesthetically.[38]

---

[37]Schmidt-Leukel, *Religious Pluralism and Interreligious Theology*, 223.
[38]Ibid., 243–45.

I do believe that Schmidt-Leukel's fractal proposal can also be fruitful for Chinese scholars and believers in their efforts to understand the diversity of religions in China's past and present. It offers us Chinese the opportunity of forging a new understanding of our religious diversity. While this is especially true for Chinese scholars of religious studies, it is also especially true for Chinese theologians as they carry on the task of constructing a harmonious theology of Christianity for contemporary China.

This task of constructing an authentically Chinese Christianity is part of a historical process that all, or most, religions have undergone. Historical studies show that whenever a "foreign" religion finds its way into a new sociocultural setting it has to undergo a process of nationalization and localization in order to be understood and accepted by the new culture. When Buddhism, Christianity, and Islam came to announce their messages to the Chinese people, they had no choice but to adopt the given cultural and religious ideas and viewpoints in order to make their message comprehensible. Through this process of inculturation, something new was added to the teachings and self-understanding of these imported religions. This does not mean that these religions lost their original identities. In my opinion, Buddhism, Christianity and Islam, in their new Chinese cultural forms, are still themselves, but at the same time, they gain a new way of being; they become Buddhism+, Christianity+, and Islam+.

In the Chinese academy of religious studies, we find some scholars who are carrying on this task of inculturation and have devoted themselves to developing a Chinese interreligious theology. Pan Chiu Li, a scholar from Hong Kong involved in Buddhist-Christian dialogue, has developed a Mahayana Christian theology that could be regarded as a living thought experiment consistent with Schmidt-Leukel's fractal interpretation of religious diversity in China.

In my opinion, Pan Chiu Lai has explored a sinicized way of doing Christian theology that very much reflects an interreligious theology. Such a pluralist interreligious theology can contribute much to interfaith dialogue. Also, some scholars from mainland China, including Zhicheng Wang, You Bin, Xinping Zhuo, Zhigang Zhang, and Rong Wang, are very active in exploring sinicized paths to enable Chinese religions to contribute to social harmony. Nowadays interreligious theology will have much to contribute to exploring how religions can address China's social needs. Schmidt-Leukel's proposals for religious pluralism and interreligious theology offer many incentives and guidelines that can enable Chinese religious believers and scholars to collaborate in meeting the challenges of globalization.

Although pluralism has been introduced into China for quite a few years and has greatly stimulated the development of Chinese religious studies, we must also face the challenge that, in China, believers and scholars have not widely accepted pluralism. Many theologians are still inclined to accept particularism, inclusivism, postmodernism, comparative studies, and so forth.[39] There is an evident need of a new theory of religious diversity that will enable scholars and believers to work together to promote harmony among religions in China today.

In conclusion, let me summarize the main reasons that I believe Schmidt-Leukel's proposals can provide such a needed new theory of religious diversity:

- China has unique conditions and resources for the construction of interreligious theology. In a sense, our history has been an actual, though perhaps not conscious, intermingling of three religious traditions learning from each other and being transformed in the process.
- The long history of *Sanjiao Heyi* offers fertile ground in which the kind of religious pluralism proposed by Schmidt-Leukel can grow and perhaps find new forms. Through the centuries, Confucianism, Daoism, and Buddhism have often clashed, but through these clashes has grown the recognition that they must live together—not only make space for and be hospitable to each other but also collaborating and learning from each other.
- In the age of globalization, the need for "religious sinicization" has been more and more recognized. All the religions of our land must become Chinese as they preserve their distinctive identities; each must make its own contribution to the well-being of our country and of the planet. Schmidt-Leukel's proposals offer distinctive, new, and useful guidelines for achieving these goals. These proposals might well be the harbinger of a transformation of Chinese religions and religious studies.

---

[39]Zhicheng Wang, *A Study*, 13.

"Infinite Paths, Infinite Doctrines"

Perry Schmidt-Leukel's Fractal Approach to Religious Diversity from the Standpoint of the Ramakrishna-Vivekananda Tradition

———

Ayon Maharaj

In his thought-provoking book *Religious Pluralism and Interreligious Theology* (2017), Perry Schmidt-Leukel breaks new ground in highlighting the pluralist tendencies in various religions and in developing an intriguing fractal paradigm for understanding religious diversity. I am honored to have been invited to respond to his book from the standpoint of my own spiritual tradition, the Ramakrishna-Vivekananda tradition of Hinduism. As a monk of the Ramakrishna Order, I fully share Schmidt-Leukel's pluralist conviction that the major world religions have equal salvific efficacy. I consider him a valuable ally in the urgent collective endeavor to combat religious bigotry and fanaticism and to promote fruitful inter-religious dialogue.

In this chapter, I try to identify briefly some of the strengths and weaknesses of Schmidt-Leukel's views on religious pluralism and interreligious theology. In the first section, I argue that his account of the pluralist and inclusivist strains in modern Hinduism is based on a selective and somewhat inaccurate interpretation of the views of Sri Ramakrishna and his famous disciple Swami Vivekananda. Contrary to Schmidt-Leukel, I contend that Ramakrishna and Vivekananda both championed a full-blown doctrine of religious pluralism that has immense contemporary relevance. In the next section of the chapter, I turn the tables on Schmidt-Leukel by critically examining his fractal model of interreligious theology from the pluralist standpoint of Ramakrishna and Vivekananda.

TOWARD A MORE ACCURATE INTERPRETATION
OF THE RAMAKRISHNA-VIVEKANANDA APPROACH
TO RELIGIOUS DIVERSITY

In chapter 5 of his book, Schmidt-Leukel militates against the monolithic view of Hinduism as an inherently and consistently pluralist religion by arguing that exclusivist and inclusivist tendencies have existed alongside "pro-pluralist" tendencies throughout the history of Hinduism. While his general argument is plausible, he also makes two specific claims about modern Hindu approaches to religious diversity that bear critical scrutiny. First, he argues that while Vivekananda claims to champion a full-blown religious pluralism, he is actually more of an inclusivist than a pluralist, since he views theistic religions as inferior stages leading to the highest philosophy of Advaita Vedānta.[1] Second, Schmidt-Leukel argues that Mahatma Gandhi hinted at an "alternative pluralism" that is more promising and egalitarian than Vivekananda's Advaitic inclusivism (*RPIT* 68–69). In this section, I challenge both of these claims by arguing that Ramakrishna and Vivekananda actually championed a consistently pluralist position that directly shaped Gandhi's own pluralist views. Moreover, I argue that Vivekananda presented a fractal account of religious diversity remarkably similar to Schmidt-Leukel's own.

Tellingly, in his chapter on Hinduism, Schmidt-Leukel only refers in passing to Ramakrishna, a pivotal figure of Hindu modernity. Schmidt-Leukel claims that Ramakrishna "clearly believed in the traditional idea of *adhikāra-bheda* (difference in spiritual capacities)," thereby implying that Ramakrishna, like Vivekananda, was more of an inclusivist than a pluralist (*RPIT* 64). In support of his claim, Schmidt-Leukel cites out of context Ramakrishna's statement that God "has arranged all these forms [of worship] to suit different men in different stages of knowledge [*adhikārī bhede*]."[2] However, Schmidt-Leukel overlooks the fact that Ramakrishna immediately goes on to provide a *pluralistic* explanation of *adhikārī-bheda* by appealing to one of his favorite analogies:

A mother cooks different dishes to suit the stomachs of her different children. Suppose she has five children. If there is a fish to cook, she

---

[1] Perry Schmidt-Leukel, *Religious Pluralism and Interreligious Theology: The Gifford Lectures—An Extended Edition* (Maryknoll, NY: Orbis Books, 2017), 55–56. Hereafter, I cite this book in the body of the essay, abbreviating the title as "*RPIT*" and then citing the page number.

[2] Mahendranāth Gupta, *The Gospel of Sri Ramakrishna*, Swami Nikhilananda, trans. (New York: Ramakrishna-Vivekananda Center, 1992), 81; Mahendranāth Gupta, *Śrīśrīrāmakṛṣṇakathāmṛta* (Kolkata: Udbodhan, 2010), 19.

prepares various dishes from it—pilau, pickled fish, fried fish, and so on—to suit their different tastes and powers of digestion.[3]

Just as a mother prepares fish in different ways for her five children with varying tastes and powers of digestion, God Himself—in His infinite wisdom—has made different religions to suit people of differing temperaments, preferences, and spiritual capacities. Just as all five children eat the same fish in a variety of forms, practitioners of various religions worship one and the same God in numerous forms and call Him by various names. For Ramakrishna, just as it would be foolish to claim that one particular fish preparation is objectively better than all the others, it is foolish to claim that one religion is objectively superior to all others. Each child's hunger is fully appeased by eating the particular fish preparation she prefers. In another dialogue in which Ramakrishna invokes the same fish analogy, he makes explicit its pluralistic thrust: "All faiths are paths. . . . One can reach God if one follows any of the paths with whole-hearted devotion."[4] Clearly, Schmidt-Leukel's inclusivist interpretation of Ramakrishna is mistaken, since Ramakrishna unambiguously held the pluralist view that all religions are direct paths to the common goal of realizing God in the particular form or aspect each person prefers.[5]

In a recently published book I have reconstructed in detail Sri Ramakrishna's sophisticated doctrine of religious pluralism.[6] For my purposes here, I briefly outline how Ramakrishna's own eclectic religious practices and spiritual experiences led him to champion a robustly pluralist view of religious diversity. Even though Schmidt-Leukel places great emphasis throughout his book on multiple religious belonging, he fails to mention that Ramakrishna was a pioneer in this regard. Ramakrishna practiced not only the theistic Hindu disciplines of Śāktism and Vaiṣṇavism but also the nontheistic discipline of Advaita Vedānta, which maintains that the impersonal, attributeless Brahman alone is real. Even more remarkably, he also practiced both Christianity and Islam and found them to be as salvifically efficacious as Hinduism. By realizing various forms and aspects of one and the same God through all of these different paths, he obtained direct

---

[3]Gupta, *The Gospel of Sri Ramakrishna*, 81; Gupta, *Śrīśrīrāmakṛṣṇakathāmṛta*, 19.

[4]Gupta, *The Gospel of Sri Ramakrishna*, 559; Gupta, *Śrīśrīrāmakṛṣṇakathāmṛta*, 577.

[5]Schmidt-Leukel opens chapter 6 on Buddhist pluralism by referring to Ramakrishna's parable of the blind men and the elephant and admits that Ramakrishna's explanation of it does have "pluralist" connotations (*RPIT* 71–72). Schmidt-Leukel's overall stance on Ramakrishna is quite confusing, since he portrays Ramakrishna as an inclusivist in chapter 5 and more as a pluralist in chapter 6.

[6]Ayon Maharaj, *Infinite Paths to Infinite Reality: Sri Ramakrishna and Cross-Cultural Philosophy of Religion* (New York: Oxford University Press, 2018), 85–116.

experiential verification of the truth of religious pluralism.[7] If dual religious belonging has only recently come into prominence, Ramakrishna was a unique—and perhaps unprecedented—case of at least *quintuple* religious belonging.

Ramakrishna's spiritual journey culminated in the unique mystical experience of *vijñāna*, his realization that the "Reality which is impersonal [*nirguṇa*] is also personal [*saguṇa*]."[8] As a *vijñānī*, Ramakrishna affirmed that "[t]here is no limit to God": the Infinite God is both personal and impersonal, with and without form, immanent in the universe and beyond it.[9] He frequently remarked that "Brahman and Śakti are inseparable . . . like fire and its power to burn," thereby indicating that the personal and impersonal aspects of the Infinite Reality are equally real.[10] On the basis of this expansive spiritual realization, he taught that theistic and nontheistic spiritual philosophies are equally effective paths to realizing God.[11]

Ramakrishna's religious pluralism, then, derives directly from his *vijñāna*-based ontology of God as the impersonal-personal Infinite Reality. Since God is infinite, there must be correspondingly infinite ways of approaching and ultimately realizing God. As he succinctly puts it, "God is infinite, and the paths to God are infinite."[12] From Ramakrishna's standpoint, God is conceived and worshiped in different ways by people of varying temperaments, preferences, and worldviews. Accordingly, a sincere practitioner of any religion can realize God in the particular form or aspect he prefers. To illustrate the harmony of all religions, Ramakrishna would frequently recite the parable of the chameleon:

> Once a man entered a forest and saw a small animal on a tree. He came back and told another man that he had seen a creature of a beautiful red color on a certain tree. The second man replied: "When I went into the forest, I also saw that animal. But why do you call it red? It is green." Another man who was present contradicted them both and insisted that it was yellow. Presently others arrived and contended that it was grey, violet, blue, and so forth and so on. At last they started quarrelling among themselves. To settle the dispute, they all went to the tree. They saw a man sitting under it. On being asked, he replied: "Yes, I live under this tree and I know the animal very well. All your descriptions are true. Sometimes it appears red, sometimes yellow,

---

[7]For details, see Maharaj, *Infinite Paths to Infinite Reality*, 17–19.
[8]Gupta, *The Gospel of Sri Ramakrishna*, 104; Gupta, *Śrīśrīrāmakṛṣṇakathāmṛta*, 51.
[9]Gupta, *The Gospel of Sri Ramakrishna*, 920; Gupta, *Śrīśrīrāmakṛṣṇakathāmṛta*, 997.
[10]Gupta, *The Gospel of Sri Ramakrishna*, 550; Gupta, *Śrīśrīrāmakṛṣṇakathāmṛta*, 568.
[11]Gupta, *The Gospel of Sri Ramakrishna*, 103–4; Gupta, *Śrīśrīrāmakṛṣṇakathāmṛta*, 51.
[12]Gupta, *The Gospel of Sri Ramakrishna*, 506; Gupta, *Śrīśrīrāmakṛṣṇakathāmṛta*, 511.

and at other times blue, violet, grey, and so forth. It is a chameleon. And sometimes it has no color at all. Now it has a color, and now it has none."

In like manner, one who constantly thinks of God can know God's real nature; he alone knows that God reveals Himself to seekers in various forms and aspects. God is personal [*saguṇa*] as well as impersonal [*nirguṇa*]. Only the man who lives under the tree knows that the chameleon can appear in various colors, and he knows, further, that the animal at times has no color at all. It is the others who suffer from the agony of futile argument.[13]

Like the chameleon that appears in various colors and sometimes has no color at all, God assumes various forms for different types of spiritual aspirants. While most people make the mistake of thinking that the chameleon only has the color that they see it as having, the man always sitting under the tree sees that the chameleon has various colors and, hence, that everyone is partially correct. The colorless chameleon corresponds to *nirguṇa* Brahman, while the chameleon with various colors corresponds to *saguṇa* Śakti, and it is clear that Ramakrishna does not privilege *nirguṇa* Brahman in any way. As we saw earlier in this section, Ramakrishna consistently maintains that the impersonal Brahman and the personal Śakti have equal ontological reality. The man sitting under the tree represents the *vijñānī*—such as Ramakrishna himself—who has realized both the personal and impersonal aspects of God and hence affirms on the basis of his own spiritual experience that all religions are salvifically effective paths.

As I have argued elsewhere, Ramakrishna played a decisive role in shaping Vivekananda's views on Vedānta and religious diversity.[14] While Vivekananda undoubtedly championed Advaita Vedānta, he interpreted Advaita philosophy in a broad, world-affirming manner that brings him much closer to Ramakrishna than to Śaṅkara. I outline briefly here five of the central tenets of Vivekananda's world-affirming Advaita Vedānta, tracing each of them to Ramakrishna's teachings.

First, just as Ramakrishna conceives the ultimate reality as both personal and impersonal, Vivekananda repeatedly asserts that "our religion preaches an Impersonal Personal God."[15] Second, Vivekananda sides with

---

[13]Gupta, *The Gospel of Sri Ramakrishna*, 149–50; Gupta, *Śrīśrīrāmakṛṣṇakathāmṛta*, 101.

[14]Ayon Maharaj, "*Asminnasya ca tadyogaṃ śāsti*: Swami Vivekananda's Interpretation of *Brahmasūtra* 1.1.19 as a Hermeneutic Basis for Samanvayī Vedānta," in *The Life, Legacy, and Contemporary Relevance of Swami Vivekananda: New Reflections*, Rita Sherma and James McHugh, eds. (Lanham, MD: Lexington Books, forthcoming).

[15]*The Complete Works of Swami Vivekananda: Mayavati Memorial Edition*, 9 vols.(Kolkata: Advaita Ashrama, 2007), 3:249.

Ramakrishna against Śaṅkara in declaring that the "Vedanta does not in reality denounce the world" but teaches, rather, "the deification of the world."[16] Third, Vivekananda was profoundly influenced by Ramakrishna's *vijñāna*-based ethical doctrine that we should serve human beings as real manifestations of God (*śiva jñāne jīver sevā*).[17] Accordingly, Vivekananda champions "Practical Vedānta" as a spiritual ethics of service based on the recognition of God in all creatures. As he puts it, "The Vedanta says, there is nothing that is not God. . . . The only God to worship is the human soul in the human body."[18] Fourth, while Śaṅkara takes *jñānayoga* (the path of knowledge) to be the only direct path to liberation, Vivekananda follows Ramakrishna in maintaining that all four Yogas—*jñānayoga, bhaktiyoga* (the path of devotion), *karmayoga* (the path of work), and *rājayoga* (the path of meditation)—"are all capable of serving as direct and independent means for the attainment of Moksha."[19]

Fifth, Vivekananda derives a robust model of religious pluralism from the fourth tenet of his world-affirming Advaita philosophy. In the context of religious pluralism, Vivekananda broadens the Hindu conception of the four Yogas to encompass all the world religions. According to Vivekananda, "each religion represents one" of the "systems of Yoga."[20] Moreover, since he takes each Yoga to be a "direct and independent" path to salvation, he concludes that all of the world religions have equal "saving power."[21] In the following passage, Vivekananda makes clear the underlying logic of his religious pluralist position:

> The ideal of all religions, all sects, is the same—the attaining of liberty and cessation of misery. . . . Though the goal is one and the same, there may be many ways to reach it, and these ways are determined by the peculiarities of our nature. One man's nature is emotional, another's intellectual, another's active, and so forth. Again, in the same nature there may be many subdivisions.[22]

Three features of this passage rule out an Advaitic inclusivist interpretation of Vivekananda's position. First, he defines the common goal of all religions broadly as "the attaining of liberty and cessation of misery," instead of defining it in more narrowly Advaitic terms as knowledge of the imper-

---

[16]Ibid., 2:146.
[17]Maharaj, *Infinite Paths to Infinite Reality*, 49–50.
[18]*The Complete Works of Swami Vivekananda*, 2:320–21.
[19]Ibid., 1:93.
[20]Ibid., 8:152.
[21]Ibid., 4:182.
[22]Ibid., 4:51.

sonal Brahman. Second, he conceives the four Yogas here as psychological types ("emotional," "intellectual," "active," and so on), thereby providing a rationale for religious pluralism. Each person is drawn toward the kind of religion that corresponds to the particular psychological type she exhibits: a predominantly emotional person will be drawn toward the religion or religions corresponding to *bhakti-yoga*, and so on. Third, Vivekananda's justification of religious pluralism on the basis of various psychological types is nonhierarchical, since it does not make sense to claim that a particular psychological type is superior to other types.

Of course, one might still object that there is a tension between pluralist passages such as this one and other passages where Vivekananda seems to claim that all religions must culminate in Advaita. The key to reconciling these two apparently conflicting strands of his thought is to recognize that when he conceives Advaita as the end point of all religions, he understands "Advaita" not in the sense of Śaṅkara's philosophy of Advaita Vedānta—which *would* entail an inclusivist hierarchy—but in the sense of the highest stage of *nondual spiritual experience*, which can be attained through *all* religions. Accordingly, Vivekananda states, "These are the three stages which every religion has taken. First we see God in the far beyond, then we come nearer to Him and give Him omnipresence so that we live in Him; and at last we recognise that we are He."[23] To Schmidt-Leukel's credit, he acknowledges passages such as this one, but he argues that Vivekananda was nonetheless an Advaitic inclusivist since he seems to hold that "not all religions contain all three levels, at least not in the same elaborate way" (*RPIT* 56). Schmidt-Leukel cites the following statement in support of his inclusivist interpretation of Vivekananda: "But I and my Father are one: I find the reality in my soul. These ideas are expressed in some religions, and in others only hinted. In some they were expatriated."[24]

The fact that some religions have only "hinted" at, or even "expatriated," Advaitic ideas does not imply that Advaita Vedānta is superior to all other religions, as Schmidt-Leukel contends. Rather, Vivekananda is making the uncontroversial *historical* claim that some religions—he likely has in mind Christianity and Islam—have downplayed or even suppressed Advaitic spiritual experience, even though Advaitic ideas are present, explicitly or implicitly, in all the world religions. Vivekananda might have been thinking, for instance, of the persecution and execution of the Sufi mystic Manṣur al-Ḥallāj, who famously declared, "I am the Absolute" (*ana al-Ḥaqq*).[25]

---

[23]Ibid., 1:331.

[24]Ibid., 1:323.

[25]Cited in *The New Encyclopedia of Islam*, Cyril Glassé and Huston Smith, eds. (Walnut Creek, CA: AltaMira Press, 2001), 166.

Vivekananda's religious pluralism, which is based not on the equal doctrinal lucidity of all religions but on their equal *salvific efficacy*, is perfectly compatible with his claim that some religions do not explicitly or clearly refer to Advaitic spiritual experience at the doctrinal level.

It is also surprising that Schmidt-Leukel overlooks the fact that Vivekananda anticipated the basic contours of Schmidt-Leukel's own fractal theory of religious diversity. According to Schmidt-Leukel's fractal paradigm, the "cultural diversity at the global level is reflected in the diversity within each culture and this again is, to some extent, reflected, on a still smaller scale, in the individual" (*RPIT* 227). Schmidt-Leukel finds in Vivekananda's work only a very limited, and Hindu-centric, fractalism. "Swami Vivekananda," he claims, "famously presented Hinduism as a religion that contains each form of religion" (*RPIT* 223). However, a more charitable and comprehensive reading of Vivekananda reveals that he taught, in fact, a full-blown fractal paradigm very much akin to Schmidt-Leukel's. At the intercultural level, Vivekananda—as we have already seen—maintains that each of the world religions "represents one" of the four Yogas.[26] Strikingly, though, he also anticipates Schmidt-Leukel in claiming that intercultural differences are reflected at both the *intracultural* and *intrasubjective* levels:

> The grandest idea in the religion of the Vedanta is that we may reach the same goal by different paths; and these paths I have generalised into four, viz those of work, love, psychology, and knowledge. But you must, at the same time, remember that these divisions are not very marked and quite exclusive of each other. Each blends into the other. But according to the type which prevails, we name the divisions. It is not that you can find men who have no other faculty than that of work, nor that you can find men who are no more than devoted worshippers only, nor that there are men who have no more than mere knowledge. These divisions are made in accordance with the type or the tendency that may be seen to prevail in a man. We have found that, in the end, all these four paths converge and become one. All religions and all methods of work and worship lead us to one and the same goal.[27]

The key to Vivekananda's fractal approach to religious diversity is that the divisions between "work, love, psychology, and knowledge" are "not very marked and quite exclusive of each other." Hence, at the *intracultural* level, Vivekananda claims that each religion, while predominantly emphasizing one Yoga more than the other three, nonetheless contains elements of the

---

[26]*The Complete Works of Swami Vivekananda*, 8:152.
[27]Ibid., 1:108.

other Yogas to varying degrees. Moreover, at the *intrasubjective* level, this same pattern reappears: although most individuals possess one faculty to a greater degree than the other three faculties, they nonetheless also have these other faculties to a lesser degree. As Vivekananda puts it in the passage cited earlier, "in the same nature there may be many subdivisions."[28] Interestingly, Schmidt-Leukel claims that the phenomenologist Hilko Wiardo Schomerus, in his 1932 study, "came fairly close to a fractal understanding of religious diversity" (*RPIT* 230). Schomerus distinguishes four major types of religion corresponding to the four Yogas found in Hinduism but also observes that "there are religious formations which comprise not only one of the said four major types but several or even all four of them, and this in a variegated mixture" (cited in *RPIT* 230). Schmidt-Leukel fails to recognize that Vivekananda, decades before Schomerus, presented an even more developed and comprehensive fractal account of religious diversity based on the key thesis that differences at the intercultural level are reflected at *both* the intracultural *and* the intrasubjective levels. It is also highly significant that Vivekananda explicitly links his sophisticated fractal paradigm to a full-blown religious pluralist position, the view that "[a]ll religions and all methods of work and worship lead us to one and the same goal." Here again, Vivekananda anticipated Schmidt-Leukel, who similarly argues that "a fractal interpretation of religious diversity . . . ultimately tends toward religious pluralism" (*RPIT* 237).

At the end of his chapter on Hinduism, Schmidt-Leukel contrasts Vivekananda's "primus-inter-pares pluralism" with the "alternative," more robust religious pluralism of Gandhi (*RPIT* 67–68). According to Schmidt-Leukel, Gandhi's alternative pluralism consists of three basic tenets. First, the "doctrinal systems" of all religions—including Hinduism—are "inevitably imperfect" (*RPIT* 68). Second, the "true essence of religion can be realized only through a *practice* that is equally available to all religions" (*RPIT* 68). Third, Gandhi champions a form of "religious equality" that does not privilege Hinduism (*RPIT* 68).

Against Schmidt-Leukel, I have argued in this section that all three of these tenets of Gandhi's allegedly "alternative" pluralism are, in fact, fully present in the pluralist doctrine of Ramakrishna and Vivekananda. Ramakrishna combines all three tenets in the following passage:

Ah, that restlessness [*vyākulatā*] is the whole thing. Whatever path you follow—whether you are a Hindu, a Muslim, a Christian, a Śākta, a Vaiṣṇava, or a Brāhmo—the vital point is restlessness. God is our Inner

---

[28]Ibid., 4:51.

Guide [*antaryāmī*]. It doesn't matter if you take a wrong path—only you must be restless for Him. God Himself will put you on the right path. Besides, there are errors in all paths. Everyone thinks his watch is right; but as a matter of fact no watch is absolutely right. But that doesn't hamper one's work. If a man is restless for God he gains the company of *sādhus* and as far as possible corrects his own watch with the *sādhu*'s help.[29]

Sri Ramakrishna likens religious fanatics to people who think that their watch alone tells the correct time. According to Sri Ramakrishna, however, "no watch is absolutely right." That is, all religions—including Hinduism—have errors, but these errors do not diminish the salvific efficacy of these religions as "paths" to God-realization. The essential attitude needed to make spiritual progress in any religion is "restlessness" for God (*vyākulatā*), which arises from sincere spiritual practice. If a religious practitioner has this *vyākulatā*, then even if she makes a mistake, God Himself will put her "on the right path." Notice also that Ramakrishna mentions Hinduism alongside Islam and Christianity, without privileging Hinduism in any way.

Gandhi himself praised Ramakrishna as a "living embodiment of God-liness" and remarked that the "story of Ramakrishna Paramahamsa's life is a story of religion in practice."[30] Indeed, it is likely that Gandhi's own pluralist view was shaped, in part, by the pluralist teachings of Ramakrishna and Vivekananda. Ironically, Schmidt-Leukel claims that contemporary American Hindu Jeffery D. Long has further developed Gandhi's alternative pluralism in *opposition* to the more Hindu-centric pluralism of Ramakrishna and Vivekananda (*RPIT* 68–69). In fact, however, Long is a prominent, for-mally initiated follower of the Ramakrishna-Vivekananda tradition who has emphasized the pluralist dimension of Ramakrishna's and Vivekananda's teachings and shown their *continuity* with Gandhi's views on pluralism.[31] Contrary to Schmidt-Leukel, then, the story of modern Hindu pluralism is not a tale of two pluralisms—the Hindu-centric pseudopluralism of Vive-kananda and the more egalitarian pluralism of Gandhi and his followers. Rather, it would be more accurate to say that Ramakrishna inaugurated a robustly pluralistic approach to religious diversity in mid-nineteenth-century

---

[29]Gupta, *The Gospel of Sri Ramakrishna*, 673; Gupta, *Śrīśrīrāmakṛṣṇakathāmṛta*, 1123.

[30]Gandhi's remarks on Sri Ramakrishna in the foreword to Swami Nikhilananda, *Life of Sri Ramakrishna* (1928; Kolkata: Advaita Ashrama, 2008), ix.

[31]See Jeffery D. Long, "*Anekānta Vedānta*: Toward a Deep Hindu Religious Pluralism," in *Deep Religious Pluralism*, David Ray Griffin, ed. (Louisville, KY: Westminster John Knox, 2005), 136–38; Long, "Advaita and Dvaita: Bridging the Gap—the Ramakrishna Tradition's Both/And Approach to the Dvaita/Advaita Debate," *Journal of Vaishnava Studies* 16 (2008): 49–70.

India that has been subsequently developed and defended in various ways by numerous pluralistically minded Hindus, including Vivekananda, Gandhi, Rabindranath Tagore, Long, myself, and many others.

A CRITICAL EXAMINATION OF THE FRACTAL PARADIGM OF INTERRELIGIOUS THEOLOGY

Equipped with a more adequate understanding of the religious pluralist framework of Ramakrishna and Vivekananda, we can now examine Schmidt-Leukel's theorization and practice of interreligious theology in the second part of his book, which comprises his Gifford Lectures proper. I am largely in agreement with the four general principles of interreligious theology he outlines in chapter 9: (1) a theological credit of trust, (2) reliance on the unity of reality, (3) the importance of interreligious practice, and (4) the processual, incomplete nature of interreligious theology. Moreover, he has made a compelling case that an important aim of interreligious theology is to discern similarities across religious traditions at three levels: the intercultural, the intracultural, and the intrasubjective. I argue, however, that the specific "fractal" paradigm Schmidt-Leukel proposes for analyzing religious diversity is not sufficiently fine-grained to serve as an effective heuristic for interreligious theology. Drawing on Hick's work as well as the Ramakrishna-Vivekananda tradition, I propose a somewhat different framework for interreligious theology that better accommodates doctrinal similarities *and* differences.

As John Hick has shown, one crucial aspect of interreligious dialogue and understanding is to recognize that there are different *kinds* of religious doctrines both within and across traditions. In particular, Hick distinguishes three fundamental types of conflicting religious truth claims.[32] First, there are disagreements about past historical events "that are in principle accessible to human observation"—such as whether Christ died on the cross.[33] Second, there are disagreements about "transhistorical" matters—such as reincarnation and the possibility of God incarnating as a human being—which cannot be verified "by historical or other empirical evidence."[34] Third, there are disagreements about "ultimate questions," such as the nature of ultimate reality.[35] According to Hick, neither historical truth claims nor transhistorical truth claims are "soteriologically vital."[36] From Hick's perspective, even if

[32]John Hick, *An Interpretation of Religion* (London: Macmillan, 1989), 362–63.
[33]Ibid., 363.
[34]Ibid., 365.
[35]Ibid., 363.
[36]Ibid., 367.

Hinduism is wrong, say, in claiming that souls reincarnate or Christianity is wrong in claiming that Christ died on the cross, the falsity of these truth claims would not diminish the salvific efficacy of these religions. As Hick puts it, "Whilst holding any or none of these theories we may still participate in the transformation of human existence from self-centredness to Reality-centredness."[37] By contrast, Hick maintains that religious doctrines about the ultimate reality *are* soteriologically vital, but he argues that such ultimate doctrines do not, in reality, conflict with each other, since the various personal and nonpersonal ultimates taught by the world religions are all different phenomenal manifestations of the same unknowable Real *an sich.*

While we might take issue with Hick's quasi-Kantian metaphysics or some of the details of his threefold classification,[38] it seems to me that Hick is essentially right that any satisfactory model for engaging in interreligious theology must be sufficiently nuanced and fine-grained to distinguish religious doctrines that are soteriologically vital from those that are not. The reason is obvious: interreligious theologians need only strive to integrate and harmonize those apparently conflicting religious doctrines that are *soteriologically vital*—doctrines concerning the nature of ultimate reality and salvation. As for soteriologically *in*essential religious doctrines, we should try simply to acknowledge and understand these numerous doctrinal differences in various religious traditions. In other words, Hick's insight helps us recognize that the acknowledgment of genuine religious *difference* is as essential to interreligious theology as the pursuit of doctrinal integration and harmonization.

As far as I can tell, Schmidt-Leukel does not distinguish between soteriologically vital and soteriologically inessential religious doctrines anywhere in his book. In chapters 10 to 13 he provides historically and theologically sophisticated discussions of conflicting doctrinal truth claims in Christianity, Islam, and Buddhism and tries to show that there are ways of interpreting their respective doctrines that minimize, or even eliminate, their mutually conflicting character. However, I believe Schmidt-Leukel's discussions in these chapters would have benefited from some prior hermeneutic groundwork. The key hermeneutic question is: which conflicting religious doctrines are soteriologically vital? Schmidt-Leukel, in his discussion of various doctrines in these three religious traditions, does not provide a clear answer to this question. In fact, he discusses both transhistorical religious doctrines as well as doctrines concerning ultimate reality, but he does not discuss the issue of whether both these kinds of doctrines are equally sote-

---

[37] Ibid.

[38] In chapter 4 of *Infinite Paths to Infinite Reality*, I criticize certain aspects of Hick's quasi-Kantian pluralist theory from a Ramakrishnan standpoint.

riologically vital. In chapter 13 he addresses one crucial doctrinal dispute that *is* soteriologically vital (according to Hick's classification): Christianity and Islam accept the reality of a creator God, while Buddhism does not. Schmidt-Leukel attempts to find theological common ground among these three religions by arguing that Buddhism is not so much atheistic as *non*theistic, since it arguably accepts a transcendent reality. His nuanced discussion of this issue is a good example of fruitful interreligious theology.

However, I find Schmidt-Leukel's discussions in chapters 10 to 12 somewhat less fruitful, because they concern primarily *trans*historical religious doctrines that are arguably not soteriologically vital. In particular, he addresses two doctrinal disputes between Christianity and Islam: (1) whether Muḥammad is the Final Prophet, and (2) whether Christ is an incarnation of God. He engages in an impressive feat of interpretive acrobatics to show that the Islamic acceptance of the eternal "Word of God" provides potential common ground for a partial rapprochement between Christianity and Islam on these issues (*RPIT* 154–58). However, I was left wondering whether Schmidt-Leukel's interpretive maneuvers were even necessary, since he did not address the hermeneutically *prior* question of whether these doctrines are soteriologically vital. Personally, I would side with Hick in taking these doctrines to be soteriologically inessential. Of course, Schmidt-Leukel can disagree with me, but as far as I can tell, he does not provide any explicit arguments in favor of their soteriological necessity.

Unlike Schmidt-Leukel, Ramakrishna *does* explicitly distinguish religious doctrines that are soteriologically vital from those that are not.[39] Like Hick, Ramakrishna takes religious doctrines about ultimate reality to be soteriologically vital, while he takes historical and transhistorical doctrines to be soteriologically inessential. Hence, Ramakrishna adopts correspondingly different stances toward different *kinds* of religious doctrines. As we saw earlier in the chapter, his unique experience of *vijñāna* revealed to him that all religious conceptions of God are true, since they all capture real aspects of one and the same impersonal-personal Infinite Reality. For Ramakrishna, then, while different religious doctrines about ultimate reality may *appear* to conflict, they are in fact complementary, since they capture different aspects of the same Infinite Reality.

By contrast, Ramakrishna would agree with Hick that the transhistorical question of whether God can incarnate as a human being is *not* soteriologically vital. During Ramakrishna's time, the Brāhmo Samāj held the view that God is personal but formless and, hence, that God cannot incarnate as a human being such as Kṛṣṇa. Ramakrishna was well aware of the Brāhmo Samāj's skepticism about Kṛṣṇa's status as an *avatāra*. While on a boat with

---

[39]For details, see Maharaj, *Infinite Paths to Infinite Reality*, 101–9.

followers of the Brāhmo Samāj, Ramakrishna—with tears in his eyes—sang an ecstatic devotional song conveying Rādhā's love for her beloved Kṛṣṇa and then told them, "Whether or not you accept the Rādhā-Kṛṣṇa *līlā*, you should accept their attraction [*tān*] for each other. Try to create that same yearning in your heart for God. God can be realized when this yearning [*vyākulatā*] is present."[40] In contrast to Schmidt-Leukel, Ramakrishna finds common ground between Brāhmos and Vaiṣṇavas not at the level of *theological doctrine* but at the level of *spiritual practice*. Recognizing that both Brāhmos and Vaiṣṇavas are theists, Ramakrishna encourages Brāhmos to try to emulate Rādhā's extraordinary yearning (*vyākulatā*) for God, since Brāhmos would agree with Vaiṣṇavas that the love of God is the aim of all devotional practices. From Ramakrishna's perspective, Brāhmos need not accept Kṛṣṇa's *avatāra* status or even his historical reality, but they can nonetheless learn a valuable spiritual lesson from the Vaiṣṇava doctrine.

Ramakrishna's stance on the specific issue of divine incarnation exemplifies his stance toward historical and transhistorical religious truth claims in general: there is simply no need to attempt to synthesize or reconcile conflicting religious doctrines that are not soteriologically vital. In fact, Ramakrishna goes even further. Since different religious doctrines suit differing temperaments and predispositions, it is important to *honor* benign forms of religious disagreement. As he was fond of putting it, "Infinite paths, infinite doctrines" (*ananto path ananto mat*).[41] From Ramakrishna's perspective, the more doctrinal paths there are, the more likely each person can find the path that most individually suitable path.

My concern, then, with Schmidt-Leukel's vision of interreligious theology is that his emphasis on doctrinal integration and synthesis might come at the cost of neglecting the equally important aim of honoring religious difference. My deeper worry is that his neglect of benign forms of religious difference may stem, in part, from his mathematically inspired fractal model, which seems to me to be too rigid and too high-altitude to register the fine-grained differences between certain *kinds* of religious doctrines that are emphasized by Hick, Ramakrishna, and Vivekananda.

From the pluralist perspective of Ramakrishna and Vivekananda, a fully adequate model of interreligious theology must not only recognize doctrinal similarities and parallels but also register *differential weightings and configurations* of religious doctrines both within and across traditions. Such an interreligious theology would be able to honor benign forms of doctrinal divergence as much as it would strive to harmonize conflicting religious doctrines of vital soteriological importance. As Vivekananda puts it, "We

---

[40]Gupta, *The Gospel of Sri Ramakrishna*, 140; Gupta, *Śrīśrīrāmakṛṣṇakathāmṛta*, 90.
[41]Gupta, *The Gospel of Sri Ramakrishna*, 158; Gupta, *Śrīśrīrāmakṛṣṇakathāmṛta*, 111.

must allow this infinite variation in religious thought, and not try to bring everybody to the same opinion, because the goal is the same."[42] According to Ramakrishna and Vivekananda, many forms of religious disagreement—far from calling for doctrinal synthesis or reconciliation—actually attest to God's infinite love and wisdom in furnishing so many different paths for God's many children.

Vivekananda's vision of fruitful interreligious dialogue remains as timely as ever: "The Christian is not to become a Hindu or a Buddhist, nor a Hindu or a Buddhist to become a Christian. But each must assimilate the spirit of the others and yet preserve his individuality and grow according to his own law of growth."[43] Vivekananda helps to remind us that at the very heart of interreligious dialogue is the dialectical endeavor to assimilate valuable insights from all religious traditions while preserving the individuality and uniqueness of one's own tradition. From this perspective, both Ramakrishna and Vivekananda should be seen as valuable allies in Schmidt-Leukel's effort to develop a fruitful interreligious theology.

[42] *The Complete Works of Swami Vivekananda*, 1:390.
[43] Ibid., 1:24.

Contrasting Tsongkhapa and Longchenpa

Buddhist Diversity, Fractal Theory, and Comparative Theology

───────

John Makransky

What often renders interreligious dialogue unproductive is the tendency for dialogue partners to essentialize their traditions, as if each were a uniform entity—for example, "Buddhism says this; Christianity says that." Dr. Perry Schmidt-Leukel argues that when we investigate the diversity of views in each religion on fundamental theological subjects, we find differences within each religion comparable to the kinds of differences we find between different religions. Schmidt-Leukel's fractal theory of religions thus de-emphasizes uniformity by highlighting the tremendous internal diversity found in each religion.[1] As a result, when we notice areas of doctrinal tension in one religion that generate competing intrareligious views of fundamental theological subjects, we may be discovering a resource to inform analogous doctrinal tensions equally fundamental in other religions. Buddhist thinkers have diverse, competing understandings of their doctrines, which can be seen to correspond to analogous doctrinal tensions in other religions.

In this chapter, I discuss contrasting ways of relating human beings to ultimate reality in several areas of Buddhist reflection, focusing on Tibetan Buddhism as an example. I focus on two major figures of fourteenth- to fifteenth-century Tibet, Tsongkhapa (1357–1419) and Longchen Rabjampa (Longchenpa; 1308–1364), who share basic doctrinal themes of Buddhism yet differ considerably in their understanding of those themes. Their views represent poles of tension in Buddhism that frame a spectrum of possible positions on each theological subject. I summarize the differing positions of these two scholars on the following Buddhist subjects: how ultimate

───────

[1] Perry Schmidt-Leukel, *Religious Pluralism and Interreligious Theology: The Gifford Lectures—An Extended Edition* (Maryknoll, NY: Orbis Books, 2017), 222–45.

reality (nirvāṇa) is related to the world (saṃsāra), how ultimate reality is related to persons (theological anthropology), how a Buddhist practitioner accesses ultimate reality to progress on the path of enlightenment (soteriology), and how a Buddhist practitioner develops enlightened forms of awareness (gnoseology).

My aim is to invite readers to explore any analogous areas of tension in your own religion in light of Tibetan Buddhism, with regard to theological anthropology, soteriology, gnoseology, and other theological topics of reflection. Many theologians who study other religions find, to their surprise, that in some areas of thought they are closer to certain theologians of another religion than they are to many theologians of their own religion. A fractal perspective on religions suggests that this condition is not an anomaly but to be expected, since intrareligious reflection often engages the same kinds of theological tensions found in other religions. If you see areas of doctrinal tension in your own religious tradition analogous to those described here in Tibet (as I expect you will), perhaps that can shine new light on your own religion.

First, some observations on diverse Buddhist ways of understanding the relation between nirvāṇa and saṃsāra—nirvāṇa as an ultimate, unconditioned reality whose realization brings freedom from inmost causes of suffering, and saṃsāra as the mundane, conditioned reality of ordinary experience that is laced with causes of suffering.

In the Indian Abhidharma Buddhist systems of Sarvāstivāda and Theravāda, which developed in the centuries after Gautama Buddha, saṃsāra and nirvāṇa are framed as a simple dualism of conditioned and unconditioned realities, respectively. For a person to fully realize the unconditioned, nirvāṇa, is to be liberated from, and ultimately to bring an end to, all conditioned causes and experiences of her suffering and rebirth in saṃsāra.[2] Indian Mahāyāna systems that emerged in the early centuries CE reframed nirvāṇa and saṃsāra as a nondualism, in which nirvāṇa is understood, in some sense, as fundamentally not separate from saṃsāra.[3] But there is a diversity of views within different Mahāyāna traditions on how that nondualism is to be understood and practiced.

Two different ways of interpreting the Mahāyāna nondualism of nirvāṇa

---

[2]Rupert Gethin, *The Foundations of Buddhism* (New York: Oxford University Press, 1998), 77; Steven Collins, *Nirvana and Other Buddhist Felicities: Utopias of the Pali Imaginaire* (Cambridge: Cambridge University Press, 1998), 141, 150, 198–99; John Makransky, *Buddhahood Embodied: Sources of Controversy in India and Tibet* (Albany: State University of New York Press, 1997), 27–28.

[3]Peter Harvey, *An Introduction to Buddhism*, 2nd ed. (New York: Cambridge University Press, 2013), 158, 161; Paul Williams, *Mahāyāna Buddhism: The Doctrinal Foundations*, 2nd ed. (New York: Routledge, 2009), 60, 185–86; Makransky, *Buddhahood Embodied*, 85–108.

and saṃsāra were taught by two leading figures of Tibetan Buddhism: Tsongkhapa, founder of the Geluk tradition, and Longchenpa, a leading theorist of the Nyingma, Dzogchen tradition. These pioneering figures, in roughly the same period and independently of each other, wrote treatises on Buddhist thought and practice, developing different systematic frameworks of understanding from the concepts and practices of earlier streams of Indo-Tibetan Buddhism.

THEOLOGICAL ANTHROPOLOGY: HOW ULTIMATE REALITY (NIRVĀṆA) IS RELATED TO THE PERSON

Tsongkhapa's anthropology is based on Indian Sarvāstivāda Abhidharma ways of systematizing Buddhist philosophy and psychology, informed by the ontology and epistemology of the Madhyamaka school of Indian Mahāyāna Buddhism. For Tsongkhapa, following Abhidharma analysis, persons are composed *only* of impermanent, conditioned phenomena that are thoroughly tainted by deluded tendencies. These conditioned phenomena are summarized in five categories, the five "aggregates" (S. *skandha*, T. *phung po*), which include all aspects of mental and physical experience:

1. The experience of our physical body and world
2. Sense consciousnesses
3. Perceptions that distinguish and label things
4. Feeling tones associated with all our experiences
5. Volitional formations, which include chains of thought, intentions, emotions and all other complex mental states.[4]

For Tsongkhapa, following Abhidharma, those five aspects of experience constitute our entire being and are inseparable from many kinds of suffering because they are the fruition of actions (S. *karma*, T. *las*) that are motivated by deluded tendencies of ignorance, attachment, and aversion (S. *kleśa*, T. *nyon mongs*). The dependent arising of sentient beings, including human beings, follows the twelve-link formula that is explained in Abhidharma traditions: *ignorance* (S. *avidyā*), the mind's deluded tendency to reify and identify with its conceptual constructs of self and others, conditions *volitional formations* in reaction to those constructs (*saṃskāra*), which imprint into *consciousness* (*vijñāna*) tendencies to construct, reify, and react in similar ways. Those karmic tendencies influence one's *physical*

---

[4]Transliterations of Sanskrit and Tibetan terms are initially signified by "S." and "T." Where two different terms are given, the first is Sanskrit, the second is Tibetan.

and mental capacities (*nāma rūpa*) and *senses* (*āyatana*), thus affecting one's *sense experiences* (*sparśa*), which give rise to pleasant, unpleasant, and neutral *feeling tones* (*vedanā*). The feeling tones of experiences bring out the mind's karmic tendencies to react with various forms of *craving* (*tṛṣṇā*), which condition forms of *grasping* (*upādāna*), which give rise to self-clinging *ways of being* (*bhava*), which condition repeated *rebirth* (*jāti*), aging, and *dying* (*jarā maraṇa*).[5]

For Tsongkhapa, then, the very source of our being is ignorance, together with the deluded tendencies it supports (which are various expressions of craving and grasping), and the karmic reactions those tendencies condition, which, together with all other factors of dependent arising, causally generate all experiences of self, others, and world as saṃsāric phenomena of suffering and repeated rebirth. As Tsongkhapa summarizes in his *Great Treatise on the Stages of the Path*, the origin of saṃsāra for all beings involves just three fundamental things: how deluded tendencies arise, how they cause beings to accumulate karma, and how karma generates the conditions for their repeated dying and rebirth.[6]

However, from Tsongkhapa's Madhyamaka perspective, the mental and physical aggregates that constitute what we are, and the delusions and karma that generate those aggregates, are all empty of inherent existence—insubstantial and illusory—even though our minds, from the force of conditioning, tend to grasp them all as if they were substantially existent. Because all phenomena appear only through the force of conditions, and are thus empty of any autonomous entity or self-existence, they can be utterly transformed or brought to an end by altering the conditions that produce them. This is done by methodically practicing all the essentials of the Buddha's teaching, which bring an end to the conditioned causes of one's aggregates of mind and body, by gradually empowering the practitioner to realize the unconditioned, empty, and liberating nature of things that is nirvāṇa.

In Tsongkhapa's understanding, then, in contrast with Longchenpa's perspective explained below, it is not the case that beings are primordially one with the unconditioned nature of nirvāṇa and have become lost from it by their identification with conditioned phenomena of delusion, karma and aggregates. Rather, for Tsongkhapa, beings are ontologically just those conditioned phenomena. Beings are simply the causal continuity of mental and physical phenomena that have taken shape in repeated saṃsāric rebirth by the causal force of delusion and karma.

---

[5]Gethin, *Foundations*, 150–51; Tsongkhapa, *Byang chub Lam rim chen mo*, in English as *The Great Treatise on the Stages of the Path to Enlightenment*, Lam rim chen mo Translation Committee (Ithaca, NY: Snow Lion Publications, 2000), 1:315–19.

[6]Tsongkhapa, *Great Treatise*, 1:298–313.

In Indian Abhidharma traditions and for Tsongkhapa, Buddhist practice ultimately aims to cut the chain of conditioned causes that produce the five aggregates, that is, to bring an end to rebirth, an end to our conditioned existence, by realizing nirvāṇa as an unconditioned dimension of reality that transcends all saṃsāric conditioning.[7] As a Mahāyāna teacher, Tsongkhapa uses these Abhidharma concepts not only to empower renunciation of saṃsāra, which is an urge to be freed from the suffering of the samsāric aggregates, but also to generate compassion for all other beings who suffer similarly. Strong compassion for others then becomes the basis to generate *bodhicitta*, the aspiration to realize nirvāṇa in its fullest form, buddhahood (*apratiṣṭhita nirvāṇa*), in order to help many others become liberated from the delusive causes of their conditioned aggregates, by helping them realize the empty, unconditioned nature of phenomena that is the realization of nirvāṇa.[8]

From Tsongkhapa's Mahāyāna perspective, to cultivate the wisdom that knows the empty nature of things, and to conjoin that wisdom with a vast cultivation of compassionate attitudes, vows, and activities, can empower a fundamental transformation of one's being that generates endless manifestation and liberating activity in the world to help others by means of the bodies of buddhahood.[9] To realize fullest enlightenment, then, is to bring an end to the impure aggregates of saṃsāra and to generate in their place a pure, enlightened set of aggregates that are composed of the qualities, wisdoms, and activities of a buddha, which endlessly benefit beings who are caught in saṃsāra.

As a Mahāyāna teacher, Tsongkhapa upholds the view that nirvāṇa and saṃsāra are nondual, but not because he understands nirvāṇa as full enlightenment with all of its qualities to be immanent in persons. Rather, in

---

[7]Ibid., 1:323–24, 335, 339.
[8]Ibid., 1:184; 3:119–22.
[9]In traditions of Mahāyāna Buddhism, the fullest form of nirvāṇa is that of a buddha. It is called "unrestricted nirvāṇa" (S. *apratiṣṭhita nirvāṇa*), because a buddha is freed both from bondage to saṃsāra and from being absorbed into nirvāṇic peace in a way that would remove him from saṃsāra (from the world). The unrestricted nirvāṇa attained by a buddha, through the force of his wisdom and compassion, manifests endlessly in the world to help other beings become freed from the sufferings of saṃsāra. This occurs through what are called the three "buddha bodies" (S. *buddha-kāyas*). A buddha's nondual awareness of emptiness is his ultimate identity, his dharma body (S. *dharma-kāya*). From that empty, aware ground of compassion, visionary forms of buddhahood manifest within pure dimensions of reality to transmit the Dharma to communities of advanced bodhisattvas. These visionary forms are called *saṃbhoga-kāya*, bodies of communal joy. From the same empty, aware ground of dharmakāya also come a vast variety of ways that qualities of enlightenment are communicated to ordinary persons in the world, through Dharma teachers, sacred art, natural phenomena, etc. This third dimension of buddhahood is called *nirmāṇakāya*, body of diverse manifestation. On this see John Makransky, "Buddhahood and Buddha Bodies," in *Encyclopedia of Buddhism*, Robert Buswell, ed. (New York: Macmillan Reference, 2004), 76–79; Makransky, *Buddhahood Embodied*, 85–108, 289–307; Tsongkhapa, *Great Treatise*, 2:86–99.

Tsongkhapa's interpretation, nirvāṇa and saṃsāra are nondual only in the sense that both are empty of substantial existence, an emptiness that provides the essential freedom for persons to be transformed by long practice of the Dharma toward the realization of a buddha's nirvāṇa that is endowed with all the powers of a buddha's enlightenment. For Tsongkhapa, then, although nirvāṇa and saṃsāra are ontologically nondual in their emptiness, they are experienced existentially as quite distant from each other. This is because buddhahood as the fullest realization of nirvāṇa needs to be generated through a vast and methodical accumulation of its own pure causes that replace the impure causes of saṃsāra.

Longchenpa, like Tsongkhapa, drew on Indian Abhidharma understandings of the five aggregates and their causal process of dependent origination. But whereas Tsongkhapa understood those aggregates to constitute the very being of persons (which is empty of substantial existence), Longchenpa understood the aggregates as obscuring what persons really are, which is pure awareness (S. *vidyā*, T. *rigpa*) primordially undivided from emptiness and endowed with all capacities of enlightenment. The experience of oneself and world as impure aggregates is what happens when one's primordially pure awareness, always undivided from emptiness and enlightened capacities, becomes identified with delusions of ignorance, attachment, and aversion that distort those innate capacities by directing their energies into narrow, self-centered patterns of reaction (*karma*), which give rise to the experiential process of dependent arising, rebirth, and redeath described above. Tsongkhapa understood beings as completely comprised by that conditioned samsāric process, which must be brought to an end and replaced by enlightenment and its qualities. In contrast, for Longchenpa, the process of dependent arising doesn't fully comprise what beings are. Rather, it represents a primordial amnesia through which beings have forgotten what they most deeply are.[10] Longchenpa's anthropology thus relies less exclusively on Abhidharma than Tsongkhapa and more on Indian Vajrayāna teachings that maintain a strong model of innate buddhahood (*tathāgatā-garbha*), as the underlying identity of beings.

For Longchenpa, unlike Tsongkhapa, the Mahāyāna principle that nirvāṇa and saṃsāra are nondual means that all qualities and capacities of buddhahood are immanent in all persons. For Longchenpa, the person is, in her deepest identity, not her conditioned mind but the unconditioned, primordial nature of her mind, which is the ground of enlightenment immanent in her:

---

[10]Longchenpa, *Rdzogs pa chen po Sems nyid ngal gso rtsa wa dang rang 'grel pa shing rta chen po*, in English as *Finding Rest in the Nature of Mind*, Padmakara Translation Group, trans. (Boulder, CO: Shambhala, 2017), 1:216–18, 237–41. This text includes a translation of the root text of *Sems nyid ngal gso* and excerpts from its autocommentary.

an innate awareness (*rigpa*) that is unconditioned in its emptiness, cognizant clarity, and enlightened capacity. The path of enlightenment for Longchenpa then, unlike Tsongkhapa, is not the new creation of a pure enlightened reality that replaces the impure reality of saṃsāra. Rather, the path is a process of recalling, and learning fully to embody, what we already are in the depth of our being. Longchenpa writes, "Whether or not the adventitious defilements [of delusion] have been purified, from the very time of one's existence as an ordinary [unenlightened] being, the essence of one's awareness is emptiness, its nature is clarity, its way of arising is ceaseless, everything [i.e., every virtue of enlightenment] is present and changeless in the nature of aware-ness. These are the aspects of the . . . [buddha] bodies, which are present in us right now, . . . without need of seeking for them from any other source."[11]

Epistemologically, then, the path of enlightenment involves recognizing how the mind's identification with its reductive, reified concepts of ignorance and delusion has hidden and obstructed its true unconditioned nature of emptiness, clarity, and enlightened capacity. Existentially, the path is expe-rienced as a return to one's primordial being, like having forgotten, and then remembering, who you really are. For Longchenpa, when the deep, empty nature of the mind is recognized, the delusive tendencies that had hidden it can no longer function, and the primordial essence of enlightenment is freed to take spontaneous expression as powers, bodies, and liberating activities of buddhahood. "The only difference between the case [of an ordinary be-ing and that of an enlightened being] lies in the complete manifestation or otherwise of the mind's nature. It is not that the qualities of enlightenment are nonexistent in the condition of ordinary beings and are generated anew later on. For these qualities are [unconditioned,] beyond all movement and change."[12] "In short . . . the bodies and wisdoms of buddhahood dwell primordially within all beings, as inalienably as sunlight in the sun itself."[13]

SOTERIOLOGY: THE PATH TO REALIZATION OF BUDDHAHOOD

Within the general Buddhist understanding that is shared by both of these Tibetan figures, mental patterns of ignorance (S. *avidyā*) make persons and phenomena appear to be self-existent, as if each were an intrinsically single, substantial, and autonomous entity. Our minds construct, reify, and fixate on

---

[11]Longchenpa, *rDzogs pa chen po Sem nyid ngal gso'i gnas gsum dge ba sum gyi don khrid Byang chub lam bzang*, in *Buddha Mind: An Anthology of Longchen Rabjam's Writings on Dzogpa Chenpo*, Tulku Thondup, trans. (Ithaca, NY: Snow Lion Publications), 314.

[12]Longchenpa, *Finding Rest in the Nature of Mind*, 206.

[13]Ibid., 219.

those appearances of self-existence, reacting to them with various forms of attachment or aversion, which bear karmic fruit as diverse forms of suffering.

To counteract those inner causes of suffering, Tsongkhapa argues, we must use precise forms of analysis and investigation (S. *vicāra*, T. *dpyod pa*) to deconstruct the false appearance of persons and things, to reveal their emptiness, their lack of self-existence. For Tsongkhapa, again, the person is composed just of saṃsāric aggregates of mind and body. But by cultivating the wisdom that realizes the emptiness of all such phenomena, one can begin to be freed from the causal process of ignorance, attachment, and karma that maintain those aggregates. Such freedom dawns when the practitioner starts to generate the supramundane, nondual awareness of emptiness that constitutes inmost liberation, nirvāṇa. However, in Tsongkhapa's Mahāyāna soteriology, unlike the normative soteriologies of Abhidharma systems, one does not thereby seek to abandon saṃsāra for a nirvāṇa that would leave behind all others who suffer in saṃsāra. Instead, together with the growing wisdom of emptiness, one cultivates compassion for all beings and generates *bodhicitta*, the urge to realize buddhahood, in order to help them all become freed from their inmost causes of suffering. The aim is to attain the fullest form of nirvāṇa, the unrestricted nirvāṇa of a buddha (*apratiṣṭitha nirvāṇa*), which is freed not just from personal attachment to the world but also from all inner obstructions that would impede vast enlightened activity for beings in the world.[14] That is the path of the bodhisattva.

To support that soteriological process, a bodhisattva makes a vow to remain in saṃsāra for the sake of beings, and to generate all the karmic merit and wisdom necessary to realize buddhahood on their behalf, through many interrelated kinds of meditative, ritual, and ethical practice that empower liberating wisdom and compassionate responsiveness (*pāramitās*).[15] The compassion for beings in saṃsāra that is embodied in all such practices becomes the "glue" that keeps the bodhisattva linked to saṃsāra, displacing the glue of saṃsāric ignorance and attachment, as he generates causes of enlightened activity for beings. Tsongkhapa uses agricultural imagery to describe the causal process that leads to enlightenment. Just as a barley seed is the specific cause of a barley sprout, while the conditions for that seed to sprout are earth and water, so cultivating *bodhicitta*, the compassionate urge to become fully enlightened for the sake of beings, establishes the causal seed of buddhahood, while cultivating the wisdom of emptiness establishes the condition for that seed to sprout in the attainment of fullest enlightenment.[16]

[14]Tsongkhapa, *Great Treatise*, 2:19–21.
[15]Ibid., 2:102–10.
[16]Ibid., 2:18.

For Tsongkhapa, freedom from attachment to the self-existent appearances of conditioned things is accomplished by realizing the ultimate, unconditioned nature of all such appearances, which is their emptiness. Yet for him, the awareness that realizes emptiness is also a conditioned phenomenon, like all forms of consciousness. As such, it provides the basis in a buddha's enlightenment for enlightened activity in the conditioned world.[17] For Tsongkhapa, then, buddhahood's vast powers of knowledge, compassionate responsiveness, and liberating activity are all a product of causes, which are generated by the bodhisattva path, and which replace the ignorance, attachment, and tainted karma that were the impure causes of one's saṃsāric experience. In sum, for Tsongkhapa, buddhahood has to be causally generated, by extensive, effortful cultivations of wisdom, compassion, and ethical activity that gradually undercut and replace the causes of saṃsāra with vast causes of enlightened awareness, manifestation, and activity.[18]

For Longchenpa, in contrast with Tsongkhapa, buddhahood is immanent in persons, so the transformation from saṃsāra to nirvāṇa does not involve an accumulation of causes for newly generating enlightenment. Rather, it involves a deep recognition of immanent buddhahood—the empty, lucid, unconditioned essence of one's awareness, which is already endowed with all capacities of enlightenment. For Longchenpa, the mind's conditioned tendencies of ignorance, attachment, and reaction (*karma*) have obscured that buddha nature, impeding its primordial capacity for unimpeded love, compassion, and wisdom. So for him, practices of the bodhisattva path cannot causally create buddhahood; rather, they attune the practitioner to the buddha nature within, making her receptive to its enlightened capacities so that they can manifest of themselves.

Longchenpa argues that we cannot create the infinite reality of buddhahood described in numerous Mahāyāna Buddhist texts—its all-pervasive wisdom, compassion, and liberating activities—by accumulating finite causes and conditions, no matter how extensively. As he writes in his *Treasury of Basic Space,* "Since pure enlightened awareness and the bodies of buddhahood are primordially established, there is no causal process for generating them by means of adventitious, conditioned phenomena. If enlightened awareness were the product of causes, it would not occur of itself, and would be a conditioned phenomenon that is subject to destruction. But [buddhahood] is described as spontaneously present, unconditioned, [and unending]."[19]

---

[17]Makransky, *Buddhahood Embodied*, 296–97, 304.
[18]Tsongkhapa, *Great Treatise*, 3:129; 2:97.
[19]Longchenpa, *Chos dbyings rin po che'i mdzod*, in English as *The Precious Treasury of the*

A buddha's all-pervading powers and activities of love, compassion, and wisdom are based not on prior accumulation of conditioned mental states but on the unconditioned nature of mind in which the infinite capacity of unconditioned love, compassion, and wisdom is primordially immanent. As Longchenpa writes, "The spontaneously present adamantine heart essence is the essence of awareness, which itself is already timelessly present as buddhahood, analogous to the sun that is [always] actually present. Those who follow other approaches hold that buddhahood is accomplished by a process of effort and achievement that involves causes and conditions. This is like holding that the sun, which is always present, shines only due to causes and conditions that dispel clouds and darkness." Thus, he asserts, "These two kinds of approach are as different as heaven and earth."[20]

To realize enlightenment, therefore, one must learn to rely not on finite, conditioned, and changeable states of mind (T. *sems*), no matter how virtuous or lofty, but on the infinite, unconditioned, empty, and cognizant essence of all such mental states, which is the ultimate nature of mind (T. *sems nyid*). As Longchenpa declares, "The truth of primordial purity is not found by striving. Buddhahood makes itself evident within the expanse of self-occurring enlightenment. Since buddhahood has already been [timelessly] accomplished, there is no need to achieve it anew. . . . This lucid expanse of primordial awareness does not stray at all from its nature, so do not stray from it!"[21]

Does Longchenpa, then, reject the many meditative, ritual, and ethical practices of Buddhist traditions, like those taught by Tsongkhapa? Not at all. He also teaches such practices in great detail. But, he argues, they promote the attainment of enlightenment not because they create enlightenment but because they purify the mind of all mental tendencies that obscure its primordially enlightened nature, by harmonizing the mind with that nature. The buddha bodies are preexistent in the experiential ground of beings, Longchenpa writes, "But they have become obscured and invisible by [mental] defilements while one remains as a living being. Thus, the accumulation of merit through development of the enlightened attitude and so forth cleanses the obscurations [that have hidden] the form bodies [*rūpakāya*] and the accumulation of wisdom through meditation on void-

Basic Space of Phenomena, Padma Translation Committee, ed. and trans. (Junction City, CA: Padma Publishing, 2001), 42, 44. The quote is my translation from the edited Tibetan text. On this point, see also Longchenpa, *Chos dbyings mdzod kyi 'grel ba Lung gi gter mdzod*, in English as *A Treasure Trove of Scriptural Transmission*, Padma Translation Committee, trans. (Junction City, CA: Padma Publishing, 2001), 119. See also Longchenpa, *Finding Rest in the Nature of Mind*, 247.
[20]Longchenpa, *Treasure Trove of Scriptural Transmission*, 105.
[21]Longchenpa, *Precious Treasury of Basic Space*, 54. This quote is my translation from the edited Tibetan text.

ness and so forth cleanses the obscurations [that have hidden] suchness, the essence body (*dharmakāya*)."[22] The so-called accumulations of virtue on the path clear away mental obscurations that have hidden preexistent virtue; they do not create virtue de novo. The increasing power of virtue on the path is like the waxing moon—it appears as if the moon is increasing in size, when actually the shadow that has hidden the already fully formed moon is lessening.[23]

GNOSEOLOGY: HOW TO ACCESS
ENLIGHTENED FORMS OF AWARENESS

Tsongkhapa's methods for realizing enlightened awareness (gnoseology) are also closely connected to his anthropology. He sets forth these methods at length in his *Great Treatise*. Since for Tsongkhapa, unlike Longchenpa, enlightened awareness is not immanent in persons, any procedures for realizing it cannot draw on it as an innate capacity. Enlightened awareness, at its core, is a nondual, nonconceptual knowing of the empty, unconditioned nature of things. To realize the emptiness of things in that nonconceptual way is to be freed from the ignorant habit of misconceiving and reifying things as self-existent—that is, to be freed from the epistemological basis of attachment, karmic reaction, and consequent suffering. But in Tsongkhapa's anthropology, human beings are constituted only by psycho-physical aggregates whose mental states are conceptually conditioned to function dualistically. So conceptual states of mind are the only possible starting point for learning to generate a nonconceptual awareness of emptiness. Tsongkhapa therefore articulates ways to employ conceptual, conditioned states of mind as the basis (and only basis) for initially accessing the ultimate truth of emptiness. When through repeated analysis and diverse forms of reasoning, one's conceptual ascertainment that everything is empty of self-existence becomes sufficiently strong, steady, and clear, it can gradually deepen into a nonconceptual, nondual awareness of emptiness that actually liberates the practitioner from the conceptual fixations of ignorance and attachment that bind him to saṃsāra.[24]

Based on the gnoseological explanations of several late Indian Madhya-

---

[22]Longchenpa, *rDzogs pa chen po Sem nyid ngal gso'i 'grel ba shing rta chen po*, in *Buddha Mind*, Tulku Thondup, trans., 240.

[23]Longchenpa, *rDzogs pa chen po Sem nyid rang grol*, in *Buddha Mind*, Tulku Thondup, trans., 333–34.

[24]Tsongkhapa, *Great Treatise*, 3:341–42. Tsongkhapa asserts that all key points of the path in their entirety (including emptiness) are within the purview of the conceptual mind that engages scripture and reasoning, and can be accessed only by means of that (2:88, 96).

maka scholars (prominently the eighth-century Indian teacher Kamalaśīla), Tsongkhapa explains that two kinds of conditioned cultivation of mind are needed to realize such enlightened awareness: calm abiding (*śamatha*) and conceptual investigation into emptiness that can lead to liberating insight (*vipaśyanā*). Without the alternation of effortful, conditioned mental states of calm abiding and insight and their eventual unification, he argues, the mind's tendency to identify with reified constructs of ignorance and attachment cannot be cut.[25]

Tsongkhapa is aware of other contemplative traditions in India, China, and Tibet that focused more exclusively on the practice of calm abiding (*śamatha*), purportedly to calm the mind so fully that it would stop engaging in activities of conceptual construction and reification that generate the appearance and attachment to self-existence that bind persons to saṃsāra. But Tsongkhapa severely criticizes that approach, emphasizing the need to balance calm abiding with precisely targeted forms of conceptual analysis into emptiness (*vipaśyanā*), in order to generate a conceptual understanding of emptiness that, with increasing stability, would become a nonconceptual, liberating insight.[26] Since in Tsongkhapa's anthropology, no innate, nonconceptual enlightened awareness is available in persons to draw upon, the only way to get to such a nonconceptual awareness in his understanding is through the conceptually conditioned procedures that he outlines.

Longchenpa's gnoseology is also closely related to his anthropology. And since for Longchenpa enlightened awareness is immanent in persons, the path to enlightenment must ultimately draw on that awareness itself as the primary means for awakening. Recall that in Longchenpa's anthropology (unlike Tsongkhapa's), persons comprise not only conditioned aggregates of mind and body. Rather, the conditioned aggregates tainted by ignorance and attachment are just distorted expressions of the unconditioned, untainted primordial unity of emptiness and cognizance that is the insubstantial, immanent ground of all experience. When a person's primordial awareness (T. *rigpa*) becomes freed from the ignorance and attachment that had obscured it, that awareness can now recognize the aggregates of mind and body as undivided from its own emptiness and cognizance, which is endowed with all powers of enlightenment, thereby permitting the innate wisdoms (T. *ye shes*), embodiments (T. *sku*), and activities (T. *phrin las*) of buddhahood that had been hidden in the aggregates to manifest of themselves.[27]

---

[25]Ibid., 3:342–44.

[26]David Seyfort Ruegg, *Buddha Nature, Mind, and the Problem of Gradualism* (London: School of Oriental and African Studies, 1989), 111–15.

[27]Longchenpa, *Tshig don mdzod*, in *Approaching the Great Perfection*, Sam van Schaik, trans. (Somerville, MA: Wisdom Publications, 2004), 68. See also Longchenpa, *rDzogs pa chen po Sems nyid rang grol* (Gangtok, Sikkim: Pema Thinley, 1999), folios 263–64 (in *Buddha Mind*,

In Longchenpa's view, then, methods for realizing enlightened awareness that draw, as Tsongkhapa does, just on conditioned, conceptual, and dualistic states of mind cannot possibly access the unconditioned, preconceptual, and nondual ground of enlightened mind. As Longchenpa states, "Primordial awareness transcends the reference points of conceptual mind, so do not make mental efforts to apprehend it. The deep nature of mind is effortless and spontaneously perfected, so do not adulterate it with antidotes of modification and transformation: let it go, of itself, in natural ease."[28]

For Longchenpa, causal methods to generate enlightened awareness, like those Tsongkhapa taught, cannot attain the state of enlightenment that is unconditioned, since enlightened awareness is not a causal creation. It is beyond the ability of conditioned mental states to generate.[29] The various kinds of mental cultivation that Tibetan Buddhism inherited from India are incorporated into Longchenpa's path system not as a means to causally generate enlightenment but to make practitioners increasingly receptive to the enlightened capacities that are already immanent in the ground of their experience: "Although the sun and moon are radiantly luminous in the midst of the sky, they can be completely hidden by clouds that prevent them from being known. So, enlightenment, though present within you, is not apparent. Thick clouds vanish naturally when left alone. Similarly, the clouds of karmic causality vanish naturally without effort or striving, as the essence of enlightenment shines of itself in the skylike expanse. But because of varying levels of readiness among practitioners, different systems of practice are provided."[30]

In Longchenpa's view, even a tremendously vast accumulation of finite causes cannot possibly give rise to the infinite expanse of nondual awareness that is buddhahood. It is the unconditioned, infinite nature of one's mind itself that realizes the infinite expanse of enlightenment as its own primordial way of being (T. *gnas lugs*). He writes, "The supreme way involves no effort of taking up or rejecting [various states of mind]. Rather, naturally occurring primordial awareness, the essence of enlightened mind, becomes evident by not wavering from its direct experience. So there is no need to strive for [enlightenment] elsewhere."[31]

Therefore, in Longchenpa's view, rather than using conceptual analysis

---

Tulku Thondup, trans., 327).

    [28]Longchenpa, *Sems nyid rang grol*, folio 258 (my translation). Also translated by Thondup, *Buddha Mind*, 321.

    [29]Longchenpa, *Treasure Trove of Scriptural Transmission*, 43, 55; Longchenpa, *Sems nyid rang grol*, in Thondup, *Buddha Mind*, 324.

    [30]Longchenpa, *Precious Treasury of Basic Space*, 130 (my translation from the Tibetan text).

    [31]Ibid., 38 (my translation). Cf. Longchenpa, *Sems nyid Rang grol*, in Thondup, *Buddha Mind*, 334.

as the primary means to undercut the reifying tendencies that bind one's mind to suffering, one must learn to rely on the unity of cognizance and emptiness that is the preconceptual ground of all experience, which is prior to all reifying and reactive tendencies and also the very essence of them, in order to heal and ultimately liberate all such tendencies: "All desired, undesired, and neutral states of mind . . . arise as a display of primordial awareness within its basic space [of emptiness]. All such mental states occur only within that basic space, not wavering from it at all. So, without attempting to change or manipulate them . . . just recognize the basic space in which they occur, and rest there. As soon as you do, those mental states subside by themselves, vanish by themselves, are liberated by themselves."[32]

For Tsongkhapa, to rest in this way would connote the mere practice of *śamatha*, calm abiding, without the necessary complementary practice of *vipaśyanā*, conceptually investigating the emptiness of things. Since for Tsongkhapa, all human awareness is ineluctably caught up in forms of fixation whether gross or subtle, even deep states of *śamatha*, "resting," would not be enough to access the liberating wisdom of emptiness. Analysis that conceptually ascertains emptiness is also essential. For Longchenpa in contrast, primordial awareness beyond all conceptual frames of reference is the very power for awakening to enlightenment. If one does not learn how to let it come to self-recognition, and rest in its capacity to liberate all conceptual fixations as empty appearances, one's application of conceptual analysis will just further impede the self-liberating power of innate enlightened awareness. Although conceptual analysis is a helpful supportive practice, it could never be the main practice for realizing enlightenment.

IMPLICATIONS FOR COMPARATIVE THEOLOGY

I have summarized a few basic tensions in Tibetan Buddhism concerning how ultimate reality is related to human beings in their basic nature, in their capacity to become aware of that reality, and in their capacity to be transformed by it. The worldviews and doctrinal frameworks of Tibetan Buddhist traditions and cultures, of course, differ from those of other religious cultures. But the Tibetan tensions noted here—between transcendent and immanent aspects of anthropology, soteriology, and gnoseology—are paralleled in other religious cultures and traditions.

Did the areas of Tibetan doctrinal tension described above point you to analogous areas of tension in your own religious tradition? If so, this becomes a basis for comparative investigation. In what different ways does

---

[32]Longchenpa, *Precious Treasury of Basic Space*, 108 (my translation).

your tradition attempt to relate an unconditioned, infinite, atemporal ultimate reality (or nature of reality) to the conditioned, finite, temporal world of human beings (theological anthropology)? In light of that, what differing viewpoints emerge on how much, and in what ways, human effort is required to align, or realign, us with that ultimate reality? Or to what extent are human beings dependent on ultimate reality itself to align us with itself, or to draw us to itself (soteriology)? What perspectives arise regarding how, and to what extent, a human being with finite, conditioned forms of knowing can become aware of an infinite, unconditioned dimension of reality (gnoseology)? Finally, as in Tibetan Buddhism, how are diverse practices of your religion understood to inform and empower all such theological understandings and possibilities, for example, practices of liturgy, prayer, contemplation, investigation, deepening faith, love, compassion, wisdom, ritual reverence, offering, repentance, ethical practices, and forms of communal life?

If we take Christianity as an example: To what extent is the image of God in the human damaged or intact (theological anthropology)? To what extent are persons saved by grace through faith, or by human disciplines and works (soteriology)? What is the beatific vision? Does it involve seeing God "face-to-face," or does it involve beginning to see beings and things as God sees them (gnoseology)? Similar questions may occur to theologically trained persons of any religion, after being exposed to analogous tensions in any other religion, like the exposure to Tibetan Buddhist tensions that we engaged in this chapter.

A Jewish Interpretation of Plurality

Some Comments on Perry Schmidt-Leukel's Fractal Interpretation of Religious Diversity

Ephraim Meir

———

Historically, relations between religions have been extremely compli-cated. They have fostered conflicts, feelings of superiority, and inimical relations. Religious identities have been built by denigrating religious others. But religions also have furthered friendly relations between human beings and cross-fertilized each other. Divine beings have transmigrated from one religion to another using altered names. Religious stories have also been adopted and adapted by more than one religion.

In our times, technology, transportation, migration, and cultural studies allow us to better know the religious other. Faraway religions have become neighbor religions. Yet progress in knowledge does not necessarily mean that we have become more respectful of the religious other, or more sensitive to otherness or to less clear-cut categories like hybrid identities, cross-border-ing, and multiple religious belonging or participation. Perry Schmidt-Leukel deems that the time is ripe to bring together multireligious perspectives and to interpret, modify, transform, and expand religious categories in order to foster a global, interreligious understanding. His new and pioneering book, *Religious Pluralism and Interreligious Theology*,[1] which contains the ex-tended edition of his Gifford Lectures, holds significant insights. A central perception is that concepts of the ultimate reality are not true descriptions of it: they are, rather, pointers and guideposts.[2] His theory is helpful in the passage from a confessional theology to an interreligious theology.[3]

---

[1] *Religious Pluralism and Interreligious Theology: The Gifford Lectures—An Extended Edition* (Maryknoll, NY: Orbis Books, 2017).
[2] Ibid., 243.
[3] Ibid.

In his interreligious theology, Schmidt-Leukel recognizes distinctiveness as well as interrelatedness. His fractal interpretation of plurality explains why and how creative theologians from different denominations may come to mutual understanding. His main argument is that since common elements are present in all religions, such an understanding becomes possible. Schmidt-Leukel gives examples of creative, interreligious thinking, arguing that primal concepts such as "Son," "Prophet" and "Buddha" are found in Christianity, Islam, and Buddhism. The three categories are present in each religion with different emphases.[4] These categories, which in fact occur in all religious traditions, express the confidence "that human beings have the potential to become vehicles of divine revelation."[5] In such a way, Schmidt-Leukel constructs a global theology that offers a fractal interpretation of religious diversity. His work makes the frontiers between religions less intractable. If one follows his argument, the different religions appear to be less separated than might be thought at first sight. Schmidt-Leukel values uniqueness, but highlights interconnection. I am in agreement with him that in the interaction between religions and in conversations with religious others, religions and religious persons evolve. Interreligious encounters lead to learning from the other, and to spiritual enrichment and transformation. Theology becomes "increasingly interreligious."[6] A view such as Schmidt-Leukel's allows for a fuller understanding of the spiritual dimensions of religious diversity. Part 1 of his book gives a positive assessment of religious diversity, and part 2 offers his interreligious theology. In chapter 14 he explains his theory on the fractal structure of religious pluralism. Chapters 10 to 13 are an impressive exercise in creative interreligious thinking; together they offer concrete examples of the fractal interpretation of reality.

Schmidt-Leukel's aim is to transform traditional thinking in view of an "interreligious reflection on different understandings of religious diversity."[7] He brings different religions together in view of a "joint and reciprocal integration of different *religion-specific pluralisms* within a process of multiperspectival exchange."[8] His interreligious theology endorses the creative interaction between religions in view of their "possible compatibility."[9] A basic premise of Schmidt-Leukel's interreligious theology is that all truth "must be compatible."[10] Following the Jain principle of many-sidedness,

---

[4]Ibid., 236.
[5]Ibid., 203.
[6]Ibid., 8.
[7]Ibid., 113.
[8]Ibid.
[9]Ibid.
[10]Ibid., 133.

he claims that there are only "apparent contradictions" between authentic truth claims and that they will "ultimately dissolve in a higher synthesis."[11] Contradictions are actually "an invitation to synthesis."[12] The search for a common platform is central in this theological construction: all religions have shared elements, with different emphases and to different degrees.

THE AIM OF INTERRELIGIOUS THEOLOGY

Schmidt-Leukel strives to overcome apparent contradictions in a higher synthesis; he looks for a common denominator. The strength of his argument lies in the fact that religious experiences are human experiences that take place in *one* world, which enables understanding. He argues that, since the truth of the Transcendent is *one*, a consensus on it must exist, notwithstanding differences in the multiple approaches. He negotiates between religions by stretching, enlarging, and transforming religious categories. He comes to surprising and challenging new insights. Consider his innovative thought on creation, which is prima facie entirely absent in Buddhism. Schmidt-Leukel creatively understands nirvana as a form of "grace," since it is unconditioned and unproduced, rather than the product of human effort.[13] The Buddha-Nature, which allows one to realize that *samsara* is unsatisfying, is called "the true creator."[14] This is a clear case of inventive, synthesizing theological reasoning. Salvation, understood in Christianity as the goal of creation (*causa finalis*), is seen as being in line with major concerns of Buddhism.[15] Schmidt-Leukel's conclusion is that salvation is conceived by Buddhists *and* Christians "in quite analogous and compatible ways."[16] He views Amida Buddhism as promising salvation by "entrusting oneself entirely to the compassion as it is represented by Amida Buddha and has become manifest or embodied in the compassionate spirit of Buddha Gautama. In essence, salvation is thus received by faith alone."[17]

Schmidt-Leukel rightly opines that pluralisms always need to be tradition-specific.[18] He takes into account tradition-bound pluralisms and discusses them in part 1 of *Religious Pluralism*. He is not interested in a metatheory independent of denominations. His own view on religious pluralism and

---

[11] Ibid.
[12] Ibid., 148, 206.
[13] Ibid., 214.
[14] Ibid., 216.
[15] Ibid., 218–20.
[16] Ibid., 220.
[17] Ibid., 177. For "sola fide" in Buddhism, see also ibid., 179.
[18] Ibid., 8.

interreligious theology is inspired by the Christian tradition and its affirmation of a God who loves all people. He finds in a variety of religions an opening to the truth present in other religions. For a Christian opening to others, he refers to the publication *The Myth of Christian Uniqueness*, and for such openness in other traditions, he refers to *The Myth of Religious Superiority*.[19]

For a Jewish openness to religious others, he mentions Michael Kogan's saying, "Instead of being *the* chosen people, my people begin to see themselves as *a* chosen people."[20] He also makes reference to Heschel's statement that religious diversity is the will of God[21] and to Raphael Jospe's thought concerning multiple perspectives on truth.[22] For Islam, openness is found in Rumi's utterance on the light, which is not different, though the lamps from which it shines may differ.[23] The Qur'an too proffers openness to religious others in the Sura on Allah's messengers to all people in the world (Sura 16.36).[24] For Hinduism, there is Swami Vivekananda's saying that different religions are like different coats; each specific coat will not fit everybody.[25] The Hindu openness to religious others expresses itself in the belief that Brahman is present in everybody as their true self, *atman*.[26] Mahayana Buddhism claims that all sentient beings participate in the common Buddha-Nature.[27] There is also the view that Bodhisattvas are active in other religions.[28] As for the religions in China, Schmidt-Leukel points to the phenomenon of multiple religious participation,[29] to the tripod of Daoism, Confucianism, and Buddhism, which cannot stand if one of the legs is missing.[30] Finally, he refers to Zhihe Wang, who works with the two principles yin and yang, which are in a relationship of dynamic complementarity: there is something of yin in yang and something of yang in yin.[31] Surely, this Chinese concept inspired Schmidt-Leukel to develop his fractal interpretation of religious pluralism.

As for me, the presence of sonship, prophethood, and awakening as "transformative, liberative experience"[32] is attested in Judaism as well. The

---

[19]Ibid., 30–31.
[20]Ibid., 37.
[21]Ibid., 33.
[22]Ibid., 37.
[23]Ibid., 49.
[24]Ibid., 131.
[25]Ibid., 55.
[26]Ibid., 132.
[27]Ibid., 82.
[28]Ibid., 131–32.
[29]Ibid., 100.
[30]Ibid., 98. He also remarks that, with this tripod, hierarchical thinking remains.
[31]Ibid., 106.
[32]Ibid., 171.

prophets put forward the idea of justice, which nowadays is also present in engaged Buddhism and in the Advaita tradition.[33] Kabbalistic meditations and practices bring about an awakening. Sonship is also attested to in Judaism. In intimate Jewish God-talk, the people of Israel consider themselves to be "sons of God" (Deut. 14:1: "You are children of the Eternal, your God"—*banim attèm la-Shem elohekhèm"*). Classical Jewish theology, of course, denies divine incarnation. Moses, for instance, is not an incarnation of God. From a historical perspective, Jesus was an observant Jew who never saw himself as God.[34] Yet in their search for a more transcendent, supernatural Jesus, the American Jews Zalman Schachter-Shalomi and Daniel Matt go beyond the historical Jesus who preached good moral behavior.[35] For Schachter-Shalomi, the Jewish kabbalist tradition offers a model of divine embodiment. In this perspective, Jesus is an "incarnate of Torah" and "axis mundi."[36] Daniel Matt likewise sees Jesus as an "axis mundi" for his apostles.[37] Jesus is for him an early Hasid, a *tsaddiq*, who became a living Torah, an intermediator between the disciples and God. He claimed an internalized redemption.[38] Schmidt-Leukel's theory on sonship, prophetic mission, and buddhahood is also valid for Judaism.

LESS THAN COMPLETE TRANSPARENCY?

Schmidt-Leukel follows Raimon Panikkar's insight that each religion "represents the whole of the human experience in a concrete way."[39] Microcosmos and macrocosmos are related. He explains diversity and commonality with Benoît Mandelbrot's theory of fractals. The term "fractal" means fragmented and irregular: Mandelbrot thought that "there is a fractal face to the geometry of nature."[40] In a parallel way, Schmidt-Leukel deems that what is true in nature is also true in culture: religions too have a "fractal face." When Bernhard Waldenfels says that the culturally known and the alien are entangled with each other, he interprets cultural diversity

[33]See Marcia Pally, *Commonwealth and Covenant: Economics, Politics, and Theologies of Relationality* (Grand Rapids: Eerdmans, 2016); Anantanand Rambachan, *A Hindu Theology of Liberation: Not-Two Is Not One* (Albany: State University of New York Press, 2015).

[34]Bart D. Ehrman, *How Jesus Became God: The Exaltation of a Jewish Preacher from Galilee* (New York: HarperCollins, 2014), 85–128. Arius held that Jesus was God's first creation.

[35]Shaul Magid, *American Post-Judaism: Identity and Renewal in a Postethnic Society* (Bloomington: Indiana University Press, 2013), 135–38, 148–56.

[36]Ibid., 150.

[37]Ibid., 155.

[38]Ibid., 52–154.

[39]Schmidt-Leukel, *Religious Pluralism and Interreligious Theology*, 222.

[40]Ibid., 224–25.

in a fractal way.[41] Schmidt-Leukel claims that no specificities are present in one religion that are totally absent in another. After summarizing some early phenomenologists, who come close to his own fractal interpretation, Schmidt-Leukel cautiously writes that "almost" everything reappears in some way in different religions.[42] From the typological endeavors of specialists in comparative religion and from phenomenologists he learns that religious diversity is "marked by fractal structures."[43] Similarities suggest that each religion is a part of the whole. On this point I would welcome further inquiry into the exact relationship between commonalities and incommensurable uniqueness.

Schmidt-Leukel's model is unity in diversity, unity in difference. His fractal interpretation is on the interreligious, intrareligious, and intrasubjective levels.[44] He rightly claims that "[r]eligions resemble each other, but they resemble each other in their diversity."[45] He also writes that "the religious other is never completely or wholly other."[46] In his fractal interpretation, what is similar is also irregular and different.[47] For Schmidt-Leukel, fractal theory allows for complementarity and enrichment. He assesses diversity and complementarity.[48] Every attempt to come to some consensus should indeed reckon with the specificity of the religious other and her undeniable otherness.

I propose an alliance between different and to a certain extent incomparable religious traditions. Of course, comparability is possible since our own experience is part of the experiences of humankind. Yet this does not mean that everything is comparable. Certain incommensurabilities preclude the translatability of all things into something else, as well as the reduction of all otherness to structurally identical or analogous elements.

Some elements in religions refuse to enter into the interreligious grid. Not everything is compatible. Just as languages possess words and expressions that are idiomatic, religions have an otherness that is not reducible to sameness. Schmidt-Leukel looks for compatibilities in order to create a communication platform. But there are also incompatibilities between the different traditions that withstand comparative efforts.

To my mind, some elements in differing cultures are not compatible with each other—not overlapping, and not parallel, but rather radically different

[41]Ibid., 226.
[42]Ibid., 229.
[43]Ibid., 230.
[44]On the intrasubjective level, people have in themselves an interreligious dialogue.
[45]Schmidt-Leukel, *Religious Pluralism and Interreligious Theology*, 233.
[46]Ibid., 235.
[47]Ibid., 233.
[48]Ibid., 236–37.

and incommensurable. Schmidt-Leukel's valid argument is that if religions are not intelligible to each other, we could not understand other cultures at all.[49] Translating religious categories is a possibility and even a necessity. But should less than complete comprehensibility not be possible? Do religions have specificities that are not present in other religions and that are part of the world experience, but are also somehow unique? Is every possibility present in everything? Schmidt-Leukel recognizes limited incommensurable elements in religions, but his emphasis is more on comparability and translatability than on incomparable uniqueness.[50]

TOWARD AN ETHICAL INTERPRETATION
OF RELIGIOUS PLURALISM

For Schmidt-Leukel, religions can correct each other or complement each other, but his endeavor goes clearly in the direction of the search for a common basis. He asks, for instance, whether Sharia law could be accepted by Christians, and writes, "The moral and spiritual values that express and are rooted in the message of God's justice and mercy are certainly to be accepted. The question of how these are to be spelled out legally is a different issue."[51] Such a view is surprisingly congruent with what I call a radically ethical interpretation of religious sources, which constitutes a common platform for all *beyond* knowledge. This leads me to the question of whether *re*cognition rather than cognition could unite religions.

For Schmidt-Leukel, following Wilfred Cantwell Smith, interreligious theologians[52] will "deliberately cross religious borders"[53] and engage in "an interreligious process of truth-seeking."[54] They remain recognizably Christian, Muslim, Buddhist, and so on, but "Christian plus," "Muslim plus," or "Buddhist plus." Truth, Schmidt-Leukel deems, cannot come from one tradition. Indeed, multiple traditions approach the ineffable truth, which is refracted in different ways in these traditions. Schmidt-Leukel follows John Hick in the idea that "the Real" is reflected in human thought and experience;

---

[49]Ibid., 243.

[50]In the introduction to the present volume, Schmidt-Leukel explains that no religion is totally other. He does not "deny that there can be partial or limited incommensurabilities," which however "can only be identified on the basis of an overarching interreligious understanding as it becomes possible by comparison and hence commensurability." See also Schmidt-Leukel, *Religious Pluralism and Interreligious Theology*, 244.

[51]Schmidt-Leukel, *Religious Pluralism and Interreligious Theology*, 163.

[52]Michael von Brueck calls interreligious theology "dialogical theology." See ibid., 133.

[53]Ibid., 137.

[54]Ibid., 139.

we experience the Real *quoad nos*. With Schmidt-Leukel's new theory, he adds that this takes place in a fractal way.

From my vantage point, doctrinal convergences could be complemented by the search for a common ethical basis. I would like to propose a deed-centered interpretation of religious pluralism, as an alternative for a more logocentric approach. Judaism is flexible on the doctrinal level, but forbids many things to Jews that are allowed for non-Jews. It is less thought-centered than deed-centered. In our times of religious fanaticism and moral indifference, an ethical interpretation of religious pluralism and the valuing of the diversity or relative uniqueness of religions in their contribution to a more humane world is a must. Theological reasoning and dialogues are vital insofar as they contribute to ethical praxis.

TRUTH AS TRUST

Schmidt-Leukel presupposes that the various religions are referring to *one* religious truth that is refracted in them. He further presupposes that, since we live in *one* world, communication on religious truth is possible. Truth in this context is attained through the intellect. It is noteworthy that, from a Jewish point of view, the word for truth, *èmèt*, first of all denotes trustworthiness and reliability, as, for instance, in the phrase *anshe èmèt* (men to be trusted) (Exod. 18:21). The word *èmèt* also means stability and constancy, as in the expression *shalom èmèt* (a durable/lasting peace) (Jer. 14:13). *Èmèt* is finally truth and reality—for example, in the verse *ve-im èmèt haya la-davar ha-zè* (and if this was true) (Deut. 22:20). Accordingly, *be-èmèt* means "truly, really" (e.g., in Jer. 26:15).[55] *Èmèt* (trust) is from the same root as *èmuna*, which is usually translated as "faith," but which basically means "faithfulness," "steadiness." There is faithfulness between God and human beings, as well as between human beings.

Schmidt-Leukel writes that "Christian theology has benefited tremendously from looking at Christianity through Jewish eyes."[56] In light of this openness to the possible relevance of Jewish views for Christianity and other religions, I would like to draw attention to a specific Jewish view on truth as "trust." This could be of special relevance for the construction of an interreligious theology. I suggest that a logocentric fractal interpretation of religious plurality be complemented by an existential, moral, deed-centered

---

[55]L. Koehler and W. Baumgartner, *Lexicon in Veteris Testamenti Libros* (Leiden: Brill, 1958), 66–67.

[56]Schmidt-Leukel, *Religious Pluralism and Interreligious Theology*, 143.

approach of religions. All religions have ethical dimensions and value good behavior of religious others.[57] Schmidt-Leukel himself gives a few examples. Sura 5:48 reads, "Strive as in a race in all virtues."[58] Anantanand Rambachan tests the quality of religions in their potential "to sustain dignity and justice for all human beings."[59] The Dalai Lama values the worth of the major religions in terms of their positive moral potential.[60] The Buddhist Lama John Makransky deems that similar ethical and spiritual qualities in the different religions are evidence to suppose that all are rooted in the same ultimate reality.[61] An ethics-centered interpretation of religious pluralities also implies a multiperspective ethical reading of religious core texts—a task that awaits creative theologians.

With my proposal, I put the emphasis upon the ethical capacity of religions and their corrective function more than on compatibility in a synthesis. Rabbi Menahem Meiri (1249–1316), a Provençal scholar and commentator on the Talmud, set the standard when he valued Christianity as a religion that required its adherents to stick to the basic moral norms of civilization. According to Meiri, a religion that did not impose basic moral prohibitions was illicit.[62] Paul Knitter, a Christian and a Buddhist, values the peace potential in religions and lays the stress on the complementarity of being peace and making peace.[63] His concern is ethical as well, which is evident in his engagement with liberation theology. A radical reformulation of truth in terms of ethics could cause a rediscovery of the peace potential in religions. Cooperation is vital for human existence, and all are chosen to realize this human potential.

THE MÖBIUS-LIKE INTERLACEMENT OF RELIGION WITH ETHICS

I greatly appreciate Schmidt-Leukel's interreligious theology from a Christian perspective. From a Jewish perspective on pluralism, I suggest the mathematical form of the Möbius strip. This explains the intertwinedness of the relation to the Ultimate with the interdependence of all human beings.

---

[57]Marcia Pally gives a list of dicta from various religions that all point in the direction of the fundamental relatedness of human beings (*Commonwealth and Covenant*, 352).

[58]Schmidt-Leukel, *Religious Pluralism and Interreligious Theology*, 46.

[59]Ibid., 69.

[60]Ibid., 85.

[61]Ibid., 86.

[62]Eugene Korn, "Rethinking Christianity: Rabbinic Positions and Possibilities," in *Jewish Theology and World Religions*, Alon Goshen-Gottstein and Eugene Korn, eds. (Oxford: Littman Library of Jewish Civilization, 2012), 195–97.

[63]Schmidt-Leukel, *Religious Pluralism and Interreligious Theology*, 184.

The advantage of this construction or scheme lies in its ability to rediscover the ethical depth-dimension in all religions, which is congruent with their dimension of transcendence. Religions, of course, also have nonethical and even antiethical dimensions. In our times, we witness the resurgence of jihad as a war in the name of Allah. For the protagonists of the Islamic State, killing is a holy duty and abuse of women is conceived as a bonus for Islamic soldiers. These and other realities highlight the Janus-faced nature of religions. Religion has negative dimensions. In this constellation, it is crucial for theologians to find a common ethical ground for religions in the endeavor to realize values such as respect for human life and the promotion of human rights. Whereas Schmidt-Leukel takes sophisticated theological thinking as a common basis for all religions, I suggest that interreligious theology takes ethics as common basis for all religions. The ethical translation of basic religious categories in the various religions is a mission for the dialogical theologian.[64]

In her reflections on Judaism and Christianity, Marcia Pally has proposed viewing these religions as a Möbius strip: they have a double covenant between God and humans and between human beings among each other, a mutual constitution of covenant between persons and God.[65] One could enlarge the horizon: in a Möbius-like interpretation of all religions, approaching the ultimate reality is inherently linked to other persons, to belonging to all. Focusing upon the humanistic kernel in religions for the greater well-being of humankind, putting the emphasis upon sharing and cooperation, one is critical of any worldview that is exclusivist and based upon self-interest. Religions share the common task of improving the quality of life for all, to promote reciprocal consideration, and to contribute to economic justice and to peaceful societies. As Franz Rosenzweig said, God did not create religions, but the world.[66] Mending the world is the task of religions. Focusing on moral deeds, one may recognize the plurality of ways of approaching the ultimate reality as intertwined with the amelioration of human society. Paraphrasing Meiri's position, one could claim that religions are a legitimate undertaking insofar as they improve the human condition. I am aware that by introducing a prescriptive moment, I leave the descriptive level. But can theology be sustained without this prescriptive moment?

In order to counter exclusivism, Schmidt-Leukel develops a highly sophisticated theological way of thinking, in which patterns of thought, present in all religions, allow them to communicate with each other. He works with

---

[64]Paul Knitter is one of the theologians to carry out this mission. See his *One Earth, Many Religions: Multifaith Dialogue and Global Responsibility* (Maryknoll, NY: Orbis Books, 1995).

[65]Pally, *Commonwealth and Covenant*, 192–96.

[66]F. Rosenzweig, "Das neue Denken," in *Kleinere Schriften* (Berlin: Schocken, 1937), 389: "Gott hat eben nicht die Religion, sondern die Welt geschaffen."

the affirmation of metaphysical truth. As for me, pluralism in intrareligious Jewish exegesis serves as a model for interreligious interpretations that are all legitimate, *on the condition* that they serve humanity as such. A radical ethical interpretation of religious sources—as eminently carried out in Judaism, for example, by Emmanuel Levinas—seems to me to provide a solid basis for interreligious cooperation. This does not exclude highly sophisticated intellectual conversations that also contribute to the sound passage from a traditional confessional theology to an interreligious theology.

TWO TYPES OF FAITH

I mentioned that *èmèt*, "trust," and *èmuna*, "faithfulness," are linked. Martin Buber wrote extensively about the Jewish concept of *èmuna*. In his "Two Types of Faith," he characterizes Jesus's call to return to God (*Ruf zur Umkehr*) in Mark 1:15 as an authentic Jewish call. However, Christianity made it a call to convert to the Christian faith (*Bekehrung zum Glauben*).[67] The Christian faith became the Hellenistic *pistis*, a belief that something is true (*ein Fürwahrhalten*), in contrast to the Jewish faith, *èmuna*, which is confidence and faithfulness. The Christian faith became faith in Jesus who redeems the world.[68] Unlike Buber, I do not think that Paul is responsible for the switch from *èmuna*, trust in, into *pistis*, belief that. But I agree with him that *èmuna* as trust typifies Judaism, whereas *pistis* is a more Christian phenomenon. Buber is alert to the fact that the Jewish concept of *èmuna* is also present in Christianity, just as the Christian concept of *pistis* is not entirely absent in Judaism.[69] But in his typology, faith as "trust" is a more Jewish concept than faith as "truth," which is more fitting for Christianity. The Jewish existential attitude, *èmuna*, trust *in*, was substituted by *pistis*, belief *that*.

Mark 1:15 puts the saying "The time is fulfilled and the Kingdom of God has come. Turn [to God] and trust the good news [*metanoeite kai pisteuete en to euangelio*]" in Jesus's mouth. Buber interprets this saying as belonging to "the very words" (*ipsissima verba*) of Jesus. He comments that the kingdom of God, *basileia tou theou* (in Hebrew: *malkhut shamaim*), asks for the return of the human being (*Umkehr*; in Hebrew: *teshuva*). To return (*la-shuv*) is translated in Greek by *metanoiein*, to think differently (*Sinnesänderung*), which is already a reduction of the Hebrew *la-shuv*. Buber

---

[67]M. Buber, "Zwei Glaubensweisen," in *Werke. Erster Band. Schriften zur Philosophie* (Munich: Kösel and Schneider, 1962), 655.

[68]Ibid., 656.

[69]Ibid., 656–57.

remarks that this "return" is degraded in Greek to *pistis*; but he also holds that behind this misapprehension rendered in the Greek, we can be confident that the intent of the text is closer to the Hebrew *èmuna*. He concludes that a person's "return," one's *teshuva*, denotes one's active "trust" (*Treue*), whereas one's "belief in" points to the receptive "confidence" (*Vertrauen*): *teshuva*, turning to others and to God, and *èmuna*, trust,[70] belong together.

I have summarized Buber's reflections on the Greek verbs *metanoiein* and *pisteuein*, which change the meaning of *teshuva* and *èmuna*, because in a Jewish perspective, belief does not mean to believe a certain content or to think differently. Underneath the Greek, Buber rightly sensed the Jewish reality of *teshuva* and *èmuna*, of turning (from one's bad ways) and trusting. I argue that his understanding of *èmuna* as an existential attitude linked to deeds rather than as a belief in utterances is useful in theology in general and in dialogical theology more particularly.

RELIGION: THE BOND BETWEEN THE SAME AND THE OTHER WITHOUT TOTALITY

This existential-ethical way of approaching the ultimate reality has consequences for one's view of religions. The various teachings and doctrines of the religious traditions are important; their moral conduct is even more so. Levinas has described revelation in terms of the ethical relation with the other.[71] For him, the prescriptive character of revelation is a "type of 'rationality,' a reason far less turned in upon itself than the reason of the philosophical tradition."[72] "Greek," which puts knowledge before doing, could learn from "Hebrew," which focuses on obedience that is neither naivety nor knowledge.[73] It is not reason but the face-to-face encounter that is the source of ethics. Levinas, of course, appreciated humanity's cognitive capacities. However, he claimed that ethics, which are not rooted in reason but must be discussed in a rational way, are a matter of *re*cognition. For Levinas, dialogue—or better, the address that the face of the other makes to the perceiver—precedes logic. This urgent appeal stemming from the other's face precedes the philosophical discourse and at the same time urges philosophical reflection. The positive disturbance for the "I" caused by the "other" comes before reason. In a very Jewish way, Levinas gives priority

[70]Ibid., 666–70.
[71]Emmanuel Levinas, "Revelation in the Jewish Tradition," in *The Levinas Reader*, Séan Hand, ed. (Oxford: Basil Blackwell, 1989), 208.
[72]Ibid., 206.
[73]Ephraim Meir, *Levinas's Jewish Thought: Between Jerusalem and Athens* (Jerusalem: Magnes, 2008), 272.

to ethical acts before thinking, a priority on which the philosopher has to reflect. "Truth arises where a being separated from the other is not engulfed in him, but speaks to him."[74] Levinas's prephilosophical, Jewish way of thinking is palpable in his philosophical discourse on truth. For Levinas, philosophy is not a humble servant to Judaism. He rather endeavored to "enounce in Greek the principles Greece did not know."[75] The work of the Septuaginta, he said to Shlomo Malka, is not finished.[76]

If one accepts Levinas's saying that philosophy is not the locus of the first meaning, the place where meaning starts,[77] this has serious consequences for our thinking on the ethical capacity of religions. Levinas writes, "We propose to call 'religion' the bond that is established between the same and the other without constituting a totality."[78] In this quotation, religion and ethics are seen as twins, as two sides of the same coin.

I have already pointed to the fact that, from a Jewish point of view, *èmèt*, usually translated by "truth," is not primarily the equivalence between thought and reality. *Èmèt* is situated first of all on the existential and ethical level: the human being lives in it and makes it true. The Greek *aletheia*, un-covering, is not the Hebrew *èmèt*, which is related to hope.[79] In other words, from a Jewish perspective, faith as the confident relation with the Higher Worlds is expressed in deeds; by performing righteous deeds, one encounters God.[80]

From Levinas I learned that all thought cannot be reduced to knowledge or experience: the meaningful is not exhausted by knowledge or experience. The command "Thou shalt not kill" coming from the other's face is an ethical command "before appearing."[81] In this radical ethical interpretation of religion, to be religious means to be ethical. All religions contain problematic utterances, but they also show their adherents an ethical path.

---

[74]Emmanuel Levinas, *Totality and Infinity: An Essay on Exteriority*, A. Lingis, trans. (The Hague: Nijhoff, 1979), 62.

[75]Emmanuel Levinas, *Beyond the Verse: Talmudic Readings and Lectures*, G. D. Mole, trans. (Bloomington: Indiana University Press, 1992), 200.

[76]Shlomo Malka, *Lire Levinas* (Paris: Ed. Du Cerf, 1998), 1.

[77]Emmanuel Levinas, *Ethique et Infini. Dialogues avec Philippe Nemo* (Paris: Fayard/France Culture, 1982); Levinas, *Biblio Essais* (Book 4018) (Paris: Hachette, 1992), 14–15.

[78]Levinas, *Totality and Infinity*, 40.

[79]Franz Rosenzweig, *Kleinere Schriften* (Berlin: Schocken, 1937), 395–96.

[80]Daniel Sperber gives the example of Rabbi Eleazar who "would give a penny to a poor man and then pray. He said: 'As for me, I will behold Your face in righteousness' [Ps. 17:15]" (Baba Batra 10a) (Sperber, *On the Relationship of Mitzvot between Man and His Neighbor and Man and His Maker* [Jerusalem: Urim Publications, 2014], 90).

[81]Emmanuel Levinas, *In the Time of the Nations*, M. B. Smith, trans. (Bloomington: Indiana University Press, 1994), 182.

FAITH AND REASON

I conclude with some remarks on the relationship between Judaism and philosophy, which is classically defined as the search for truth. Throughout the ages, starting with Philo Judaeus of Alexandria, Judaism was brought into contact with philosophy. Although tension arose from time to time and although the universal philosophical inquiry was also seen as detrimental to faith, faith and reason were brought together and synthesized. Spinoza broke with this "double faith" in reason and revelation and opted for philosophy as the only legitimate source of knowledge.[82] Fortunately, Schmidt-Leukel's work is a refined attempt to bring reason and faith of diverse religions into balance again.

Today's academic discipline of Jewish philosophy no longer conceives of philosophy as the "handmaiden of revelation," as in the case of Philo.[83] It is no longer theology that verifies Judaism.[84] What makes Jewish philosophy Jewish is not one's biography or the language in which one writes (Hebrew), nor is there any "essence" that makes Jewish philosophy Jewish. Jewish philosophy is rather the encounter between philosophy and Judaism. Not content, but context makes Jewish philosophy Jewish.[85] What happens when Judaism meets philosophy?

Today's challenge for the Jewish philosopher is to describe the specific contribution of Jewish thought to philosophy. Since Jewish thought is also thinking, one cannot separate it from philosophical investigation. Beyond apologetic defenses, Judaism still waits for the formulation of its specific philosophy. As Levinas said, the work of the Septuaginta is not finished. One of the contributions of Jewish philosophy as the meeting between Judaism and philosophy is the idea that ethical acts precede thinking, and as such, they require thinking. On the level of dialogical theology, that implies that the common denominator between religions is foremost ethical conduct, understood as preceding all thought: "*na'ase ve-nishma'*" (we will do and hear) (Exod. 24:7). In a dialogical theology and philosophy from a Jewish vantage point, religious pluralism is appreciated as a multitude of ways in which to mend the world.

Schmidt-Leukel's creative fractal interpretation of religious pluralism greatly contributes to a global, interreligious theology. He perceives similarities in all religions and highlights their comparability, since the

---

[82]Raphael Jospe, *Jewish Philosophy in the Middle Ages* (Boston: Academic Studies Press, 2009), 551–54.

[83]Ibid., 38.

[84]Ibid., 34.

[85]Ibid., 33–35.

truth is *one*. A Jewish view on truth as existential "trust" emphasizes the ethical depth-dimension as common ground for all religions. This allows for a deed-centered, more than a logocentric, interpretation of religious pluralism. For Schmidt-Leukel, similar patterns of thought are present in all religions. In the view presented here, ethics precedes thinking, and the common denominator of all religions is foremost the ethical conduct and the amelioration of society.

The Fractal Proposal and Its Place in the Christian Theology of Religions

Alan Race

This chapter sets out to explore how the fractal interpretation of religious diversity, as advocated by Perry Schmidt-Leukel, offers further reasons for the theological mind to adopt a pluralist perspective in the theology of religions. I propose to explore this, first, by setting the fractal interpretation in the wider context of Schmidt-Leukel's advocacy for what he calls interreligious theology, and second, by examining how it might relate to the theology of religions of two Christian theologians. Finally, I offer a brief set of reasons why pluralism in the theology of religions, in light of the fractal proposal, can be considered to be a Christian position. But I begin by recalling prescient recognitions from forty to fifty years ago of what the future promises.

THE PROMISE OF INTERRELIGIOUS THEOLOGY

In the epilogue of his masterly book *The Analogical Imagination*, theologian David Tracy threw down the following gauntlet to Christian theologians:

> Christian systematic theology of the future cannot afford the traditional luxury of first interpreting Christianity and then quickly noticing and even more rapidly interpreting, via principles of Christian self-understanding, the "other religions."[1]

This challenge, announced in 1981 by one of Catholicism's foremost theologians, echoed an earlier sentiment from 1966 by one of the foremost Protes-

---

[1]David Tracy, *The Analogical Imagination: Christian Theology and the Culture of Pluralism* (London: SCM Press, 1981), 449.

tant theologians, Paul Tillich, when he averred toward the end of his life that were he to begin his theological career again, it would be the dialogue among religions that would supply the data for theological reflection. The future of theology, Tillich came to see, lay in the "interpenetration of systematic theological study and religious historical studies."[2] These were prophetic words.

Even now, however, many Christian theologians remain nervous about surrendering systematic theology's "traditional luxury." Yet, as Tracy himself observed, without a surrender the alternative is to retreat into either a "brittle univocity" or a "relaxed pluralism of privacies."[3] In other words, the plurality of religions, each presenting live options for orientating life, requires self-conscious engagement, understanding, and interpretation. To the extent that both Tracy and Tillich anticipated a new phase in Christian self-understanding, they were (ecumenically) prescient of Perry Schmidt-Leukel's controversial call for what he names interreligious theology.[4] Underlying this call is the assumption that inquiry into the relationship between ultimate transcendent reality and the contingent realities of humanly experienced life is best pursued as a shared, comparative, dialogical endeavor between different religious traditions.

Still, the need for such a mutually accountable theology is not obvious to everyone. The religions, based on their differing core experiences of the sacred, have developed over time their narratives of self-sufficiency in terms of the salvific potential they have declared in the face of the world's negative deficiencies. Yet self-sufficiency is no longer either religiously satisfying or theologically adequate. Under the impact of globalization (where everyone and everything is everywhere), the last sixty years, at least, have witnessed an exponential growth in the awareness of the world's religious plurality, manifesting as both a phenomenon and a challenge. As a result, interreligious dialogue and comparative theology (dimensions of what Schmidt-Leukel terms interreligious theology), together with the intricately related area of theology of religions, have emerged as components of a dramatic shift in theological awareness.

However, any new development in whatever sphere of human inquiry always precipitates reaction in the form of disagreement, argumentation,

---

[2]Paul Tillich, "The Significance of the History of Religions for the Systematic Theologian," in *The Future of Religions* (New York: Harper & Row; London: Greenwood Press, 1966), 91.

[3]Tracy, *Analogical Imagination*, 451.

[4]Perry Schmidt-Leukel cites Tillich's final lecture (1965) as an anticipation of the fractal proposal in his *Religious Pluralism and Interreligious Theology: The Gifford Lectures—An Extended Edition* (Maryknoll, NY: Orbis Books, 2017), 223–36. See also Schmidt-Leukel's mention of Tillich's Bampton Lectures, delivered four years earlier, in 1961, indicating Tillich's growing shift in theological perspective, in *Religious Pluralism and Interreligious Theology*, 114–17, and commentary by Wilfred Cantwell Smith the same year.

and accusation, and this has proved no less the case in relation to each of my three areas: interreligious dialogue, comparative theology, and theology of religions. Each is a heavily contested sphere: for some, their impact is *minimal* in so far as there seems little reason to reimagine that "traditional luxury" that Tracy was already lamenting in 1981; for others, their impact is *maximal* insofar as they create the conditions that are destined to lead to a differently configured interreligious future, both culturally and theologically. Given the depth of disagreements about the significance of the shift in theological awareness, it is worth briefly specifying further how the impact of my contested spheres is felt.

At the level of *minimal* impact we can identify the following strategies in relation to my three areas:

- *Interreligious dialogue* essentially advocates for the search for clarity of understanding *about* the religious other, together with respectful listening so as not to misrepresent or bear false witness against the dialogue partner.
- *Comparative theology* is accepted as a mechanism for deepening the appreciation of the other, with the potential for being able to absorb new insights from the comparative encounter into one's own outlook, yet without disturbing the fundamental disposition of that outlook.
- Although the imperative to interpret the fact of religious plurality remains a theological necessity, the current shape of the *theology of religions* debate is said to have reached an inconclusive impasse, especially in relation to the typology of exclusivism, inclusivism, and pluralism—an assessment, moreover, that is also often accompanied by accusations that the types are based on an essentializing of the religions rather than being reflective of existentially lived practices.

At the other *maximal* end of the spectrum of responses, the implications of the impact of my three related areas are more far-reaching:

- *Interreligious dialogue* is accorded the honor of being a vehicle for forging complementarity between traditions—as in the following statement from the Thirteenth Annual Meeting of the Indian Theological Association in 1989: "When religions encounter one another in dialogue, they build up a community in which differences become complementarities and divergences are changed into pointers to communion."[5]

---

[5]"Towards an Indian Christian Theology of Religious Pluralism," in *Religious Pluralism: An Indian Christian Perspective*, ed. K. Pathil (Delhi: ISPCK, 1991), 347–48.

- *Comparative theology* is capable of yielding more than increased in-depth theological understanding in relation to different elements of different traditions but can lead to deeper enrichment, such as that envisaged by John Thatamanil's recommendation: "The time is at hand (and now is) for Christians not merely to speak and think positively about religious others but also to learn from them and let that learning enable Christian communities to rearticulate how we understand the meaning of God, world, and the human condition."[6]
- The need to venture an explanation for the persistence of many religions in the world, each with their salvific solutions for ailing humanity, remains as pressing as it has always been, and if the three options in the *theology of religions* are indeed the only logical options,[7] then there is no escape from deciding between them on the basis of relevant theological arguments. The suggestion of an impasse is merely a strategy for avoiding necessary theological judgments.

The idea of interreligious theology inevitably embraces the maximal interpretation of my three contested spheres. Interreligious dialogue is based on the assumption that the religions not only search for truth but also find it; comparative theology harbors an incipient pluralism insofar as the different manifestations of religious practice and theory between traditions assume an authenticity in the way of truth; and pluralist theory is more convincing than either exclusivism or inclusivism, once the ultimate mystery of the sacred, combined with Wilfred Cantwell Smith's judgment that faith is a "global human quality,"[8] is realized.

If Schmidt-Leukel's interreligious theology represents a step too far for some, there remains one further proposal to explore, one that has the potential for tipping the arguments in his favor, and this is his argument for a *fractal interpretation of religious diversity*, borrowing from the observations of the mathematician Benoît Mandelbrot (1924–2010). This is set out

---

[6]John Thatamanil, "Learning from (and Not Just about) Our Religious Neighbors: Comparative Theology and the Future of *Nostra Aetate*," in *The Future of Interreligious Dialogue: A Multireligious Conversation on* Nostra Aetate, Charles L. Cohen, Paul F. Knitter, and Ulrich Rosenhagen, eds. (Maryknoll, NY: Orbis Books, 2017), 298. Thatamanil advocates comparative theology as a way to overcome the impasse in theology of religions. For other examples of the in-depth "mutually critical and enriching relationship" that is possible with comparative theology, see, for example, Paul Knitter and Roger Haight, *Jesus and Buddha: Friends in Conversation* (Maryknoll, NY: Orbis Books, 2015); Michelle Voss Roberts, *Dualities: A Theology of Difference* (Louisville, KY: Westminster John Knox Press, 2010); John J. Thatamanil, *The Immanent Divine: God, Creation, and the Human Predicament: An East-West Conversation* (Minneapolis: Augsburg Fortress, 2006).

[7]This is the strongly maintained position of Perry Schmidt-Leukel, repeated in summary form in *Religious Pluralism and Interreligious Theology*, 3–4.

[8]Wilfred Cantwell Smith, *Towards a World Theology* (London: Macmillan, 1980), 171.

in the final chapter of his Gifford Lectures[9] and in the opening essay of this book. From my point of view, my question is: are there features within this proposal that strengthen the case for interreligious theology, and in particular the case for the pluralist approach in theology of religions? I wish now to examine this question in one of my three areas: the bearing that the fractal proposal has on the theology of religions. I do this by exploring two analogical models in the theology of religions, one Anglican and one Protestant.

TWO EYES (AT LEAST) ARE BETTER THAN ONE

My first example was pressed forty years ago by the Anglican theologian John A. T. Robinson in his dialogically oriented book *Truth Is Two-Eyed*, following theological travels in India.[10] Robinson, a relatively self-confessed newcomer to the interreligious field, invoked the analogy of an ellipse, an oval figure encircling two centers (or eyes), each center occupying the central space at either end of the oval shape, and making for what he called a "two-eyed vision of reality." Each of the two eyes represented a cluster of religious types that he labeled "mystical" and "prophetic," or "nondual" and "dual," or "unitive/impersonal" and "relational/personal." Robinson's proposal was that within each cluster the dominant theme of one religious apprehension also embraced the dominant theme of its partner (other eye) apprehension yet as a minor element in tension with the main elements of its own cluster. So "prophetic religions" contain elements of "mystical religions" and vice versa—the elliptical analogy being employed to yield explanatory power for how religions might reflect differentiated truth in relation to the unity of transcendent reality. Robinson spelled out the intention within his analogy as follows:

> I am interested rather in exploring the polarity, the tension, between two centers which are to be found in different degree within all our spiritual traditions and indeed within each one of us. This is in part a dialogue between West and East, but only in the sense that there are clusters of ideas or presuppositions which are more dominantly associated with one geographical or religious tradition than another.[11]

It is unlikely that we would divide "East" from "West" today in the manner of Robinson's formulation, commonly accepted a generation ago

---

[9]Schmidt-Leukel, *Religious Pluralism and Interreligious Theology*, 222–45.
[10]John A. T. Robinson, *Truth Is Two-Eyed* (London: SCM Press, 1979).
[11]Ibid., 8.

(he was also aware of its potential to mislead). Moreover, the phenomeno-logical assumptions behind it are also less popular today under postmodern pressures that emphasize particularities over generalities. Nevertheless, his analogical picture has direct relevance in discussions of fractal theory: Robinson hinted that the putative theological polarity and experienced spiritual tension between two dominant visions exist at three levels—the macrophenomenological between religious types, within single traditions, and in the mind of the believing individual—and Schmidt-Leukel has em-bodied the same observation in his fractal proposal:

> A fractal interpretation of religious diversity proposes that the dif-ferences that can be observed at the *interreligious level* are, to some extent, reflected at an *intrareligious level* in the internal differences discerned within the major religious tradition, and that they can be broken down at the *intrasubjective level* into different religious pat-terns and structures of the individual mind.[12]

I suggest that what Robinson first hinted at in 1979 stands to gain firmer foundations with Schmidt-Leukel's fractal proposal. But there is more: the pluralist theological ramifications inherent within a fractal view become more explicit in a manner that Robinson was unable or unwilling to grasp.

For all of his theological aspiration that "truth is two-eyed," Robinson did not espouse a pluralist conviction. This was essentially for broad theo-logico-ethical reasons: the analysis of the *material, historical,* and *personal* dimensions of life-processes (dimensions analyzed in three central chapters of his book) in Christian terms, he believed, was more affirmative of human meaning and flourishing than religious visions associated with the mystical East. Robinson did not want to appear dogmatic about this conviction—far from it—this was simply how things seemed to him, given his best attempt at dialogical honesty, and made without any supersessionist intentions. He summed it up in the open inclusivist statement: Christ, he averred, "offers the profoundest clue to all the rest."[13]

My contention is that the fractal patterns explored by Schmidt-Leukel, especially in bringing the themes of "Son," "Prophet," and "Buddha" into comparative alignment, supplies precisely the perspective leading to pluralism that was not available to Robinson forty years ago but to which Robinson had opened his own door.

---

[12]Schmidt-Leukel, *Religious Pluralism and Interreligious Theology*, 233.

[13]Robinson, *Truth*, 129. This is a form of Christian inclusivism "from below"—the view that seeks to use historical research to demonstrate how it is that Christian faith completes or fulfils the aspirations to holiness, goodness, and truth, within other traditions.

Schmidt-Leukel outlines three dialogical relationships between "the Son and the Buddha," "the Prophet and the Son," and "the Prophet and the Buddha." These three relationships have had, to say the least, a checkered history, where each side of the relationship has promoted itself as superior to the other, and has often involved violence between them. Yet under Schmidt-Leukel's careful analysis, a fractal pattern can be detected whereby what it means for Jesus to be "the Son" finds an echo in some strands of Buddhism and Islam, what it means for Gautama to be the Buddha finds an echo in some strands of Christianity and Islam, and what it means for Muhammad to be the Prophet finds an echo in some strands of Christianity and Buddhism. Given the history of negative relationships, it might be expected that to bring these three traditions into positive relationship would represent a tour de force. Yet there are voices, in both history and the present, that counteract the usually perceived inevitability of theological antagonism between the three traditions, and especially as this has often been focused on the central figures within each.

In other words, there are complementarities between pairs of traditions in comparative engagement that balance commitment to real life change (Robinson's material, historical, and personal dimensions of life)—a "Western" emphasis—with forms of spiritual centeredness that both inspire contemplative awareness and warn against the dangers of ego-attachment—an "Eastern" emphasis—in all processes of human living. Why one emphasis ought to provide "the profoundest clue to all the rest" in hindsight seems more confessionally determined than Robinson wanted, or was able to recognize.

In the end, Robinson counted the complementarities as unequal: between the two eyes on reality, one had greater capacity and clarity of vision. Somehow, the threefold affirmation of the embodied realities of the material, the historical, and the personal worlds was more convincing for human flourishing in a Christian framework than in all others. Yet, following a period of extended theological dialogue between traditions since the publication of *Truth Is Two-Eyed*, and in the light of Schmidt-Leukel's fractal proposal, is it not surely the case that the bilateral dialogues between Schmidt-Leukel's three pairs of traditions address Robinson's concerns directly by rendering his case for Christian inclusivist superiority (however sensitively and dialogically Robinson wanted to hold to it) arbitrary? That is to say, while the three issues of the value of the material world, the concept of creation, and the pursuit of moral change through historical processes are constantly debated in dialogue, with varying degrees of theological sophistication, under the spotlight of fractal comparability no one tradition can finally demonstrate a monopoly on the truth. In turn, this entails that the fractal proposal has no need of Robinson's hesitation over pluralist thinking in the theology of religions. At least I contend that there is a prima facie case for rethinking Robinson's hesitation.

COMPLEMENTARITIES REINFORCED

Let me turn now to my second example of how the fractal proposal might illuminate the pluralist option in the theology of religions debates. It was John Hick who most famously employed the analogy of the Copernican revolution from astronomy to explain his shift in theology of religions toward a pluralist position. Prior to Copernicus (1473–1543), astronomers imagined the earth to be at the center of the universe, with suns and planets rotating around it. Further observations by Copernicus initiated a major shift in perception, such that the positioning and movements of the planets were better explained by placing the sun at the center of the universe. By analogy, said Hick, the facts of religious diversity were better explained by placing God or the divine at the center of the religious universe rather than Christianity or the church, which had been the theological picture to date. New research about the world religions, their persistence among whole peoples and civilizations, their intellectual impressiveness and spiritualities did not fit with inherited Christian assumptions that hitherto had counted other religions as either theologically erroneous or at best requiring the fulfilling superiority of the Christian dispensation. It was time, asserted Hick, for a Copernican revolution in how Christian theology interpreted the fact of persistent religious diversity. It is worth recalling Hick's early formulation:

> Copernicus realized that it is the sun, and not the earth, that is at the center, and that all the heavenly bodies, including our own earth, revolve around it. And we have to realize that the universe of faiths centers upon *God*, and not upon Christianity or upon any other religion.[14]

It was an arresting image, challenging theologians to broaden the range of data rather than the appeal to one tradition only for ascertaining the truth about divine reality. But such a bold move also raised further issues: in particular, how might very different phenomenal traditions, studied under the scrutiny of religious studies, be reflecting the sunlight that stems from the same transcendent source? Since Hick's bold move, students of the religions have emphasized more forcefully the phenomenological differences between the culturally shaped religious doctrines and the experiences that

---

[14]John Hick, "Whatever Path Men Choose Is Mine," in *Christianity and Other Religions*, John Hick and Brian Hebblethwaite, eds. (Glasgow: Collins, Fount Paperbacks, 1980), 182. In later writing, Hick substituted the category of the "transcategorial Real" for "God" in order to indicate the inclusion of nontheistic traditions in his overpluralist hypothesis.

inform them, and for some, under the protective wing of postmodernism, to the point of total incommensurability between them.

. Hick's "Copernican revolution" formed part of his well-known turn toward a pluralist *hypothesis* (as he always called it) in the theology of religions. The hypothesis was not formulated on the basis of phenomenological samenesses between traditions, as some critics have accused him, but on the distinction between transcendent reality as being beyond categories (transcategorial) and transcendent reality as known and experienced in terms of differently developed cultural traditions. This was the key distinction, which later more purposefully included nontheistic manifestations as part of the revolution. Transcendent reality was manifest within differently experienced this-worldly forms. Still, more needed to be said, and in *The Rainbow of Faiths*,[15] his important rejoinder to critics, Hick turned to three further analogies for illustrating how phenomenological religious differences might nevertheless be related to the one transcategorial transcendent reality.

The first analogy was employed in order to explain how the different concepts associated with ultimate reality in the religious traditions—Yahweh, Holy Trinity, Allah, Shiva, Brahman, Tao, Dharmakaya, and so on—indicate several personae and impersonae (as Hick called them) corresponding to different experiences associated with the different traditions. Appealing to Wittgenstein's use of the psychologist Jastrow's famous line drawing of a duck-rabbit to explain how the ambiguity of human perception leads us to experience the same phenomena "as" either a duck or a rabbit, Hick suggested that in the religions we similarly experience ultimate reality "as" Allah, Brahman, the Tao, and so forth. "The analogy that I am suggesting here," wrote Hick, "is with the religious experience component of religion."[16] Notably, Hick is not suggesting that the religions report the same experience of ultimate reality in differing words, but that the same ultimate reality is manifest in the different experiences that animate the hearts of the religions.

The second analogy Hick employed was an appeal to the well-known complementary wave-particle explanation in physics of how light exhibits different properties depending on the experimental conditions set up for investigation. Sometimes light can be said to have wavelike properties and sometimes particlelike properties, depending on the nature of the experiment and how the observer acts in relation to the light that is under review. Hick used this analogy to explain how spiritual practices and forms of worship

---

[15]John Hick, *The Rainbow of Faiths* (London: SCM Press, 1995); also published as *A Christian Theology of Religions: The Rainbow of Faiths* (Louisville, KY: Westminster John Knox Press, 1995).

[16]Hick, *Rainbow*, 25.

could be said to be actions, as it were, under different experimental conditions in relation to the light of ultimate reality. We pray in theistic religion from the perspective of an I-Thou relationship; we meditate in nontheistic religion from the perspective of nondual awareness; yet each is an authentic practice, as wave or particle explanation is an authentic result under different experimental conditions.[17]

The third analogy suggested by Hick related to cartography. As differently conceived maps traced in two-dimensional space assist navigation of a three-dimensional globe only by distorting it for the purposes of orientation, so the theologies and philosophies of the religions, mapping the journey of religious commitment, cast their necessarily distorting picturing of ultimate reality according to the limitations inherent in any form of mapping. "And it could be," remarks Hick, "that the conceptual maps drawn by the great traditions, although finite picturings of the Infinite, are all more or less equally reliable within their different projections, and more or less equally useful for guiding us on our journey through life."[18]

As is often said, analogies might illuminate an argument but they also have limitations. What is required for further convincing is some theological work filling out the analogical connections. So I ask, in what sense might Hick's three analogies enlist further support from appeal to Schmidt-Leukel's fractal proposal? Unlike the case with Robinson, where Schmidt-Leukel's work can be said to supply the comparative theological work that was lacking in the "two-eyed vision," with the Hick case it complements and compliments the pluralist hypothesis by providing further religious detail to render the pluralist case more convincing. In order to demonstrate how this might be, let me now turn to some of Schmidt-Leukel's creative observations.

From my point of interest, Schmidt-Leukel's most engaging—even seminal—work occurs in part 2 of *Religious Pluralism and Interreligious Theology*. Here he pulls together the many dialogical experiments and engagements, speculations and intriguing suggestions from theologians and philosophers of Buddhism, Christianity, and Islam, with the purpose of demonstrating how each tradition, when paired with either of the other two traditions, contains echoes or elements of the other. Overtures from Christianity to Buddhism and Islam, from Buddhism to Christianity and Islam, and from Islam to Buddhism and Christianity, respecting the dialogical rule of remaining open to truth from wherever it comes, have yielded remarkable fruits. The suspicions, disputatious prejudices, and oppositional polemics of history are slowly being replaced by a spirit of mutual learning that allows a new interreligious future to emerge.

---

[17]Ibid., 25–26.
[18]Ibid., 27.

From a Christian-Buddhist dialogue perspective, let me give one example of this mutual learning by way of illustration from Schmidt-Leukel's account, citing from either side of the divide. Viewing first from the Christian side, there is no reason to suppose that Buddhist teaching was conjured up or created by virtue of Buddha's own human capacities; rather, it is clear that it was discovered in the experience of enlightenment, which in turn generates the wisdom of knowing and compassion for acting. But something analogous to this is reflected in the central Christian affirmation of salvation in Christ. The experience of salvation is a form of knowing that the world is loved from eternity and this is the source of all our enactments in human loving. Aloysius Pieris, the well-known Sri Lankan theologian, has brought the two experiences together in the following observation: "Deep within each one of us there is a Buddhist and a Christian engaged in a profound encounter."[19] Schmidt-Leukel then draws our attention to the implication of the complementarity: "But Jesus and the Buddha represent different manifestations of this complementarity, because this complementarity is expressed in two different idioms."[20] It is not that the "Son" represents love and compassion and "Buddha" represents knowing and experiencing. Both participate in both realities but from within their different emphases and in different degrees. If this is the case, there is no reason why the Buddha and Buddhist experience cannot be integrated with a Christian outlook.

Viewing now from the Buddhist side, Schmidt-Leukel cites the views of the Theravadin monk Bikkhu Buddhadasa. By equating "dharma" with "God," both terms being expressive of the transcategorial formlessness of ultimate reality, Buddhadasa is able to incorporate "the Son" into his Buddhist outlook insofar as "the Son" (Jesus) is the mouthpiece of divine truth. Schmidt-Leukel cites Buddhadasa's equating of Buddha with the Son of God: "What is known as 'God' is neither physical nor spiritual in nature, it is bodiless, without a mouth, without any faculty of speech that we know of, but it can cause a body to be formed, with a mouth and a voice to speak what God wishes him to speak. That speaker may therefore be called the son of God."[21] The main point is that Jesus preaches and achieves in his own person and impact the values of nonattachment and ego-transcendence (the goal of Buddhist spirituality)—as witnessed, for example, most wonderfully in the Gospel of Matthew's Sermon on the Mount. There seems no reason, from a Christian point of view, why Christian faith should object to this assessment.

Admittedly, I have cited only one example here but more could have

---

[19] Cited by Schmidt-Leukel, *Religious Pluralism and Interreligious Theology*, 175.
[20] Ibid.
[21] Ibid., 180.

been canvassed. But still there remains the pressing question of how these pluralist tendencies might square the circle in relation to claims to finality or uniqueness. In answer to this, Schmidt-Leukel draws attention to the revelatory role played by the three seminal religious figures. In tune with the approach by Catholic theologian Roger Haight, Schmidt-Leukel adopts a symbolic view of their status. That is to say, Jesus, Buddha, and Muhammad each *mediates* ultimate reality to the world. "Since God is both present to and transcendent of any finite symbol," says Haight, "the symbol both makes God present and points away from itself to a God who is other than itself."[22] Again, it is important to be reminded that it is not the case that the seminal figures record the same experience in different cultural terms; they are rather *different manifestations of different experiences in different cultural terms* stemming from the one ultimate transcendent reality.

This framing of the category of revelation in symbolic fashion does not suffer the category error of a conflation of terms, as some might complain. Schmidt-Leukel sums up the comparative rapprochement between the three traditions like this:

> We may conclude that prophethood, sonship, and buddhahood can be seen as different categories in which humanity has given expression to its confidence that human beings have the potential to become vehicles of divine revelation. They can be living promises of ultimate mercy in the face of human guilt and failure, and mirrors, symbols, or images of those qualities and values of human life that ultimate reality elicits and sustains.[23]

Schmidt-Leukel even goes so far as to claim that such a framing falls within the scope and meaning, for traditional orthodox Christianity, of the Council of Chalcedon's incarnational language.[24] It is permissible, however, to retain a degree of skepticism about this without necessarily undermining the value of the symbolic approach as such.[25] That said, the central thrust of Schmidt-Leukel's analysis makes it clear that the "Son" contains within its potential the capacity to recognize the authenticity of the "Prophet" and

---

[22]Ibid., 154.
[23]Ibid., 203.
[24]Ibid., 154.
[25]I have argued elsewhere that asking the question of how historical figures achieve symbolic status leads us in the direction of a bottom-up approach that has less need of traditional incarnational language than is usually imagined in an age vastly different from Chalcedon's fifth century. See "The Value of the Symbolic Jesus for Christian Involvement in Interfaith Dialogue," in *Religious Pluralism in the Modern World: An Ongoing Engagement with John Hick*, ed. Sharada Sugirtharajah (New York: Palgrave Macmillan, 2012), 83–94.

the "Buddha," without supersessionism or theological snobbery. Likewise, the "Prophet" and the "Buddha" are capable of having their theological frameworks stretched in order to encompass the value of the "Son" and each other. All three are fractally related!

It has been necessary to undertake this brief excursus into Schmidt-Leukel's proposals in order to locate how fractal patterning might be relevant for pluralist thinking. Schmidt-Leukel proposes that elements of religious expression from one tradition reappear in others in different degrees and with different emphases in different frameworks, and over different levels (between traditions, within single traditions, and within individual persons). This suggests that the traditions somehow belong together, such that the identity of one cannot fully be known without the others. How then do we explain this? The answer comes: in terms of the three analogies put forward by Hick, which envisage complementarities across what seem like prima facie contradictions.

For some, Hick's analogies might seem rather abstract or speculative, and stretch theological credulity too far in the absence of any sort of phenomenological leverage. Schmidt-Leukel's fractal observations in religious histories and narratives of development provide some of that leverage via comparative research in his analysis of the three seminal symbolic figures of "Son," "Prophet," and "Buddha" and the capability of each of the three traditions for seeing dimensions of the meaning of the other two as—at least potentially, if not wholly—repeated as a minor theme within their own apprehension. In this way, the fractal proposal provides some grounding in phenomenology for the pluralist hypothesis in the theology of religions.

Observations about fractal patterning are not the only developments in comparative studies that help to flesh out pluralist approaches. Further support for it could be evinced, for example, from recent comparisons in the area of spirituality and ethics by Paul Knitter. After noting how a certain nondual isomorphism exists between the religious orientation and dependency on the love or compassion of ultimate reality, on the one hand, and the concomitant necessity to be a channel for that love or compassion, on the other, Knitter draws the following implication:

> This isomorphism between loving the human and loving the divine, and the hermeneutical priority given to loving the human, implies a further philosophical or theological conclusion: while all the traditions affirm that one can never adequately know or speak of God or the Absolute, they do seem to hold that one can adequately act like God and the Absolute.[26]

---

[26]Paul Knitter, "Love and Desire—Human and Sacred," *Interreligious Insight* 16 (2018): 10–17.

If this is a correct insight by Knitter, then "acting like God or the Absolute" is a function of all traditions—which in turn leaves theologians with the conundrum of how to square the "acting" across traditions with their different conceptions of God or the Absolute. This of course is the central question for theology of religions and for which the pluralist hypothesis provides a satisfactory resolution. For my purpose here, I think Knitter's insight also yields further support for the expectation that a fractal relationship between traditions is wholly unsurprising. The fact that it may not have been observed before now has more to do with past relationships of antagonism and straightforward religious/theological prejudice than with pluralist preferences.

The fractal approach acts both as a summary of what is possible in comparative studies and a spur to reinvigorating theology of religions discourse. In his book, Schmidt-Leukel sets out the new possibility in the context both of a study of emerging pluralist ideas in a number of traditions and of a comparative analysis of his themes of "Son," "Prophet," and "Buddha." In both areas the most immediate impact might well be felt in the debates in the theology of religions. Schmidt-Leukel makes his point in a matter-of-fact manner:

> Within a religious interpretation of religion, a fractal interpretation of religious diversity will work best in conjunction with a pluralist theology of religions, that is, with the assumption that there is a diversity of different but in principle equally valid ways of experiencing and relating to ultimate reality, a diversity that reflects the diverse nature of humanity.[27]

Pluralist thinking is not the prerogative of so-labeled liberals in Christian faith only but has champions across a number of traditions, and the comparative analysis points us in the direction of pluralist interpretations in the theology of religions. Of course, exclusivists and inclusivists in the theology of religions are likely to be less excited by the fractal picture than pluralists. But the fractal image places the *onus probandi* more on the exclusivists and inclusivists to explain their reservations against pluralism in the light of it. Put simply, those reservations begin to look more and more arbitrary than might otherwise have seemed the case. For example, the fractal picture undermines the exclusivist case against non-Christian religions on the grounds of their idolatry or that they are reflective of "religion" and not "revelation." The fractal picture also questions the inclusivist ambiguity with regard to other faiths because the "good and true and holy" elements

---

[27]Schmidt-Leukel, *Religious Pluralism and Interreligious Theology*, 245.

within others—as specified, say, by *Nostra Aetate*—become shared elements (albeit under different scales and with differing emphases) rather than one tradition rendering a clearer and more potent version of them over others.

There is one area, however, where the impact of the fractals interpretation might be less convincing for critics of pluralism, and that is in its recommendation that traditions let go of their hold on the finality of their tradition. The reticence to let go of clinging to claims of finality might have more to do with the psychology of religious conviction—the felt need to hold on to a sense of certainty in a world culture of uncertainty—than with, strictly speaking, what rational inquiry reasonably finds plausible. If the concept of a tradition's finality is perceived to be an integral part of that tradition's dynamic historical life, then it will be hard-pressed for believers to abandon it. The complaint is sometimes made that to adopt pluralism is to so change a tradition's self-understanding that the felt loss of identity represents a step too far. At this point John Hick's rejoinder to critics remains relevant: in the light of the comparable fruits of the traditions, "we really do have to make a choice between one-tradition absolutism and a genuinely pluralistic interpretation of the global religious situation."[28] And further, "There's a sense in which religious pluralism does ... give a different status to the various traditions and their teachings from that which they give themselves. But I want to claim that in the sense in which this is so, it is a virtue and not a vice."[29] There is an ethical as well as theological gain, it seems, in the move to pluralism. Major shifts in religious perception have generally always been accompanied by resistance, as history has shown. It might help to view the embrace of pluralism as part of a broader cultural change—even evolution—that is taking place in relation to debates surrounding cultural values studies.[30]

IS IT CHRISTIAN?

One final question remains for this essay: in what sense is it possible to say that the endorsement of pluralism in the light of the fractal proposal can be supported as a Christian position? My contention is that the fractal picture discloses more keenly what has been intuited through Christian history and yet functions also to create a new framework for Christian commitment.

Let me set this out in a series of propositions:

1. Wilfred Cantwell Smith's estimation/observation, from the perspective

---

[28]Hick, *Rainbow*, 43.

[29]Ibid., 45.

[30]Cf. Alan Race, *Making Sense of Religious Pluralism: Shaping Theology of Religions for Our Times* (London: SPCK, 2013), 75–87; also printed as *Thinking about Religious Pluralism* (Minneapolis: Fortress Press, 2015).

of the historical study of religions alluded to earlier in this essay, that "Faith is a global human quality,"[31] resonates with the New Testament emphasis that trust in God need not be confined to the Jewish matrix in which Christian faith was born. Indeed, the acceptance that it is to be found outside of that matrix was in large measure part of the reason for the Christian mission among the pagans of the gentile world.[32] Although the Christian Gospels were written down in the thirty- to fifty-year period following the Roman sacking of Jerusalem in 70 CE, and reflect disputes that arose between different Jewish and gentile groupings within the churches, it may be that the recognition of "faith" as distributed among Jews and gentiles alike was already recognized astutely by Jesus himself.[33]

2. This broader prevalence of faith was acknowledged in the Greek philosophical tradition of the Church Fathers through the *logos* doctrine, which stated that all human beings participate in God's embrace of the world through the seed of divine reason that resides within them. While never fully eclipsed, particularly by the development of the doctrine of original sin with Augustine and by its later continuance in Reformation theology, the *logos* idea was revived more intentionally especially by Vatican II. In religious studies, Smith's evaluation had an earlier variant in the German history of religions school in ideas such as Rudolf Otto's "religious *a priori*."[34] The religious impulse is part of human nature, a factor also assumed by research in religious experience associated with the zoologist Alister Hardy.[35]

3. In their efforts to recognize the presence of God throughout human experience, theologians have made use of various devices—observational, analogical, philosophical—to explain how that presence might be envisaged. Images from the natural world and ordinary human experience have been an integral part of the theological endeavor, given the belief in the presence of God in and to the world as the essential meaning of the doctrine of creation. The fractal proposal nudges this acceptance of "faith" into an enlarged space: what Christian history had perceived from its own origins has been, in truth, a global phenomenon.

4. Where "faith" might unite, "cultural traditions" definitely divide—or so it has seemed throughout history. The cultural traditions that divide religions are substantial and have seemed insurmountable, creating a nervous-

[31]Smith, *Towards a World Theology* (London: Macmillan, 1980), 171.

[32]This is not to say that Judaism was wholly exclusivistic in relation to gentiles, as the acceptance of God-fearers who were attached to synagogues testifies. But the Christian movement pushed for the equality of ethnicities under Christ as a matter of principle.

[33]Cf. Bob Robinson, *Jesus and the Religions: Retrieving a Neglected Example for a Multicultural World* (Eugene, OR: Cascade Books, 2012).

[34]Rudolf Otto, *The Idea of the Holy* (Oxford: Oxford University Press, 1923).

[35]Alister Hardy, *The Spiritual Nature of Man* (Oxford: Oxford University Press, 1979).

ness about "crossing the theological Rubicon"[36] from either exclusivism or inclusivism to pluralism. In spite of the fact that the pluralist hypothesis, properly understood, has never been advocated on the basis of theological or philosophical phenomenological comparabilities or similarities between traditions, and that it has been misleading to suggest that that has been the case, the substantial differences at the level of cultural manifestations have continued to prop up suspicions about it. This suspicion was inherent in the way John Robinson developed his analogy of the ellipse and was not overcome completely even with John Hick's three separate analogies—duck/rabbit experiencing-as, wave/particle experimentation, and perspectival cartology—insofar as critics might well complain that they apply only at a somewhat abstract level. Schmidt-Leukel's analysis of the seminal figures—"Son," "Prophet," and "Buddha"—addresses this nervousness by demonstrating that even central elements within traditions need not be configured in incommensurable ways. The Christian "Son" is not alien to the "Prophet" or to the "Buddha," even at culturally developed doctrinal levels. In the light of the fractal proposal, this entails that pluralism in the theology of religions can be embraced as a Christian option for the present times, without the accusation that serious differences are being willfully ignored.

5. Calls to reinvent interreligious dialogue for social, political, or other purposes, thereby pushing theological dialogue into a specialist niche activity, together with theological diversions into "comparative theology" or "global ethics"—each of these moves being admirable in their own terms and for their own purposes—represent further stalling at the shore of the pluralist Rubicon. Schmidt-Leukel's fractal proposal has the advantage of inviting many different and hitherto separated endeavors—religious studies, interreligious dialogue, comparative studies, theology of religions—into a space where interreligious theology might thrive to the advantage of each of the disciplines. It will be a new territory in which Christian faith has much to both offer and learn as part of its dialogical responsibilities.

Pluralism has been canvassed to date essentially as a *hypothesis*—that is, as a provisional theological explanation for the persistence of the global diversity of religions. For a hypothesis to be elevated to a plausible *theory*, further investigation and evidence is required. Would it be in order to say that the fractal observation applied to religious diversity invites us now to move the pluralist outlook from provisional hypothesis to plausible theory?

---

[36]See *The Myth of Christian Uniqueness: Toward a Pluralistic Theology of Religions*, John Hick and Paul F. Knitter, eds. (Maryknoll, NY: Orbis Books, 1987).

Exploring the Possibilities and the Limitations of Interreligious Theology

A Muslim Response to Perry Schmidt-Leukel's Proposal

————

Maria Massi Dakake

Within the academic discipline of religious studies or theology, inter-religious dialogue and interreligious theology constitute a subfield that has attracted both well-meaning and sincere academic proponents, as well as a host of academic critics. Some critics argue that those working in this field go too far in their attempts at interreligious engagement, and so compromise the integrity of the individual traditions; while others suggest that attempts at interreligious engagement have gone as far as they can, and have proved, in the end, to be largely ineffectual in achieving their broader social goal of encouraging greater religious tolerance and appreciation for religious diversity. Those engaged in interreligious exchange have also been criticized for a lack of self-reflection and an insufficient awareness of their own theoretical biases and conceits—particularly with regard to acknowledging the perspective from which interreligious theologians theorize their own religion, as well as those of others. At times they may seek to "bracket" their own beliefs in order to assume a transcendent perspective independent of any one religious tradition. At other times, they may speak self-consciously from within their own tradition, thereby viewing other traditions with the lens of their own tradition, which, by this very process, becomes the benchmark for evaluating and understanding the other.

The field has also had to contend with polarizing tendencies: either to consider the various religious traditions as so fundamentally and substantively similar (differing only in outward form) that they lose their distinctiveness and independence as self-contained traditions, or else to view religions as too fundamentally and substantively different to be in meaningful conversation with one another. Holding the middle ground in this contested and, I would dare say, vexed, field is not easy. But Perry Schmidt-Leukel's book makes an energetic, and largely successful, attempt not only to find the elusive middle ground, but from there to break through the field's previous limitations and find new theoretical ground for a more rigorous and meaningful conception of pluralism. His book *Religious Pluralism and Interreligious Theology*[1] accomplishes this by making three distinct but related interventions into the field of interreligious theology.

First, he argues for a fully and properly pluralist approach to other religions that is committed to the idea that there can be multiple, equally true religious traditions. Importantly, though, the acceptance of the equal validity of these other traditions is not predicated on the scholar standing and assessing the various religious traditions from a position beyond *all* of them, that is, from a point of epistemological transcendence and an ultimately fictitious "view from nowhere." Rather, in this pluralistic, or more precisely, interreligious theology, scholar-theologians self-consciously speak from within their own traditions, finding resources for an indigenous construction of pluralism within their own traditions as they look outward toward the other traditions.

Second, he aims to demonstrate the potential such an approach can have by taking the reader through an exercise in interreligious theology that attempts to construct a mutually acceptable and comprehensible understanding of the categories of "Son (of God)," "Prophet," and "Buddha" in the three major traditions of Christianity, Islam, and Buddhism. He does this by noting that these seemingly irreconcilable "confessional" categories of spiritual authority and manifestation, each of which is dominant in one of these three traditions, have counterparts, if minor ones, within the other two traditions that can be drawn upon in facilitating greater understanding and acceptance of these categories among all three traditions.

Third, and finally, the findings of this exercise, and what is learned from the process itself, informs a new theoretical paradigm for interreligious theology—Schmidt-Leukel's "fractal" theory of interreligious theology. In this response I address what I consider to be the book's three central claims in reverse order: beginning with the fractal theory, then addressing Schmidt-Leukel's analysis of the concepts of "Son of God" and "Prophet" in Christian-Muslim theological encounter, and finally rethinking the possibilities (and limitations) of a confessionally grounded, but fully pluralistic reading of religious diversity.

---

[1]Perry Schmidt-Leukel, *Religious Pluralism and Interreligious Theology: The Gifford Lectures—An Extended Edition* (Maryknoll, NY: Orbis Books, 2017).

SIGNIFICANCE AND USEFULNESS
OF SCHMIDT-LEUKEL'S FRACTAL THEORY

In the final chapter of his book, Schmidt-Leukel outlines his fractal theory of interreligious theology and identifies several key benefits of his theory, some of which are significant for broader issues in the field of religious studies, beyond methodological approaches to pluralistic, comparative, or interreligious theologies. Schmidt-Leukel argues that his fractal theory facilitates a move from theology (located within a single tradition) to interreligious theology by making the religions "less strange" and more comprehensible to one another and provides a compelling alternative to some postmodern assertions of the "radical incommensurability" of the religious traditions.

At the same time, the theory promises to revive phenomenological approaches to the study of religion, and to place such study on firmer ground by eliminating the requirement that scholars "bracket" their own subjective confessional commitments. This allows such phenomenological analyses to be engaged in from a variety of individual and confessional perspectives (rather than a singular and supposedly "objective" or neutral position), including even those who have no traditional religious commitments who seek to analyze the religious traditions from a purely secular or even atheist perspective. The fractal theory also suggests that "the notion of religion is not an empty concept"—that is, it is not, as J. Z. Smith and others have indicated, a term "invented" by religious studies scholars themselves—but rather, "religion" is a concept with real, if variable, meaning. Finally, Schmidt-Leukel argues that the fractal theory—which discerns in the different religious traditions a set of uncanny resemblances and a host of recurring features, scaled to different levels of prominence in each tradition but apparent in various ways in all of them—points toward a "transcendent origin" for all of the religions.

In short, the fractal theory aims to avoid the excesses and pitfalls of three currents in the study of religions: (1) those that propose both impersonal and purportedly objective modes of comparative or interreligious theology; (2) those that endorse subjective and postmodern approaches to religion that suggest that the traditions are too fundamentally different for meaningful dialogue, much less collective theological construction; and (3) those for whom "religion" as a concept is essentially meaningless.

As a scholar of Islam, I find the fractal theory immensely helpful for a number of reasons—particularly its ability to read and recognize minor or less central concepts and views within the Islamic tradition and normalize them within that broader tradition. For example, given the prominence of religious law in Islam, more mystical or even antinomian strands of thought in Islam—which in the case of some forms of Sufism, for example, may be practiced by a minority of Muslims, but are certainly not "negligible" or "marginal" phenomena—were typically read by Orientalist scholars as a "countercultural" element within Islam, and as a critique from within, rather than as an organic and integral part of the tradition. These scholars seemed unable to recognize (at least in the case of Islam) that such phenomena can emerge naturally from the theological and religious issues that arise, as in any religion, from its particular formulations of doctrine and practice. The fractal approach to discerning, understanding, and normalizing religious diversity not only *among* religious traditions but *within* them allows elements of a given religious tradition that might lie outside the religion's "mainstream" but that are nonetheless spiritually important and intellectually influential to be seen as organic developments within that tradition itself; such outlying elements facilitate balance and comprehensiveness within the tradition, and in some cases are logical and necessary outgrowths of its more central tenets. This allows for the Islamic tradition to be understood more accurately and comprehensively from outside of the tradition and may well enhance the appreciation of diversity from within it as well. All of these benefits are, of course, in addition to the particular usefulness Schmidt-Leukel sees in the fractal theory as a basis for, and as a means of, facilitating, interreligious theology.

While the use of the mathematical/scientific concept of fractals may initially seem an odd choice for explaining the very human phenomenon of religious diversity, the real genius of its application in this context lies in the fact that it is a mathematical model that explains the repeated and scalable configurations one finds, not only in clearly and obviously structured phenomena like crystals and snowflakes, but also in the apparently random and serendipitous development present in living organisms and organic systems, such as forests. In forests the growth and positioning of trees seems to be influenced by a host of independent environmental and biological factors; but upon closer analysis using fractal theory, the trees actually reveal distinct patterns of formation and development (in individual trees and among the different trees themselves) according to repeating mathematical ratios. In other words, fractal patterning is fully organic in nature, allowing for the possibility of perpetual irregularity and diversity, and for growth and development (as well as death and decline over time). In this way, the fractal perspective may be particularly applicable to what appears to be the chaotic richness of many of the world's religious traditions. It allows religions to retain their substantial identity as certain aspects or elements within the tradition grow or decrease in importance or change in various ways; but at the same time it offers the religions a means of finding common ground with other traditions without compromising their own unique configuration.

SON, PROPHET, AND BUDDHA: A FORMIDABLE
CHALLENGE TO INTERRELIGIOUS THEOLOGY

We can imagine the elements that typically constitute religious traditions along a continuum: from the more abstract/transcendent elements, on the one hand, to the more human, communal, and ethical manifestations of the traditions, on the other. We might locate, on one end of this continuum, the oneness/nonduality that characterizes the concepts of absolute reality found in many religious traditions, and on the other end, the multiplicity of human rituals and ethical practices found in these traditions. On both ends of this continuum, one often finds enough similarity between the various religious traditions to effect a substantial dialogue, to recognize and appreciate common elements, and even to come to some tentative interreligious theological insights.

It is often what lies between these two ends of the continuum—that is, the means by which a tradition-specific path of communication and connection is forged between the transcendent and the human—that is more contentious. These "connections" usually take the form of a human founder/messenger and authoritative constructions of divine or spiritual truth manifested in "revelations" composed in human language. What makes this issue especially thorny is that it entails very particular, and not always translatable or mutually comprehensible, claims for why a particular *human* being or revelation in a particular *human* language should have the authority to offer communication between the transcendent and human realms. How and why is this human being or this human language endowed with such authority? Is the authority communally situated, or presumed to be "universal"? Can such a claim be accepted by those outside of the tradition? And if so, does this not impose on these outsiders a particular set of obligations (intellectual or spiritual) deriving from a tradition not their own?

In his book, however, Schmidt-Leukel takes on this exact issue, proposing to find a basis of understanding between Christians, Muslims, and Buddhists regarding the very particular claims each tradition makes about its authoritative founder and the seemingly irreconcilable constructions of that authority as Son (of God), Prophet, and Buddha. Importantly, Schmidt-Leukel approaches this interreligious theological challenge as a set of consecutive dialogues (Christian-Islamic, Christian-Buddhist, and Islamic-Buddhist), rather than as a trialogue, properly speaking. I comment here primarily on the Christian-Islamic engagement on the question of the "Son" and the "Prophet," with some brief remarks also offered on the Islamic-Buddhist understanding he suggests.

Schmidt-Leukel recognizes the seemingly insurmountable barrier between the Christian tradition, which has traditionally and doctrinally considered Jesus to be the "Son" of God and an incarnation of God in human form, and the Islamic tradition, which strenuously rejects such notions as absolutely unacceptable conceptions related to God. To affirm a "Son of God," from this perspective, is to compromise God's transcendence by attributing a specific and limiting human relationship to God; it is also to conceive of God as embodied (however ambiguously) in a human material form. The Qur'an suggests in places that such views come close to the unforgivable sin of polytheism/idolatry/"associationism" (*shirk*), if not *shirk* itself.

Yet Schmidt-Leukel proposes a path to mutual understanding on this issue by finding resources within both the Christian and the Islamic traditions that are consistent in their understanding of the person of Jesus. From the Christian perspective, Schmidt-Leukel observes that the doctrines of sonship and incarnation in relation to Jesus are not substantially supported by the Gospel accounts of Jesus's own words about himself in relation to God. This observation is very much in line with the critique of Christian religious developments found in the Qur'an itself, which advises and at times admonishes Christians to observe more carefully and faithfully the teachings found in their own revealed scripture, the Gospel.[2] This involves arguing that it was only through a later and false interpretation of this scripture, or ignoring Jesus's own instruction to his followers to worship God (rather than himself), that they eventually went theologically astray, despite the genuine virtue that the Qur'an observes among Christians.[3]

Furthermore, Schmidt-Leukel seeks to turn the discussion away from "incarnation" toward other, if more minor, conceptualizations of Jesus's relationship to God—in particular, the idea of Jesus as the "image" of God and as identical with "revelation" itself. For sure, these two concepts are far more acceptable within the particularities of Islamic doctrine than notions of sonship or incarnation. The idea of Jesus as the "symbol" or "image" (he uses both terms) of the invisible God is quite consistent with the Qur'an's description of Jesus (and in one instance, Jesus and his mother

---

[2]See, for example, Qur'an 5.47: "Let the people of the Gospel judge by that which God has sent down therein"; 5.68: "Say, "O People of the Book! You stand on naught till you observe the Torah and the Gospel, and that which has been sent down unto you from your Lord"; and also 5.66: "Had they observed the Torah and the Gospel and that which was sent down unto them from their Lord, they would surely have received nourishment from above them and from beneath their feet."

[3]See, e.g., Qur'an 5.82: "And thou wilt find the nearest of them in affection toward those who believe to be those who say, 'We are Christians.' That is because among them are priests and monks, and because they are not arrogant"; and 57.27: "Then We sent Our messengers to follow in their footsteps, and We sent Jesus son of Mary and We gave him the Gospel and placed kindness and mercy in the hearts of those who follow him."

Mary together) as a "sign" (*ayah*) of God.[4] The word *ayah*, or sign, is always associated with revelation in the Islamic tradition, being the term that is used in the Qur'an itself for verses of the Qur'an, for powerful and supernatural displays of God's power through the prophets, and for regular, natural phenomena that the Qur'an regularly invokes as "signs" or pointers toward the existence, oneness, and benevolence of God. Indeed, as a demonstration of the usefulness of the fractal approach to religious difference, we can see that invoking the alternative notion of Jesus as "image" of God correlates well with the Qur'anic conception of Jesus, not only as prophet but as "sign" (i.e., a form of revelation) of God; thus, a reliable and mutually agreeable path toward understanding has been outlined.

Two questions immediately arise, however. First, does emphasizing Jesus as symbol or image of God—which is surely different from the doctrinally central concept of incarnation—for the purposes of interreligious pathfinding and "synthesis"[5] not constitute a compromise on some level of the Christian tradition itself? An image is not simply a different aspect of or perspective on incarnation, but something quite different. How does the idea of Jesus as an image or symbol of God, rather than God's son or an incarnation of the divine itself, square with the fundamental tenet in the Nicene Creed that as the second person of the Trinity, Christ was "begotten and not made"—indicating a profound ontological differentiation between Christ and all of God's other creatures? In other words, while religions might find similar or matching fractals at different levels of emphasis in other traditions that are helpful for interreligious theological thinking, how important are the differences of scale? Has forging this conceptual path between these two traditions made real progress, or merely skirted around and avoided (rather than confronted) the larger obstacles of the doctrinal centrality of "incarnation" to Christianity and the radical and uncompromising rejections of sonship in relation to God (or filial imagery in any form) that one finds in Islam?

Second, even if the concept of finding common ground in the way in which both Christianity and Islam associate Jesus with revelation itself works well in a Christian-Muslim interreligious encounter, does the same concept work when Buddhist views are similarly considered? Are interreligious pathways constructed between two traditions always, or often, limited to those two traditions? *Other* pathways may be constructed between two *other* religions, but the fact that such constructions are most fruitful in bilateral, rather than trilateral or multilateral engagements (as Schmidt-Leukel's separate treatment of the religions in pairs suggests)

---

[4]Qur'an 19.21; 21.91.
[5]This is Schmidt-Leukel's term. See *Religious Pluralism and Interreligious Theology*, 148.

seems to indicate a certain limitation on the usefulness of this theory for a more broadly and universally construed form of "interreligious theology." I return to this point in my conclusion.

From the Islamic perspective, Schmidt-Leukel's attempt to strike a path toward synthesis that relies on engaging the concept of "revelation" is highly perceptive and effective, for there are many explicit and implicit ways in which Jesus is associated with revelation as such in the Qur'an. He is, as Schmidt-Leukel notes, identified as a "word" from God that is cast upon or into Mary by the Angel Gabriel—an idea that is richly explored in his chapter, and which he supports, not only with Qur'anic evidence, but also through the respected opinions of notable contemporary Islamic scholars and theologians. Indeed, one can find further support for adopting this focus of Jesus as "revelation" in order to build interreligious theological thinking between Christians and Muslims. For example, the Angel Gabriel, the angel of revelation in general and for Muhammad in particular, is also referred to in the Qur'an as the *Ruh al-Quddus* (lit., "the Spirit of Holiness," but often translated as "the Holy Spirit"); although this is indeed quite different from the Christian notion of the Holy Spirit as the third person of the Trinity, we might note that the Nicene Creed describes the Holy Spirit as "the one who has spoken through the prophets." Pursuing this idea further, we would note that Jesus is likewise referred to in the Qur'an and Islamic tradition as *Ruh Allah* (the "Spirit of God"), indicating some symbolic, if not ontological, connection between the Angel (the "Holy Spirit") and the person of Jesus. And of course, the claim that the understanding of Jesus as revelation is a useful basis for Christian-Muslim mutual consensus about his status is further strengthened by the Qur'anic description of Jesus as a "sign (*ayah*)" of God, as noted above.

If Schmidt-Leukel's fractal theory works as I understand it should, then we would expect the pathway forged between these traditions on the basis of these common (if differentially "scaled") elements of the two traditions' views on Jesus to work in both directions. If the dominant Christian notion of incarnation can be de-emphasized in favor of speaking about Jesus as image and revelation in interreligious conversations with Muslims, then one should find some way in which the concept of incarnation in relation to Islamic revelation—or the confluence of messenger and message in the case of Muhammad (as well as Jesus)—can be detected in the Islamic tradition as well.

Indeed, we find that this is the case, for we see that the Qur'anic revelation is not so much an "inlibration" of God's word (as Schmidt-Leukel conceives it), but rather a kind of "incarnation" on the human tongue as it is spoken. The Qur'an is, as its literal meaning "recitation" suggests, first and foremost an oral revelation that resides in the hearts and manifests on the tongues of those who recite its words. The Qur'an is revealed first to Muhammad's heart, and then conveyed as physical sound emitted by the workings of the human tongue to his followers, and thereafter it lives and manifests upon the tongues of the Muslim believers who utter it day after day, and generation after generation. With regard to the second idea—namely the conflation of message and messenger in the person of Jesus, we might note (again as a "minor key" within the Islamic tradition) the fact that both the Qur'an and the Prophet Muhammad are identified in the Islamic tradition as *"dhikr Allah,"* or "the remembrance/reminder of God." There is a way in which both Muhammad and the message that he brings can be seen as functionally equivalent insofar as they both serve as means for the remembrance of God. On a more ontological note, the Prophet's wife 'Ā'ishah famously said, Muhammad's character was the Qur'an.[6]

Despite the usefulness of Schmidt-Leukel's exploration of Jesus as "revelation" as a site for interreligious common ground between Christians and Muslims, it has its limitations. I have already suggested (as an outsider) the particular problems I see with this approach from a Christian perspective. The critique I would offer from a Muslim perspective is that Schmidt-Leukel's attempt to soften the sharp edges of the Qur'anic rejection of the sonship and divinity of Jesus seems to rest heavily, at times, on the assumption that part of the problem for Muslims in accepting the doctrine of Jesus's sonship (at least as a position different from their own formulation of Jesus as prophet, but understandable as an alternative perspective) is that they have taken the doctrines of incarnation and sonship too literally; and he points out that many if not most Christian theologians themselves would bristle at overly literal interpretations of these doctrines. If Muslims could only be made to see this doctrine in its metaphorical sense, he suggests, it would be much easier for them to accept.

But this does not give enough credit to Muslim theologians, even in the medieval period, who seem to have had (at least in some well-known cases) a fairly sophisticated understanding of such Christian doctrines, and certainly could appreciate the difference between metaphorical and literal ways of speaking about God and God's attributes, as this formed an important area of inquiry and debate in both Islamic theology and Qur'anic exegesis. It is true that the Qur'an does often seem to critique the Christian doctrines of the Trinity, or the sonship and divinity of Jesus, in ways that suggest a highly literal reading that is not consistent with Christians' own formulations of these doctrines—for example, suggesting that the Trinitarian conception of God makes God "the third of three" and might lead to polytheism.[7] This

---

[6]Ahmad b. Hanbal, *Musnad*, v. 10, h. 25240, Damascus: *Mu'assasat al-Risalah*, 1995–2001.
[7]Qur'an 5.72–73.

should not, however, necessarily be understood as a failure of understanding or lack of sophistication, but rather as a purposeful polemical restatement of the Trinitarian doctrine intended to warn Christians that such a doctrine came dangerously close to polytheism. This is an argument that would have been all the more persuasive to Christians precisely because they *did not* view themselves as polytheists, and the Christians in the Qur'an's original audience in Arabia would likely have abhorred the idea.

More importantly, though, the idea that the metaphorical nature of titles suggesting a "filial" relationship between God and creation was misread by or lost on Muslims has little basis. For it is not only in the case of Jesus that the Qur'an rejects notions of divine "sonship"; elsewhere the Qur'an criticizes Jews and Christians for claiming to be the children of God themselves:

> And the Jews and the Christians say, "We are the children of God, and His beloved ones." Say, "Why then does He punish you for your sins?" Nay, but you are mortals of His creating. He forgives whomsoever He will, and He punishes whomsoever He will, and unto God belongs sovereignty over the heavens and the earth and whatsoever is between them, and unto Him is the journey's end.[8]

The Qur'an's initial audience, as well as later Muslim thinkers, almost certainly knew that this Jewish-Christian claim to be children of God was not meant literally. Even as a metaphor, then, attributions of filial relationships between God and human beings were problematic, with the Qur'an suggesting in the passage cited above that to claim such a unique relationship with the Creator could lead to the conceit that one was exempt from the ordinary modes of human accountability. Of course, Christians (and Jews) who invoke God as "Father" or consider themselves to be God's "children" do not see this as the basis of a preferential relationship for them with God to the exclusion of other people, but the Qur'an suggests (as it does in likening Trinity to forms of polytheism) that such ideas have the potential to lead naturally in those directions.

At the end of this section, Schmidt-Leukel asks if the idea of Jesus as the "Son of God" could be acceptable to Muslims if it was viewed "as a legitimate attempt at expressing the dynamics of revelation in that case in which revelation assumes the form of a person" (158). I would argue that, from an Islamic perspective, one might be able to accept that the Christian doctrine of the "sonship" of Jesus can be read as purely metaphorical (although I wondered above whether a purely metaphorical understanding would be acceptable to most Christian theologians) and that it is therefore

---

[8]Qur'an 5.18.

not a form of polytheism or idolatry. However, I am more skeptical about the possibility of accepting it as a doctrinal expression about the nature of Jesus that is consistent with Qur'anic conceptions of Jesus as prophet and servant (like all of the other prophets) while remaining true to the Qur'an's emphatic rejection of the attribution of filial relationships to God in any form.

PLURALISTIC THEOLOGY FROM WITHIN

Schmidt-Leukel's careful and insightful exploration of pathways of understanding between the concepts of Son, Prophet, and Buddha in Christianity, Islam, and Buddhism demonstrates both the great potential and the limits of his fractal theory of religious diversity. This brings us back to the question of what it means to do interreligious theology, not from a monocentric perspective, but from a variety of centers and perspectives, and from within each of the traditions themselves. Fractal theory suggests a way of looking at religions, theoretically and theologically, as composed of "parts" that recur in a variety of patterns both between and within individual religions. An appreciation for this, Schmidt-Leukel argues, allows us to see sameness and difference between and within traditions without doing harm to the integrity of any individual religious tradition or to the meaningfulness of the category of religion itself. Yet it is not only the recognizable and helpful similarities among various elements and strands of thought in different religious traditions that matters, but their variable scale and function within a particular tradition, and the extent to which they are an integral part of a greater and unified whole. To give a minor aspect of one religion particular prominence or a distinctive function in order to build common ground for doing interreligious theology with another religious tradition might be helpful in a limited or tentative way in the direct encounter or interface between two traditions; but to alter the scale of different elements within a tradition in a more permanent way is indeed to change and alter them fundamentally, in a way that Schmidt-Leukel himself seems to want to avoid.

Schmidt-Leukel's fractal theory of religious diversity and religious commonality is both deeply insightful and practically very useful in situations of interreligious engagement. It allows for the shifting of perspective that makes interreligious understanding and appreciation possible, while preserving the uniqueness and integrity of the religions themselves. But I am more skeptical about the idea that this approach can be the basis of a properly interreligious theology—that is, a constructive theology built outside the confessional confines of the individual traditions. I say this in part because I conceive the space in which interreligious engagement takes place to be liminal and temporary in nature—formed by the meeting of two particular religions in a nonnormative context and shaped by the particularities of these two traditions. In other words, the liminal space of Christian-Muslim encounter will not be the same as the equally liminal spaces of Christian-Buddhist or Muslim-Buddhist encounter. They are places where one meets the other for relatively fleeting moments of mutual or "reciprocal" illumination and theological exchange.

In response, or perhaps in addition, to Schmidt-Leukel's fractal theory, I would here offer another metaphor for interreligious encounter—and one that comes directly from the Qur'an: the idea of the "barzakh," that is, the meeting point between two realms or realities that can never merge, or lose their distinctiveness, but which can meet and dwell briefly with one another. The concept of *barzakh* is rich in the Qur'an and Islamic theology, wherein it is variously used to describe or refer to the meeting point between this world and the next, between individual death and universal resurrection, and between the spiritual and material aspects of the soul.

Perhaps most useful for our metaphorical purposes here, however, is the Qur'an's description of the *barzakh* as the point of the "meeting of the two seas" (that is, freshwater rivers and the salty ocean). At their point of meeting the two seas do indeed "mingle" and can cohabitate in this space, for they are both water; and indeed, in this liminal space the water is less salty than the ocean and more brackish than the river. But the "junction" of these two seas is as much a barrier as a meeting point, in that their mingling is limited to this liminal space, and is never allowed to compromise the integrity of the two bodies of water themselves—the salty ocean remains salty, and does not lose its saltiness, nor is the freshwater made brackish for its encounter with the sea. In interreligious encounter, each tradition can understand and learn from the other, but only in a limited space and for a limited time, for there is value in Islam being Islam and Christianity being Christianity, for example, even if they are both "religions" and mutually understandable as such, just as there is value in the sea being the sea and the river being the river, even if both are water.

The religions may have much to learn from one another, not only for the practical and ethical purpose of facilitating interreligious tolerance and understanding between the religions, but also for the deepening and nuancing of their own theologies and self-understanding. Yet, as I see it, the insights gained through such limited and liminal encounters need to be turned back toward the individual religious community as the central site for theological exploration and construction, rather than made the permanent basis of a collective interreligious theology. Interreligious theology is, ultimately, theology from the edge, rather than from some central point between all of the traditions. But it is precisely this location on the edge that makes its fruits extraordinary and invaluable.

PART FOUR

CONTINUING
THE CONVERSATION

Fractal Patterns in Religious Diversity: What to Make of Their Discovery?

A Response

Perry Schmidt-Leukel

Through their support, critical comments, and pointing out open questions, the contributors to this book explore and test the value of the theory that religious diversity exhibits fractal patterns and that such patterns are particularly significant in view of an "interreligious theology" (an umbrella term that covers various types of interreligious theology, including different versions of "comparative theology"). The wealth of their reflections will be beneficial to the wider community of all those who still gaze at human religious diversity with a sense of awe, wonder, and puzzlement. Such exchange between scholars is—despite occasional reciprocal misunderstandings—one of the blessings of the academy, and I am very grateful to each contributor and the two editors for the time and effort they invested in this discussion and in making it available to a larger readership.

COMPARATIVE THEOLOGY, INTERRELIGIOUS THEOLOGY, AND THEOLOGY OF RELIGIONS

The discourse in this book rests on the broad consensus that today theological (or theology-like) reflection—whether of a Hindu, Buddhist, Daoist, Confucian, Jewish, Christian, or Muslim nature—cannot do without taking into account far more seriously than in the past the insights found in other religious traditions. Part and parcel of such "taking into account" is to engage in interreligious comparisons and ask what we may learn from such comparisons regarding religious truth claims.

The proposal that there are fractal correspondences between interreligious and intrareligious diversity is of a phenomenological nature. As such, this proposal is independent of a religious or nonreligious stance in the interpretation of religious diversity. Moreover, *if* one looks at religious diversity from a religious perspective, the discernment of fractal structures does not in itself conclude the debate between exclusivists, inclusivists, and pluralists (17–19).[1] Yet the discernment of fractal structures is important to interreligious theology, especially if interreligious theology is practiced on the basis of a pluralist understanding of religious diversity. But note that I do not take religious pluralism as a position above or beyond the religions. I see "religious pluralism" as an approach that can be taken from within each of the religious traditions: the approach that regards at least some other religions as equally valid paths of salvation and as mediating equally valid recognition of ultimate reality despite—or, better, through—the religions' diversity. This is one of the main points in the first part of my *Religious Pluralism and Interreligious Theology*, as is highlighted earlier by Rong Wang (88) and Maria Dakake (163).

One important implication of this understanding of "religious pluralism" emerges from Ayon Maharaj's critique that I do not sufficiently reflect on the question of which type of religious beliefs or doctrines are to be considered as "soteriologically vital" and which as "soteriologically inessential (111)." Although I agree with him (and John Hick, to whom he refers) that such a distinction needs to be made, I think that it needs to be made from within the different religious traditions and must become part of the discourse that I call "interreligious theology."[2] Although as a Christian theologian I do have an opinion on what should count as "soteriologically vital,"[3] it is not my intention to prejudge by which criteria pluralists from various religious traditions should assess other religious paths as equally salvific or liberative. Such a prejudgment would either express a covert superiority claim for one's own tradition (being deemed to know the suitable criteria for this type of judgment) or would assume a position beyond and above all the religions—a position I consider as illusory and self-refuting.

The intention of the first part of my book on religious pluralism and interreligious theology was to show that at least the major religious traditions are indeed equipped with the resources that enable them to develop their own specific versions of religious pluralism, even if all of the major religions are traditionally dominated by either exclusivist or inclusivist approaches. Maharaj—perhaps rightly so—holds that in my discussion of Hinduism I

---

[1] Numbers in parentheses refer to page numbers in this volume.

[2] See Perry Schmidt-Leukel, *Religious Pluralism and Interreligious Theology. The Gifford Lectures—An Extended Edition* (Maryknoll, NY: Orbis Books, 2017), 112–14.

[3] See Perry Schmidt-Leukel, *God beyond Boundaries: A Christian and Pluralist Theology of Religions* (Münster: Waxmann, 2017), 222–69.

have underestimated the strength and consistency of the pluralist orientation in the work of Ramakrishna and Vivekananda, although he admits
that Vivekananda's speeches can give the impression of "two apparently
conflicting strands" (106). I would be delighted if Maharaj's reading turns
out to be correct. And my delight would be even greater if he joins the so
far still small crowd of contemporary Hindu pluralists who actively challenge the primus-inter-pares pluralism of the Hindutva movement and its
antipluralistic politics of religions that is so hostile toward Muslims and
Christians in India.[4]

Some contributors, especially Francis Clooney, inquire more deeply
into the relationship between my conception of interreligious theology
and comparative theology. Unfortunately, Clooney mistakes my view of
comparative theology in several respects, so that some rectifications are in
place. I never suggested that the kind of comparative theology that Clooney
practices is "short-lived, because deep down it relies on a very bad theology
of religions" (44). Nor have I ever held—as he alleges—that "comparative
theology without a (pluralist) theology of religions is no theology at all"
(46). And "demolishing much of comparative theology" (40) is certainly
not—and never has been—my intention. In *Religious Pluralism and Interreligious Theology*, as in other publications,[5] I have criticized one aspect,
namely the proposal of some comparativists that comparative theology could
keep its fingers out of the theology of religions jam-pot and avoid the kind
of issues that are debated between exclusivists, inclusivists, and pluralists
without reducing itself, by means of such abstention, to the nontheological
discipline of "comparative religion." I hold that "the consistent exclusion
of the theology of religions discourse from comparative studies would
deprive such studies of their theological nature."[6] Hence I am pleased with
Clooney's own admission "that comparative theology without theology
of religions might end up as a nontheological mode of study" (43). Given
Clooney's and James Fredericks's endorsement of an inclusivist position,
and given that some among the "next generation" of comparative theologians have also criticized a concept of comparative theology that would
evade questions of a theology of religions, I have argued that a conception

[4]I have not, as Maharaj misreads me (109), set Jeffery Long's pluralism against Ramakrishna
and Vivekananda but against the Hindutva movement, which is—explicitly—the target of Long's
critique (see Schmidt-Leukel, *Religious Pluralism and Interreligious Theology*, 68–69). But may
I suggest that Hindu pluralists need to self-critically ponder the question of how it is possible that
people such as M. S. Golwalkar (who came from the Ramakrishna order) could transform the
ideas of Ramakrishna and Vivekananda into the ideological basis of the Hindutva?

[5]Perry Schmidt-Leukel, *Transformation by Integration: How Inter-Faith Encounter Changes
Christianity* (London: SCM Press, 2009), 90–104; Schmidt-Leukel, *God beyond Boundaries*,
80–87.

[6]Schmidt-Leukel, *Religious Pluralism and Interreligious Theology*, 30.

of comparative theology without theology of religions was probably only a short-lived phase in its development.[7]

Thus, if comparative theology remains sensitive to the theology of religions issues, it is—from my point of view—"a formidable instrument for doing interreligious theology."[8] I have sketched succinctly, but hopefully clearly, the methodological role of the confessional dimension and the nature of comparison within interreligious theology.[9] Furthermore, I do *not* think that interreligious or comparative theology can only be practiced on the basis of a pluralist position. But I hold that an exclusivist cannot engage in interreligious theology as that kind of collaborative work draws on more than one religious tradition for theological insight.[10] Interreligious theology—and comparative theology as one of its forms—is different from "theology of religions" (in the *genitivus objectivus* sense), but intrinsically interrelated. Interreligious theology is theology of religions as a *genitivus subjectivus*.[11]

I do criticize inclusivism, though, not the hermeneutical inclusivism, which inevitably (!) employs one's own religious ideas and categories in the evaluation of other religious traditions, but "inclusivism" defined as the claim that one's own tradition is uniquely superior in mediating salvific knowledge of ultimate reality.[12] I do not say that comparative theology per se is bound to this inclusivism—several comparative theologians actually do not subscribe to such superiority claims. Yet, how can Clooney, on the one hand, endorse such inclusivist theologies as those of Karl Rahner and Jacques Dupuis (43), and, on the other hand, hold that Hindu traditions are not "inferior or insufficient" because of their difference from his (Clooney's) Catholic position (45)? To Rahner and Dupuis the inferiority of other traditions consisted precisely in their lack of the full and correct recognition of Christ as it is allegedly only found in Christianity (or, as Rahner held,

---

[7]Ibid., 29–30. Was this type of comparative theology (that presented itself as an alternative to the theology of religions) related to the Vatican's condemnation of both religious pluralism and a broad-minded inclusivism à la Dupuis, as for example in its 2000 declaration *Dominus Iesus*? Well, see James Fredericks's revealing remark about Catholic comparative theologians: "These Catholics are approaching the question of religious diversity in a way quite different from the way *Dominus Iesus* approaches the question and, for that matter, the way those criticized by the declaration approach the matter" (Fredericks, "The Catholic Church and the Other Religious Paths: Rejecting Nothing That Is True and Holy," *Theological Studies* 64 [2003]: 225–54, 253). In other words, comparative theology is presented as a safe haven from the condemnations declared in *Dominus Iesus* because of its abstention from the thorny theology of religions questions.

[8]Schmidt-Leukel, *Religious Pluralism and Interreligious Theology*, 30. See also the discussion at 116–19.

[9]Ibid., 140–41, 143–44.

[10]Ibid., 135.

[11]See Wilfred Cantwell Smith, *Towards a World Theology: Faith and the Comparative History of Religions* (Maryknoll, NY: Orbis Books, 1989), 124.

[12]See Schmidt-Leukel, *Religious Pluralism and Interreligious Theology*, 3–5; *God beyond Boundaries*, 68.

Catholic Christianity); that is, other religions are seen as inferior or insufficient because of their being different from the supposedly superior Christian/ Catholic faith.[13]

One of my main critiques of inclusivism is its inability to appreciate religious diversity in more than a preliminary sense. If someone is honestly convinced that redemptive revelation or liberating insight is exclusively found in her own religious tradition (as in exclusivism)—or is found there in a uniquely superior way (as in inclusivism)—the wish that ideally all should become partakers of this unique, or uniquely superior, truth is morally good and ethically obliging.[14] Hence I do not share Kenneth Rose's position that religious pluralism is "the only ethical basis for the academic and theological study of religion" (36) because I cannot rule out the possibility that some exclusivist or inclusivist position may ultimately be correct. I wholeheartedly agree with Rose that pluralism is the only approach that tries to combine religious diversity with the idea of theological equality. But we cannot know for sure whether religious pluralism is actually closer to the truth than the alternative options. It might be so and perhaps even quite probably so. At least this issue is worth being explored as much as possible. Rose is entirely right in stating that "some metaphysical situation is in fact the case" (36), which involves also the possibility that the naturalist denial of any transcendent reality might be true. I understand interreligious theology as a scholarly enterprise in search of truth—even if we are (under pre-eschatological conditions) not in a situation in which we will ever know the truth beyond any rational doubt.

However, the persistence of this skeptical caveat should not entice us to the "radical reformulation of truth in terms of ethics" (138) that Ephraim Meir, though from a different point of view, suggests. I agree with Ephraim's important reminder that from a religious perspective "the ethical capacity of religions" (138) is an essential criterion in assessing their validity as liberative, righteous, or straight paths. I also take this "prescriptive" element as indeed indispensable (139). However, reducing the interreligious exploration of the possible truth in the religions' messages to their ethical potential would all too easily leave us with a view in which "the religion of the other might be seen as generating positive ethical values despite the religion's falsity, rather than because of the religion's truth."[15] When

---

[13]For their analysis see Schmidt-Leukel, *God beyond Boundaries*, 120–22, 131–46.

[14]It is a major inconsistency of Dupuis's theology that he wants to retain the unique superiority of God's revelation in Christ while accepting religious diversity not only as a matter of fact (*de facto*) but as divinely willed (*de iure*). His position amounts to an inclusivist version of double predestination: the majority of humanity being predestined by God to live with deficient forms of divine revelation.

[15]Reza Shah Kazemi, *Common Ground between Islam and Buddhism* (Louisville, KY: Fons

Meir speaks of a complementarity between doctrinal convergences and the search for ethical commonalities, I have no objections. I fully agree that what comes across as descriptions of the Ultimate needs to be understood as orienting us in a meaningful way to a reality that as such escapes human conceptual understanding and description. Yet I suggest that such orientation should not be reduced to ethics—and Meir himself underlines the spiritual significance of trust, which clearly transcends pure ethics.

THE FRACTAL INTERPRETATION OF RELIGIOUS DIVERSITY IN ITS RELATION TO RELIGIOUS PLURALISM AND INTERRELIGIOUS THEOLOGY

As stated above, the claim that religious diversity displays fractal patterns is a phenomenological claim and as such bound neither to a particular position in the theology of religions (exclusivism, inclusivism, pluralism) nor to a religious interpretation of religious diversity at all. The naturalist can understand such fractal patterns as inherent features of human illusion, and the exclusivist too can take the parallels either as illusory or irrelevant and the differences as variations of falsehood. But how does the discernment of fractals contribute to the project of interreligious theology, especially if carried out on pluralist premises?

In this respect I find the observations by Kenneth Rose, Hans Gustafson, and Alan Race most helpful. First, as Rose says, the fractal patterns in religious diversity may imply that "the full potential of religion *as religion* is present to all historically and culturally produced religious traditions," even if each of these "can express but a finite range of the available religious goods" (34). This shows that and how different religions can be equally true and thus illuminates how religious pluralism is possible without falling into relativism. Second, the hidden potential in each religious tradition is waiting only for the challenge of interreligious interactions to be stimulated into actuality, and therefore "the encounter between two or more religions can awaken cross-religious attraction" (33). I couldn't agree more. Furthermore, Rose holds that through these two observations "the hidden relatedness that secretly relates all religions as channels, sacraments, or bearers in their diverse ways of the full plenitude of being" (34) is uncovered. This resonates strongly with Gustafson's impression that the discovery of fractal patterns in religious diversity strengthens his "pansacramental worldview," according to which all things can be "potential mediators (symbols) of the sacred" (69)—a view that presupposes the reciprocal interpenetration of the sacred, the world, and the person (74).

The underlying idea that a diversity of things and people can make the sacred present substantiates the need for both ecumenical and interreligious theology, and this, naturally, creates an interest in the correspondence between the two theological enterprises of ecumenical and interreligious theology. This is where the discovery of fractal structures becomes relevant. Inasmuch as the human subject is at one end of sacramental mediation, the awareness of a legitimate diversity of mediations at the inter- and intrareligious levels refers back to the intrasubjective level, that is, the "interior reflection, or intrapersonal dialogue" (77). Conversely, the interior reflection triggered by the diverse religious predispositions can foster the engagement with intra- and interreligious diversity. Pansacramentality suggests that the mediation of the sacred occurs within the fractal patterns that permeate all three levels—an idea that implies that the elements constituting diversity are compatible as sacraments of the sacred and that fractality has something to do with this complementarity.

As an example of such fractal compatibility I have analyzed the three central religious and confessional categories of incarnation, prophecy, and awakening in terms of their reciprocal co-inherence (21–22).[16] Race, Rose, and Meir accept my analysis. To Christians, it recommends an understanding of incarnation that remains faithful to the prophetic component. The idea of prophetic proclamation in itself already implies some kind of incarnational thinking: If the prophet speaks the word of God, the word of God is incarnate in human words. And if the word of God can be incarnate in a human message, why should the word of God (the Logos) not also be seen as incarnate in a message that is expressed not in words but in the life of a human being? Then, however, we may and must ask whether a number of human beings have probably embodied the divine word, and hence whether the life of a prophet is also part of the prophetic message.

Race raises the question of whether the discernment of fractal patterns in religious diversity strengthens the case for a pluralist theology of religions. His answer is "yes," provided that the key differences that make up diversity, such as the mystical and the prophetic, nondual and dual, impersonal and personal, and so on, can be interpreted as complementary instead of contradictory. Such complementarity is one of the presuppositions of a pluralist approach. A fractal perspective, which argues that such polarities not only mark the differences among but also within the religions, and that they are rooted in structures of the human psyche and mind, strengthens

---

[16]Schmidt-Leukel, *Religious Pluralism and Interreligious Theology*, 235–36.

religious pluralism only under pluralist premises. Hence there is a certain circularity, which may appear not that impressive to the nonpluralist. Nevertheless, the argument puts some pressure on nonpluralists regarding the diversity within their own religious traditions. If the nonpluralist admits that *intra*religious diversity is legitimate and good, at least to some extent (no pluralist holds that all aspects of religious diversity are compatible or of equal value), then the question arises why this should be less true for *inter*religious diversity. This explains why there is an inclination of a fractal interpretation of religious diversity toward a pluralist position.[17]

As Race shows in his discussion of John A. T. Robinson, the issue hinges upon the question of combining difference with equal value. The strength of John Hick's analogies, as Race recalls, lies in the demonstration that in a number of cases we can and have to admit precisely this combination of equality and difference. The inclusivist, however, even if he admits the existence of fractal patterns, could still argue that one particular constellation and combination is superior to all other combinations, for example, in that it provides "the profoundest clue to all the rest," as Race quotes from Robinson (150). Yet this inclusivist attitude is less congenial to interreligious learning and would presumably link the practice of interreligious theology to the expectation that in the long run such practice will demonstrate this unique superiority—not just of one's own religion but of one particular, highly special manifestation of it.[18] Hence it seems to me that although the discovery of fractal patterns does not demonstrate the truth of religious pluralism, it nevertheless works best with it, especially if pluralism is not understood as a goal in itself but as a position most favorable to interreligious learning.

I am most grateful to Maharaj for pointing out that a fractal interpretation of religious diversity can be found in Vivekananda's lectures in a more elaborate way than I have been aware of. I find very persuasive Vivekananda's suggestion that of the four different paths of liberation (based on the traditional four *yoga*s or *mārga*s: works, love of God, meditation, and knowledge), "each blends into the other" (107). Hence, if we distinguish religious communities by means of that path to which they give priority, the other paths are to some extent also present. As Maharaj points out, Vi-

---

[17]See also ibid., 237.

[18]The Christian inclusivist could certainly argue that even if the three elements of prophetic proclamation, incarnation, and awakening all combine in specific ways in each of the three categories of the Prophet, the Son, and the Buddha, one could still hold that the particular combination that these elements assume in the category of the Son is superior to the other two. But then the inclusivist will be confronted with the huge diversity of different interpretations of incarnation within the Christian tradition and will have to presuppose such unique superiority in the end only for one highly specific Christological model.

vekananda obviously understands this diversity of salvific paths as rooted in the religious potential of the individual person. This is indeed a fractal view comprising the three main scales of interreligious, intrareligious, and intrasubjective diversity. At least structurally, this model is very similar to Bhikkhu Buddhadāsa's suggestion of three complementary ways of wisdom, faith, and willpower. Here too the underlying idea is that each of these three spiritual features implies *in nuce* the other two.[19] But can such fractal complementarity also be extended to spiritual paths that appear to be far more opposed to each other? As I suggested (19–21), this is indeed possible.

John Makransky's case study deals with such a difference, namely that between self-help and other-help in the process of salvation/liberation. He asks his reader to look for analogies in other religious traditions regarding the need for either "human effort . . . to align . . . us with that ultimate reality," or, in contrast, our dependency "on ultimate reality itself to align us with itself" (129). It will not be difficult to comply with his request: the polarity of self-help and other-help can be discerned in one way or the other in all the major traditions. However, Makransky's case is more complicated inasmuch as it does not relate to the wide field of inner-Buddhist diversity, but to the far more subtle branching within one section of Buddhist subtraditions, here within the web of the Mahāyāna-Tantrayāna schools of Tibetan Buddhism. The diversity encountered at that sub-sub-level of intrareligious diversity develops within the framework of a good deal of common presuppositions, which in themselves are already highly specific if seen within the broad spectrum of Buddhism and even more so against the background of global religious diversity. Nevertheless, recurring themes of fractal patterns can still be discerned. The differences between Tsongkhapa's and Longchenpa's understandings of their joint Mahāyāna heritage is an early version of the long controversy in Tibetan Buddhism between the *rangtong* (self-emptiness) and *shentong* (emptiness of other) interpretation of emptiness, that is between the affirmation of the reality of universal emptiness and the affirmation of a reality that is empty of everything other than itself. At times this debate has become fierce and even violent, while some Tibetan pundits took a more ecumenical approach trying to harmonize the two contrasting views.

Understanding the different positions in this debate as part of a recurrent fractal pattern, and therefore taking it as more than merely an intra-Tibetan doctrinal issue but as a challenge for a global interreligious theology, prompts us to inquire into the possible complementarity of the two views exemplified by Tsongkhapa and Longchenpa. One possible line of this inquiry might start from the agreement among both masters that at the end

---

[19]See Schmidt-Leukel, *Religious Pluralism and Interreligious Theology*, 80–81, 223.

of the day (and the end of all dispute), ultimate "truth/reality" (one and the same word in Sanskrit: *satya*) is beyond all our concepts, that it is ineffable or, to use John Hick's term, "transcategorial." Thus, what appears at first sight like an ontological or metaphysical debate may actually be more akin to two different pastoral strategies—in Buddhist parlance: two different "skillful means" (*upāya kauśalya*)—with the question of which of the two is more "skillful" or "wholesome" (*kauśalya*). In talking about ultimate reality, Buddhism in general seeks to avoid the two extremes of "eternalism" and "nihilism," and one can easily read Tsongkhapa as averting the first and Longchenpa fighting the second—though with the suspicion, among the followers on both sides, that the other party fell precisely into the opposite trap. The suspicion that the radical refusal to conceptualize the Ultimate in any way whatsoever is nothing but atheism or nihilism in disguise, and the reciprocal allegation that any talk of some unconditioned and eternal reality is at best an illusion and at worst human self-aggrandizement are also known to the ideological and theological debates of the West. As far as the intra-Buddhist conflict is concerned, one aspect is the long and bitter history of Buddhism's distancing from the Hindu Vedāntic tradition, that is, the never-ending conflict over *ātman* (self) and *anātman* (no[t]-self).[20] This aspect shows how much an issue, by which the Hindu and the Buddhist tradition used to demarcate their differences, nevertheless reappears in transformed ways within both of them—and hence, how much interreligious and ecumenical theological efforts are intertwined. And it can take a long time until complementarities between what appears as outright contradictions are finally established. Within Christianity it took more than four hundred years before Lutherans and Catholics agreed that justification by works and justification by faith can indeed be understood as two sides of the same coin.

FRACTAL PATTERNS
AND THE QUESTION OF UNIQUENESS

The case of Tsongkhapa and Longchenpa illustrates rather well the critical caution advanced by Clooney and Meir. "Not everything is compatible," says Meir (135). I agree, but given the vast range of different interpretations held within the religions in view of their own teachings, another caution is

---

[20]How much this conflict is present in Tsongkhapa's critique of the Buddha-Nature teaching can be seen in his tract *The Great Essence of True Eloquence* (*Legs bshad snying po*); see the translation in Robert A. F. Thurman, *The Speech of Gold: Reason and Enlightenment in the Tibetan Buddhism* (Delhi: Motilal Banarsidass, 1989), esp. 346–51.

also in place: don't be too hasty in judging that two teachings are incompatible simply because two among the vast range of possible interpretations turn out to be irreconcilable. But Meir and Clooney go further and hold that there can or could be incommensurabilities that balk at being part of a fractal pattern. What, Meir asks, if "religions have specificities that are not present in other religions . . . , but . . . somehow unique" (136)? Somewhat similarly, Clooney speaks of "loose ends" (52) or "of the enduring presence of the particular," which "can be an affront to the guardians of generality" (50). His defense of the particular against its systematization seems to have a special thrust that becomes more visible when he states that "particularity . . . is often at the heart of what really matters" and then poses the rhetorical question: "Is not Jesus Christ an irreducible particularity, a scandal, and a stumbling block" (50–51)?

I suggest that uniqueness or particularity neither stands in opposition to the discernment of fractal patterns nor is it something that would fall necessarily outside of such patterns. The kind of fractal patterns that can be discerned in inorganic and organic nature differ from fractals in abstract geometry in that no geometrical form ever has an exact counterpart in nature. Nothing in nature would ever be an immaculate circle or a flawless triangle, let alone such a complex figure as the Sierpinski triangle. In a fractal fern leaf none of the smaller leaves duplicates exactly the larger leaf and no two of the small leaves are exactly identical. In coastlines we never find two bays or spits of fjords that are perfectly identical or cases where the larger structure is precisely replicated at the smaller level. Maria Dakake rightly underlines that the discernment of fractal patterns in religious diversity does not compromise the reality of "unique configuration(s)" (165).

Uniqueness and particularity are pervasive throughout and within the fractal patterns. This is neatly illustrated through the sample provided by Makransky. In no other religion would we find exactly the same constellation as in the comparison of Tsongkapa with Longchenpa. But we do find features in that comparison that have their recognizable parallels in configurations that are contained in other religious traditions. The particularity and uniqueness of individual phenomena and especially of individual persons does not mean that they would stand altogether beyond any pattern. Decades ago, Aloysius Pieris, a fellow Jesuit of Clooney, had given the right answer to Clooney's question about the uniqueness or particularity of Jesus Christ when he wrote,

> That Jesus is unique is obvious even to Buddhists, just as Christians would hardly question the uniqueness of Gautama. Is not each one of us unique? The issue is whether Jesus' uniqueness consists in his absoluteness as conveyed by certain Christological titles; and whether

the uniqueness of Gautama should be understood in terms of the absoluteness that the word *dharma*—or in certain schools, *Buddha*—seems
to convey.[21]

Pieris had clearly seen the fractality in the relation between Buddhism
and Christianity in his diagnosis that although "gnostic detachment" may
be at the focus of Buddhism and "agapeic involvement" at the focus of
Christianity, both attitudes are found, and commended, in both traditions
and display an inner complementarity to a degree that goes down to the
level of intrasubjective diversity: "In other words, deep within each one of
us there is a Buddhist and a Christian engaged in a profound encounter."[22]
My suggestion that the categories by which Christians confess Jesus as the
incarnate Son of God, and Buddhists affirm Gautama as the Awakened One
("Buddha"), and Muslims proclaim Muhammad as the final Prophet show
in themselves a fractal interrelatedness (inasmuch as each one of the three
categories implies the other two as central elements) expands on Pieris's
insight by bringing in not only Islam (and, by implication, Judaism) but
also by widening the scope of the key spiritual features. I cannot see how
this analysis should be invalidated by pointing to the individual uniqueness
of Gautama, Jesus, and Muhammad. Nor would it be invalidated by the
understanding that the configuration of the three components of prophetic
revelation, incarnation, and awakening is rather different in each one of the
three epithets of Prophet, Son, and Buddha. It is rather part of the strength
of a fractal perspective that it helps us to get a better understanding of the
nature of such differences as well as of their interweaving.

A different issue, however, is the application of uniqueness to a particular
religious figure or teaching or institution in the sense of constituting the
only or uniquely superior vehicle of salvation/liberation. In this case we
are back to the theology of religions debate and the inbuilt problems that
exclusivism and inclusivism create for a theological appreciation of religious
diversity. That these are vital issues in the interaction between people of
different faiths emerges forcefully from Wang's discussion of the place of
Christianity in contemporary China. She describes the pluralist attitude as
crucial for a sinicized Christianity, and sinicization seems to be essential
for the future of Christianity in China and perhaps even for all religions in
China. I agree with Wang in seeing the traditional idea of the "harmony of the
three teachings" (*sanjiao heyi*) as a precursor of interreligious theology on
which contemporary religious thinkers can build. But the traditional model

---

[21] Aloysius Pieris, *Love Meets Wisdom: A Christian Experience of Buddhism* (Maryknoll, NY: Orbis Books, 1988), 131.
[22] Ibid., 113.

stands also in need of further development in order to serve an ongoing interreligious dialogue. If there is a tension between faithfulness to one's own religious tradition and the need to openly and seriously engage with others, a fractal interpretation of religious diversity can certainly help to see that both are compatible because the religious other is never wholly other.

INTERRELIGIOUS THEOLOGY: WHY AND WHEREFORE?

Should interreligious theology be confined to the exploration of only those questions that are considered "soteriologically vital"? This is what Ayon Maharaj suggests, and he combines this suggestion with the critique that I have wasted too much intellectual effort or "acrobatics" (112) in exploring possible commonalities between apparently contradictory religious beliefs that Maharaj deems to be soteriologically inessential. Now as I said before, I think that the decision of what is or isn't seen as soteriologically essential should be left to the theologians within the different traditions and then be made a matter of interreligious theological conversation. And if we take seriously what I describe as the third principle of interreligious theology, namely that it has to be done interreligiously lest it become a theological "no-man's-land," we cannot avoid asking about the possible truth in the different traditions' central confessional stances. Moreover, the different concepts of salvation or liberation that we find across the religious traditions, informing and shaping the criteria by which the theologians of different religions assess other religions as being either paths of salvation or paths of perdition, are deeply imbedded in the respective webs of various doctrinal concepts and a whole range of possible interpretations. Interreligious theology—especially if based on a pluralist position—explores the possible truth within such conceptual webs and hence does not ignore, neglect, or even reject the kind of arduous, detailed exploration of religious differences that comparative theologians rightly regard as indispensable. Leading pluralists have produced masterpieces of comparative (or interreligious) theology long before the label of the "New Comparative Theology" had been coined, as, for example, Raimon Panikkar's second edition of *The Unknown Christ of Hinduism* (1981), John Hick's *Death and Eternal Life* (1976), or Wilfred Cantwell Smith's *Faith and Belief* (1979) and *What Is Scripture?* (1993).[23]

---

[23]The accusation—widespread among some critics of religious pluralism—that pluralist theologians "display a lack of interest in the concrete and empirical details of what religious communities and their adherents actually tend to believe, value, and practice" (as Marianne Moyaert says, based on F. Clooney and J. Fredericks) is just false propaganda that does not become truer by frequent repetition. Religious pluralism cannot and should not be divorced from interreligious

This kind of extensive comparative effort cannot and should not be put aside by focusing too narrowly on soteriological issues.

Maharaj worries if my analysis of fractal patterns in religious diversity is not at the expense of "honoring religious difference" (113). Yet I do not think that this is the point. The question is not one of either honoring or neglecting difference but rather how to understand and interpret differences: Can they be understood, legitimately, as compatible differences (though still differences!) or is the only legitimate interpretation the one that reads them as incompatible (which always seems to be a possibility)? The fractal perspective points toward the correspondence between inter- and intrareligious differences. If a particular kind of intrareligious difference is understood as compatible, why should that not also apply to the structurally similar difference at the interreligious level? And if—and this needs further exploration—at least some of the major types of religious differences are rooted in particular features of the human mind and psyche, further light may be shed on why and how they can be comprehended as complementary instead of contradictory.

Dakake provides a fine example. She accepts that the understanding of Jesus as the revelation or word of God provides "a reliable and mutually agreeable path toward understanding" (168). But this understanding of Jesus is the basis of the category of "incarnation." If a revelation of God is really a revelation *of God*, then in some way God must be present, manifest, or "incarnate" in the revelation. If the word of God is really the word *of God*, God must be somehow "incarnate" in that word—be that the Qur'an or Jesus or both. If this is so, ʿĀʾisha's confession, quoted by Dakake, that "Muhammad's character was the Qur'an" shows that the idea of "the word becoming flesh" is not that alien to the Muslim universe of meaning as the polemics on both sides (Islam and Christianity) usually claim. And why should it be impossible for Muslims to understand the category of a "son"—if taken in a metaphorical sense—as equally valid to that of a "servant," if the true son is the one who is obedient (like a servant) to the will of the father (Matt. 21:28–32)?

The category of *a* or *the* "Buddha" emphasizes the awakening to what is eternally true and real. But what turns someone into a Buddha (and not merely an awakened being) is the proclamation of the eternal truth of the Dharma in such a way that it leads people to liberation. Such proclamation can be legitimately seen as an act of revelation.[24] Moreover, on Buddhist

---

theology. See Marianne Moyaert, "Christianity as the Measure of Religion? Materializing the Theology of Religions," in *Twenty-First-Century Theologies of Religions: Retrospection and Future Prospects*, Elizabeth Harris, Paul Hedges, and Shanti Hettiarachchi, eds. (Leiden: Brill, Rodopi, 2016), 238–66, 248–49.

[24]As did Peter Masefield when he gave his study on the formation of early Buddhism the title

premises, the Buddha embodies (or "incarnates") the truth of the Dharma. Given this interweaving of prophethood, incarnation, and awakening, every new insight generated in bilateral dialogues between Muslims, Christians, and Buddhists has its implications for all three traditions.[25] Hence I think that dialogue in its internal scope is far less limited than Dakake assumes. I indicated this by drawing a sort of conceptual circle (Prophet and Son, Son and Buddha, Buddha and Prophet), which finally turns out to follow the pattern of a Poincaré chain.[26] And so I would like to stretch Dakake's metaphor of *barzakh* (173): The rivers contain more of the sea, and the sea more of the rivers, long before they mingle at their meeting point. How can we know this? By looking at the internal diversity of each religious tradition. None of them displays the kind of purity and homogeneity that exist only in the brains and books of the self-declared orthodox. Not "to compromise the integrity" of different religions means not to ignore their rich internal diversity.

So far I had not thought about the possible usefulness of a fractal interpretation for feminist concerns. Much of Jerusha Tanner Rhodes's discussion seems to be more pertinent to my understanding of interreligious theology in general rather than to the particulars of a fractal interpretation of religious diversity. That religious traditions should not be mistaken as homogeneous entities is indeed crucial and now confirmed by many scholars. But this insight is only the basis for the further claim that the relation between inter- and intrareligious diversity displays fractal patterns. Comparative feminist theology is an important strand of interreligious theology. But the range of interests informing interreligious theology cannot be reduced to the far more specific interests of interreligious feminist theology. As Rita Gross once said, "Buddhist teachings on suffering help feminists remember that basic human suffering and existential anxieties are not patriarchy's fault and will not be eliminated in post-patriarchal society."[27] In other words, interreligious learning involves much more than what is of a specific feminist interest. Not all problems in and of life can be reduced to the kind of problems that the feminist critique addresses.

I do not want to exclude the possibility that the discernment of fractal patterns might be useful in view of the more particular aims of feminist theology. But I think the main relevance of a fractal perspective consists in providing the religious interpretation of religious diversity with a clearer

---

Divine Revelation in Pali Buddhism (Colombo: Sri Lanka Institute of Traditional Studies; London: Allen & Unwin, 1986).

[25]See Schmidt-Leukel, *Religious Pluralism and Interreligious Theology*, 138, 235–36.

[26]See ibid., 230.

[27]Rita Gross, *Buddhism after Patriarchy. A Feminist History, Analysis, and Reconstruction of Buddhism* (Albany: SUNY Press, 1993), 133.

conception of the nature of the diversity that they are interpreting. Conversely, could the discovery of fractal patterns be an obstacle for feminist concerns? I don't think so. Would the insight into the reciprocal inherence of confessional categories such as buddhahood, incarnation, and prophethood really "reinscribe and further reify androcentrism, patriarchy," or both as Rhodes asks? This, I suggest, does not depend on the fractal pattern as such but on the theological application and elaboration of the three categories. I do not see any good theological reasons why buddhahood, incarnation, and prophethood should apply only to males, even if Buddhism, Christianity, and Islam have made, and continue to make, this restriction. Yet the possibility of changing such a restricted understanding does not hinge on the fractal constellation itself but on tradition-specific arguments that critique such privileging of the male gender. Despite the dominance given to the male gender in each of the major religious traditions, they do contain scattered insights of a more egalitarian sort. Why this particular instance of intrareligious diversity has not materialized at the macro level of global interreligious diversity (at least none of the major religious traditions is predominantly gender egalitarian) is an interesting question. But this may change in the future, given that at least some branches within major religions—such as Protestants in Christianity, Shin-Buddhists in Buddhism, some liberal Jewish synagogues or Islamic Mosques—have opened ministry to women.

However, I strongly hold that the search for fractal patterns and the discussion of their validity should not be instrumentalized for ideological reasons. I do not buy into the theory—or, better, suspicion—that every search for, discovery of, and statement about truth is merely part of a power game and serves "in truth" a hidden political agenda. I am not sure if Rhodes herself would subscribe to such a radically constructivist view, for it would undermine the legitimate claim by feminists that—as a matter of fact/truth—there is so much gender injustice in the different cultures of the word, being to a significant extent fostered and sustained by religious beliefs and institutions. If the statement of this fact would itself have to count as merely an expression of power interests, feminist theologians would subvert their own basis; they would do likewise if they rejected "claims that assert any universal norm" (63), for, as Rhodes seems to admit, feminists do make the claim of a universal norm of gender justice.

AN INTERIM CONCLUSION

A fractal interpretation of religious diversity pays strong attention to the often neglected fact that religions are far from being homogeneous and static entities—something that Wilfred Cantwell Smith emphasized in his

1962 classic *The Meaning and End of Religion*. But the fractal theory goes beyond merely recognizing the reality of wide-ranging and thoroughgoing intrareligious diversity. It suggest that this diversity displays discernible patterns and structures reappearing at the macro level of global religious diversity and the micro level of intrasubjective diversity. The fractality of such patterns prompts the conclusion that there might be some deeper sense or inner logic behind them. At least to some extent, this inner logic may turn out to be one of different but compatible and complementing features or elements within particular clusters of human experience with the divine in the midst of human existence. But this intuition will need a much larger number of specific investigations before it may become more substantial. Interreligious theology is clearly the locus where one will appropriately expect the kind of findings that will either weaken or substantiate the fractal theory.

But what if theologians and their counterparts in the various religions just turn a blind eye to the challenge of religious diversity, withdrawing to a pious form of disinterestedness? What if they just avoid and refuse the challenging project of doing theology together? I agree with Kenneth Rose that such an example of nonengagement rests, intellectually, on very shaky grounds—even though its proponents apparently are not very worried about that. Nevertheless, their self-contained attitude may be opened up once they realize the fractal correspondence between the diversity within their own tradition—or even within their own hearts—and the diversity we meet at large on our planet. The fractal theory, if it should indeed be further consolidated, can function as such an eye-opener.

Contributors

Francis X. Clooney, SJ, is the Parkman Professor of Divinity and Professor of Comparative Theology at Harvard Divinity School, where he joined the faculty in 2005. After earning his doctorate in South Asian Languages and Civilizations (University of Chicago, 1984), he taught at Boston College for twenty-one years before coming to Harvard. His primary areas of Indological scholarship are theological commentarial writings in the Sanskrit and Tamil traditions of Hindu India. He is also a leading figure globally in the developing field of comparative theology, and has written on the Jesuit missionary tradition, particularly in India. He is the author of *Thinking Ritually: Retrieving the Purva Mimamsa of Jaimini*; *Theology after Vedanta: An Experiment in Comparative Theology*; *The Future of Hindu-Christian Studies: A Theological Inquiry*; and *Learning Interreligiously*. Forthcoming is *Slow Learning in Fast Times: On Reading Six Hindu and Christian Classics and How It Matters*. From 2010 to 2017, Francis was the director of the Center for the Study of World Religions at Harvard. He was elected to the British Academy in 2010.

Maria Massi Dakake researches and publishes on Islamic intellectual history, Qur'anic studies, Shi'ite and Sufi traditions, and women's spirituality and religious experience. She has recently completed work on a major collaborative project to produce the first *HarperCollins Study Qur'an*, a verse-by-verse commentary on the Qur'anic text. This work draws upon classical and modern Qur'an commentaries, making the rich and varied tradition of Muslim commentary on their own scripture, written almost exclusively in Arabic and Persian, accessible to an English-speaking audience for the first time in such a comprehensive manner. She is also currently working on a coedited volume, *The Routledge Companion to the Qur'an*, as well as a monograph on the concept of religion as a universal phenomenon in the Qur'an and Islamic intellectual tradition.

Hans Gustafson is the director of the Jay Phillips Center for Interfaith Learning at the University of St. Thomas in Minnesota, where he teaches and researches in the areas of (inter)religious studies and theology. He holds two M.A. degrees (philosophy and theology) and a Ph.D. in the study of religion. His most recent publications include the edited volume *Learning* *from Other Religious Traditions: Leaving Room for Holy Envy* and *Finding All Things in God: Pansacramentalism and Doing Theology Interreligiously.*

Paul Knitter is the Emeritus Paul Tillich Professor of Theology, World Religions, and Culture at Union Theological Seminary, New York, as well as Emeritus Professor of Theology at Xavier University in Cincinnati, Ohio. He received a licentiate in theology from the Pontifical Gregorian University in Rome (1966) and a doctorate from the University of Marburg, Germany (1972). Since his 1985 book, *No Other Name?*, he has been exploring how the religious communities of the world can cooperate in promoting human and ecological well-being. More recently, his writing and research have focused on Christian-Buddhist dialogue, which is the topic of *Without Buddha I Could Not Be a Christian* (2009) and the coauthored book with Roger Haight, SJ, *Jesus and Buddha: Friends in Conversation* (2015). Since 1986 he has been serving on the board of directors for CRISPAZ (Christians for Peace in El Salvador).

Ayon Maharaj is assistant professor and Head of Philosophy at Ramakrishna Mission Vivekananda Educational and Research Institute in West Bengal, India. He is also an ordained Brahmacārin, with the name of Buddhacaitanya, in training to be a Sannyāsin monk of the Ramakrishna Order. Holding a doctorate from the University of California at Berkeley, he has published over fifteen articles on Indian, German, and cross-cultural philosophy. He is the author of two books, *Infinite Paths to Infinite Reality: Sri Ramakrishna and Cross-Cultural Philosophy of Religion* (2018), and *The Dialectics of Aesthetic Agency: Revaluating German Aesthetics from Kant to Adorno* (2013). He is the editor of the forthcoming *Bloomsbury Research Handbook of Vedānta*, and he serves as a section editor for the *International Journal of Hindu Studies.*

John Makransky is associate professor of Buddhism and comparative theology at Boston College; senior academic adviser for the Centre for Buddhist Studies at Rangjung Yeshe Institute, Nepal; cofounder of the American Academy of Religion's Buddhist Critical Reflection Group; and former president of the Society of Buddhist-Christian Studies. John's writings have focused on concepts and practices of Indian and Tibetan Buddhism, ways of adapting such practices to address current problems and needs, and theoretical issues in interfaith learning. He is author of *Awakening through Love: Unveiling Your Deepest Goodness; Buddhahood Embodied: Sources of Controversy in India and Tibet;* coeditor of *Buddhist Theology;* and author of many articles. He is also the developer of the Sustainable Compassion Training (SCT) model, and cofounder of the Foundation for Active Compassion and Courage of Care Coalition, organizations that provide contemplative trainings in sustainable, inclusive compassion and awareness for people in caring professions and activism.

Ephraim Meir is Professor Emeritus of Modern Jewish Philosophy at Bar-Ilan University, Ramat Gan, Israel. He is president of the International Rosenzweig Society. His published books include *Dialogical Thought and Identity: Trans-Different Religiosity in Present-Day Societies*; *Interreligious Theology: Its Value and Mooring in Modern Jewish Philosophy*; *Becoming Interreligious: Towards a Dialogical Theology from a Jewish Vantage Point*; and *Old-New Jewish Humanism.*

Alan Race is a priest-theologian in the Anglican Christian tradition, whose research interests are in the areas of the theology of interfaith dialogue and theology of religions. He has taught Christian theology and interfaith dialogue in university, seminary, and adult study center settings. He is the author of the classic text *Christians and Religious Pluralism: Patterns in the Christian Theology of Religions* (1983 and 1993), which first set out the threefold typology of exclusive, inclusive, and pluralist Christian responses to religious plurality. Other books include *Interfaith Encounter: The Twin Tracks of Theology and Dialogue*; and *Making Sense of Religious Pluralism: Shaping Theology of Religions for Our Times.* He has also edited numerous books, including the SCM Core Text, with Paul Hedges, *Christian Approaches to Other Faiths.* Alan is chair of the World Congress of Faiths and editor of the journal *Interreligious Insight.*

Jerusha Tanner Rhodes is a Muslima theologian, scholar, and public educator. She is assistant professor of Islam and interreligious engagement and director of the Islam, Social Justice, and Interreligious Engagement Program (ISJIE) at Union Theological Seminary, New York. Her work and writing focus on Islamic feminism, interreligious engagement, religious pluralism, and social justice. She has a Ph.D. and M.A. in theological and religious studies with a focus on religious pluralism from Georgetown University; an M.A. in Islamic Sciences from the Graduate School of Islamic and Social Sciences; and a B.A. in anthropology and religion from American University. She is author of *Never Wholly Other: A Muslima Theology of Religious Pluralism* and *Divine Words, Female Voices: Muslima Explorations in Comparative Feminist Theology.*

Kenneth Rose is senior research fellow at the Graduate Theological Union and emeritus professor of philosophy and religion at Christopher Newport University. His degrees include an M.Div. from Harvard Divinity School and an M.A. and Ph.D. in the study of religion from Harvard University. At Harvard, he was a Fellow at the Center for the Study of World Religions. He teaches and publishes in the areas of comparative religion, the theology of religions, comparative mysticism, religious pluralism, and the philosophy of meditation. He developed and led the online course "Wisdom from World Religions," which was funded by a Templeton World Charity Foundation grant (https://radianceofawareness.com/course/). His publications include *Yoga, Meditation, and Mysticism: Contemplative Universals and Meditative Landmarks; Pluralism: The Future of Religion*; and numerous academic articles, reviews, and popular publications.

Perry Schmidt-Leukel is professor of religious studies and intercultural theology, director of the Institute for Religious Studies and Intercultural Theology, director of the Center for Religious Studies, and one of the principal investigators of the Cluster of Excellence "Religion and Politics," University of Muenster/Germany. He holds degrees in theology (Diploma; Ph.D.) and philosophy (master's). His *Habilitatio* (1996) was in systematic theology, ecumenical theology, and religious studies. Before he came to Muenster (2009), he taught at the Universities of Munich, Innsbruck, and Salzburg, and was professor of religious studies and systematic theology at the University of Glasgow (2000–2009). His main research interests are in the fields of interfaith relations, Buddhist-Christian dialogue, theologies of religions and interreligious theology. He has published more than thirty books. Among his more recent English books are: *God beyond Boundaries: A Christian and Pluralist Theology of Religions* (2017); *Religious Pluralism and Interreligious Theology: The Gifford Lectures—An Extended Edition* (2017); and *Buddhist-Christian Relations in Asia* (2017).

Rong Wang is associate professor in the School of Marxism, Guizhou University of Finance and Economics, Guiyang, People's Republic of China. Her research fields are philosophy of religions, religious pluralism, and dialogue. For doctoral studies at Zhejiang University she focused on Paul Knitter's pluralism and religious dialogue. After graduating from Zhejiang University in 2009, she spent six years in Sichuan University researching Perry Schmidt-Leukel's work on religious pluralism. She has published more than twenty papers in Chinese academic journals such as the *Journal of Zhejiang University, Religious Studies*, and *LOGOS & PNEUMA: Chinese Journal of Theology*. She has also translated seven books into Chinese.

Index